TEXTS
IN
CONTEXT

CRITICAL DIALOGUES ON SIGNIFICANT EPISODES IN AMERICAN POLITICAL RHETORIC

With newly-edited speech texts
by Anna E. Dickinson and
by Martin Luther King, Jr.

EDITED BY
MICHAEL C. LEFF
AND FRED J. KAUFFELD

Hermagoras Press
1989

7 - 6 - 90

This book is gratefully dedicated to
Donald K. Smith:
teacher, scholar, benefactor, friend,
vir bonus peritus dicendi.

TABLE OF CONTENTS

PREFACE

The origin of this book can be traced to one of David Zarefsky's ideas. Some years ago, sensing a revival of interest in public address, Zarefsky proposed holding a conference devoted to that subject. As he conceived it, the conference was to be a modest affair — small, informal, and uncommitted to any grand schemes about the course of future scholarship. It would simply provide a time and place for the like-minded to gather and talk.

As so often happens with good ideas, this one circulated for a time without anyone acting on it. Eventually, however, it was energized through that unofficial but familiar institution — the convention coffee-klatch.

In the Spring of 1987, the joint meeting of the Southern and Central States Speech Communication Associations featured a program devoted to Lincoln's "Second Inaugural Address." Four speakers presented different interpretations of that address, and a lively discussion followed. Afterward, over coffee, several of the participants and observers shared their enthusiasm about the session and resolved to organize future opportunities for the same kind of exchange. At that point, Zarefsky's proposal came back to mind, and the first steps were taken toward organizing a public address conference the next year in Madison.

In keeping with the original conception, we did not plan a systematic agenda for the conference. Rather, our method was, as Claude Raines said at the end of *Casablanca,* "to round up the usual suspects." We sought to locate scholars actively engaged in the study of public address and identify work in progress that could be turned into a finished paper on relatively short notice. We did engage in one act guided by programmatic considerations: we reserved a session for a review of the "state of the art" in public address scholarship and persuaded David Zarefsky, Martin Medhurst, and Jim Aune to present papers on that theme. Otherwise, the program took shape as we talked to potential contributors. We asked people to write about a "case study in public address," and the content of our sessions resulted from the choices made by the participants.

The conference convened at Madison June 3-6, 1988, under the title, "The Wisconsin Symposium on Public Address: Case Studies in Political Rhetoric." The format was designed to allow maximum concentration on the case studies and to promote as much open discussion as possible. For each session, a main speaker was allotted forty-five minutes. A draft copy of every paper was sent to an assigned respondent about a month before the conference, and the respondents delivered fifteen-minute presentations immediately after the main papers. Thereafter an hour was devoted to general discussion of both the paper and the response.

The discussion periods proved lively and stimulating, and they contributed greatly to the vitality of the conference. Unfortunately, we could find no way to reproduce these conversations in a form that would interest or make sense to a reader. But we have made an effort to retain something of the spirit of exchange and controversy that marked the conference. For that reason, we have published the papers and responses in paired sets, each one forming a chapter of this volume. Almost all of these contributions have been revised significantly as a result of comment and criticism generated at the conference. Nevertheless, the basic pattern remains unchanged. The responses all suggest alternative interpretations of the same text or texts, and the reader perhaps can sense how subsequent discussion might follow from a consideration of these differing perspectives. Moreover, Dilip Gaonkar's epilogue, in some measure, follows from his close attention to the points raised during the discussions.

The conference, then, had its origin in conversation and much of its business was conducted through that medium. We present this volume in the hope of enlarging the conversation and engaging others in it. Nevertheless, the process of turning the proceedings into the more static medium of print raises some special problems — matters that may seem puzzling either to the original participants or to those who did not participate and can only know what is in the text. A few of these matters deserve notice here.

The sub-title of this book announces that its subject is American political rhetoric. Yet, one of the chapters deals with Edmund Burke's "Speech on Conciliation," an address by an Englishman delivered in the British Parliament. On the surface, this chapter may seem out of place. We believe, however, that Burke's speech deserves an important place in the American rhetorical tradition. It concerned America; it had an important immediate effect on this side of the Atlantic, and for more than two centuries, it has continued to attract and influence American readers. As John Lucaites elegantly puts the point, Burke's address "is of America and America's history as much as if it had been spoken by George Washington, Thomas Jefferson, or Abraham Lincoln."

Five of our six case studies deal with a single speech text, and appreciation of the critical effort obviously demands a reading of the speeches themselves. Although generally we have not included the speech texts within the book since they are readily available in other sources, there are two notable exceptions.

The paper by Karlyn Campbell and the response by Wil Linkugel and Robert Rowland represent a special case, since their subject is Anna Dickinson's "Joan of Arc" lecture, a previously unpublished work. Fortunately, Karlyn Campbell has provided us with a transcription of that lecture based on a holographic manuscript found in Dickinson's papers. We are pleased to present the first printed version of the lecture in this book, and we express our thanks to Karlyn Campbell for her special contribution to this book, and more generally, for her continuing effort to recover the female voice in American rhetoric.

In the case of Martin Luther King's "I've Been to the Mountaintop" speech, we have been fortunate enough to secure permission to publish here the first complete text of the speech. It is a transcription made by Michael Osborn from an audiotape recorded during the speech.

Those who attended the conference, or who had access to the program, will note that there are omissions, additions, and organizational changes in this publication. One of the conference sessions, the paper by Christine Oravec and the response by Jim Jasinski, is not represented in this book. Oravec previously had committed her paper to another publication, and so she and Jasinski voluntarily limited their contribution to the conference alone. We wish to acknowledge the importance of that contribution and thank them for their participation.

We have also added an epilogue by Dilip Gaonkar, which provides an after-the-fact assessment of the papers and their significance. One of the functions of this epilogue is to frame issues that emerged during the discussions, and, as indicated above, we hope that it helps to convey some sense of the interchange that animated the conference.

Robert Scott's paper originally was presented at the conference banquet, and since we believe that it captured the spirit of the occasion, we have printed it as the foreword to this volume. The title of this paper includes the phrase "against rhetorical theory." Yet, we believe that Scott's message is not one of opposition or complaint. Instead, it is a positive celebration of concrete occasions and of the concrete ties that bind those who join in the conversation about our subject. This spirit of friendship suffused the conference, and we hope that we have helped to preserve some part of it in this book.

Finally, we must acknowledge our gratitude to those whose help made this book possible: to the Rhetoric faculty at the University of Wisconsin-Madison for their cooperation in planning and hosting the public address conference; to Greg Lampe, Andrea Dolan, and Amy Slagle for cheerful assistance in running the conference; to Michael Weiler, Ray Dearin, Jim Darsey, Tom Rosteck, and Robert Iltis for chairing conference sessions and for their efforts to keep the conversation going; to Sharon Dario for her patient work as copy-editor; to Jerry Murphy for his unflagging support and expert advice in preparing the book for publication; to Susan and Christine for putting up with late nights and grumpy editors, and, of course, to Donald K. Smith, to whom this book is dedicated and without whom it never would have appeared.

Michael Leff
Fred J. Kauffeld
Madison, November 1988

FOREWORD

AGAINST RHETORICAL THEORY: TRIPPING TO SERENDIP

ROBERT L. SCOTT

I have decided that "theory" is a pernicious concept, at least in some contexts. Of course people use the word in different senses and, for me, a number of these senses are benign. Nonetheless, I am here to warn you against theory. You may think that strange for a rhetorical theorist or even for a rhetorical critic who is used to the justification of the critical activity on the grounds that it may contribute to theory. In any case, theory is not only seen as a proper basis for fruitful (in this context "fruitful" means orderly) criticism but also has high status in the world of justification. Should we want to give all that up?

To do so is to stand with Cicero against Aristotle. If not that, then to reinvent Aristotle. But there is nothing fresh about reinventing Aristotle, that is the broad road that our field embarked on in 1917, or soon thereafter and, with some wanderings to be sure, it has been our highroad ever since.

Of course what I am doing has about it the odor of true confession. If so, then I confess. However if this insight is personal, even idiosyncratic, it may be particular to me. So I might as well deal with it in its particularity. If it has some general value, you will have to give it that. Sometimes the particular, even the personal, does have general value.

I did graduate work at the University of Illinois. I learned

Editor's note: Professor Scott delivered this paper at the conference banquet on June 3, 1988. Among other things, it was intended as a tribute to Donald K. Smith, to whom this volume is dedicated. We print the paper here in its original form.

from and respect the names of Karl R. Wallace, Marie Hochmuth Nichols, Richard Murphy, Ray Nadeau, and Otto Alvin Loeb Dieter. However the person who had the greatest impact on me while I was a graduate student, and for a long time after, was my fellow student Wayne Brockriede.

I doubt that my experience as a graduate student was unique. Some years ago a graduate student at the University of Minnesota asked me, "Do you know who here has had the greatest influence on me?" And he answered his own question, as I guessed he was longing to do, by naming another graduate student. I think he expected to surprise me. He surprised me no more than I surprised you. I suspect that each of us in crediting the patterns of our work as scholars would be as likely to name student colleagues who have remained close to us as we would our professors. That should humble us as professors, but what was it about those experiences? Rather than answering the question, let me compound the problem.

I count my blessings further, as I would guess each of you do. When I went from Illinois to the University of Houston in 1953, I was fortunate to find Otis M. Walter there. And when I moved to the University of Minnesota in 1957, I met the person who probably has had the greatest impact on what I've learned and certainly on my attitudes toward learning—Donald K. Smith.

Now D.K. Smith was a good man fallen among thieves; that is to say, he became a high ranked university administrator. I am delighted that Don Smith is here tonight. I am downright joyous to assure you all that he repented in his later years right here at the University of Wisconsin and that our colleagues in the Wisconsin department, ever convinced of the fine belief that it is never too late to save a fallen brother (or sister, I would imagine), took him in, dressed his wounds, nourished him, and set him once again on the path of professorial righteousness. I tried while D.K. was still a vice president at the University of Minnesota. Let me tell you that story.

One day we invited Vice President Smith to step back in his old, professorial shoes and address our department's Wednesday Noon Research Meeting. He did so, speaking on "The Rhetoric of Confrontation." The speech was witty and winsome, given Smith's natural charm, but it was filled with justifications for the military-industrial-educational complex as one might expect from a university administrator in those days of the latter 1960s. Feeling called to battle, as I generally am when Smith's voice disturbs the stirrups and anvils in my inner ears, I undertook to set him aright. My efforts went from the oral to the written, and memoranda flashed back and forth between Folwell and Morrill halls. It was easy for me to understand, reading what Smith wrote, why we referred to the place of his abode on our campus as imMorrill Hall. Finally in my desperation I was driven to author a complete essay under the title of "The Rhetoric of Confrontation" intended to go to the editor of *The Quarterly Journal of Speech*.

Before sending it away, however, I sent it to Don Smith. He returned it promptly, copiously marked, sheets turned over with scribbles on the reverse sides, pages added, and a note saying that most of what was in the essay he had said in the first place, although often I had misunderstood him, and what did I mean by not giving him credit. As I read what Smith wrote, and thought about what he had said, I began to admit to myself at least that not everything from that source was errant, Platonistic nonsense emanating from a Guardian of the University with purported superior memories of glimpses of pure truth. Much of it was sublime sophistry.

Take for example famous footnote number two in which Smith and I claim to have discovered a sense of rhetoric not indicated as recently as 1953 by Donald C. Bryant in his well-known "Rhetoric; Its Functions and Its Scope,"[1]—in which he notes the useful ambiguity of the word "rhetoric" in its three faces of teaching, theorizing, and practicing. We suggested that there are palpable rhetorics that those who interact in any culture, and especially in the great social movements within a culture, create and that are instantiated in audiences as they actively respond to those in their environments who purport to make messages. Auditors become, as it were, participants in rhetorical transactions, not simply recipients of messages. In arguing as we did, it seems to me that we anticipated in 1969 much that has marked the best work of the almost two decades that have followed. Of course my celebrated modesty does not permit me to go much further in indicating our prescience. But I hereby lay claim to all the territory

---

[1]Donald C. Bryant, "Rhetoric; Its Functions and Its Scope," *Quarterly Journal of Speech* 39.4 (Dec. 1953): 401-24.

lying between the ideograph and the narrative paradigm.

The upshot was the publication of the essay and an award by the SCA in 1970. The essay was reprinted twelve times in five years, and then I stopped counting. You can probably get a current figure from D.K. Smith who is much less modest than I.

My story is illustrative. And it is your story, too. What I insist is that the tradition of rhetoric in which we are all steeped is more accurately a tangle of traditions. If those traditions are in part theories, and they are at least what many people have called theories, we have ingested these with our morning oatmeal and breathe them into life as we work with students and one another and as we write. It is the sprawling, but living, tradition of rhetoric I praise in favor of the tepid claim to improve rhetorical theory. Allow me to develop this notion a little further.

"All the rhetoricians's rules/teach him but to name his tools"? It seems to me that in an important way Samuel Butler's jibe is accurate. But we make several errors in responding to it. In the first place, there is nothing wrong about naming one's tools. In fact, there are a good many things right about doing so, especially if one works with others. When repairing automobiles it may be better to say, "Hand me the 9mm box-end wrench, please" than to say, "Gimme that thing over there." Even when working alone, the person who knows that there are box-end wrenches, open-end wrenches, ratchet wrenches, as well as adjustable wrenches is apt to do a better job of matching tools to work.

The fault lies in having *rules,* at least in the sense of the word before "rules-theory" came onto the scene. In the sense of "go immediately to jail; do not pass Go, do not collect $200" the rhetorician's rules that Butler remarked on are apt to be super-fluous—even misleading, that is, not at all *good* ways to name one's tools.

People often use the word "theory" to mean "hunch" or "a tentative solution to a puzzle," as when Miss Marple says, "What's my theory? Well, my dear, there is only one person who had access to the poison and also to the room in which the deceased slept." Or use the word to claim their authority: "I've been speaking in public for twenty-five years now, and, I add modestly, with some degree of success. My theory is that if you speak loudly enough so that you can be heard easily, most people will at least listen."

But even these rather common and benign uses of the word begin to call to mind the aura of a formula; the algorithmic lust, once born, is difficult to extinguish. And certainly it is more than recently born in modern, Western culture. It has perhaps a few wrinkles and gray hairs, but it is still a rather lusty adult.

Our field as a behavioral science, nee social science, gives us adequate examples. There is something beguiling about the equals sign with letters, especially Greek, and numbers on either side. Taken as metaphor, such representations of what people are pleased to call "reality" are probably useful. Taken as more than that, I'm inclined to think we get the opposite of what we bargain for, unreality. But I shouldn't use the terms I have, since I believe that "reality" is another pernicious concept.

Of course "rhetorical theorists" may think of their pronouncements as hunches or experience as well as algorithms, but I fear the shadow of the latter, nonetheless, since the implication is that the former are approximations that should tend toward perfection, that is the latter. We sometimes take what we do, especially when we do rhetorical criticism, as being proto-theoretical or, worse, as art. A stock question for editors to put to the behavioral/social scientific scholars of communication is "what theoretical import does this have?" More and more frequently, that question is becoming the litmus test for rhetorical critics as well (personal testimony to the author by several editors—believe me; you'd better believe me).

But why in the world did I say "or worse, art"? To arrest your attention, of course. But also to make a point: in modern, Western culture "art" is important only in its own venue—that is, as detached from the serious business of life. We countenance it, even welcome it, as a respite from the world of work or worry (recognizing that it might be work or worry for those who do it, but they are akin to entertainers). No. We do not sort out our lives quite as simply as I have suggested, but there is that tendency. Particularly scholars who label their work as *art* should be careful since they do not live in the real world to begin with, and therefore are apt to be twice devalued.

In short, what I am talking about are some very basic attitudes. These are attitudes that we share in some ways and in some ways both relish and suffer from. What I recommend are some very basic attitude changes, not that I think for a moment

that these will be quick coming, even for myself, let alone my colleagues, the academic world at large, or the still larger *real* world.

Hence, Cicero. My favorite passage in *De Oratore*[2] is the one
in which Sulpicius asks Crassus, if "you hold that there is such a
thing as an 'art' of oratory?" You remember Crassus' reply of
course, "Do you think I am some idle talkative Greekling, who is
also perhaps full of learning and erudition, that you profound me a
petty question on which to talk as I will?" (I.xxii. 102). After
some discussion of the use of labels in this context, Crassus agrees
(since he has been praised as the wisest and most eloquent of men,
not merely writing pamphlets but active in the "most momenteous
causes") that there may be an *art* in a sense. H. Rackham, in his
introduction to the Sutton translation, comments (in a footnote,
p. xvii) that "it must be remembered that *ars* means a systematic
treatment of a subject and conveys the sense that we attach rather
to the word 'science'." The sense of *art* or *science* or even *techné*,
if we wish to be Greeklings, may all be taken as essentially caught
by the admonition to be systematic. Who can argue against that
admonition?

The difficulty, as it often does, rests in interpretation. Shall we
look at the admonition as to be *systematic persons* or as to be
persons committed to a system?

We are living in an age that can be described in one of its
facets as an era of bureaucratized knowledge. The goal of the
knowledge industry (one can utter such phrases these days without
setting too many people's teeth on edge and that in itself is
significant), the goal of the knowledge industry is "system," at best
system that is self-extending and self-justifying. As bureaucrats in
such a system, we operate in defined circumstances. These
circumstances make demands that may be responded to sensibly
only in terms set by the system of which we are parts. Thus our
roles are defined and circumscribed. The goal is for the steady
production of dependable products, the products being such that
they become in turn part of the system; that is, they help sustain
the system.

The bureaucratic ideal has definite attractions. Among these

---

[2]Cicero *De Oratore,* trans. E.W. Sutton and H. Rackham (Cambridge: Harvard
University Press, 1959).

attractions is the confidence generated by the system itself. After all, in theory, it is dependable. Dependability rests not simply in production but also in the justification of product: means and ends are both built in; judgment is minimized if not obviated and likewise the often awesome burdens that go with judgment — these are depersonalized. Of course we are depersonalized, too; that is, in a bureaucratic system it makes no difference who does the work.

Our goal, then, as persons committed to system is to bring the system to the point that we do not count. Perfect rhetorical criticism in this mode should be produced anonymously. That end of anonymity, if generalized throughout academia, would have at least one concomitant almost making it a consummation devoutly to be desired: it would play hob with promotion and tenure procedures.

In contrast, being a systematic person means to work carefully and thoroughly. More importantly, however, being a systematic rhetorical critic means working alertly within a tradition of rhetoric.

What is the tradition to which I refer? It is well over 2000 years old and composed of elements that are by no means wholly consistent with one another. Inconsistency may be its glory, since we are constantly puzzled by the variety of suggestions pulling us in different directions particularly when we try to get our bearings in the currents of argument flowing relentlessly around us. In short, that ubiquitous term "it" once again turns out to be a harlequin laughing at our vain effort to capture a sense of something, a singularity in the plurality of being and becoming. What we may call the tradition of rhetoric is many-voiced, many-valued, and directed toward many ends. None of us can touch every aspect of this tradition within which we work, and, although we may interpret it, we cannot fix its further evolution. We may, however, contribute to that evolution, perhaps most often unwittingly.

CONCLUSION

I said just a minute or so ago that the inconsistencies in our tradition may be its glory. Aside from pricking your flagging attention, why did I say such a thing? Because I believe that our tradition is filled with inconsistencies and because I believe that that should delight us. We can be arrested by the dissonances we sense. We can try to make the elements that we sort out harmonize with one another. And we may succeed — at least in momentary sorts of ways. Our tasks of sorting and resorting are the tasks of teaching and scholarly interpretation — writing histories of our discipline or portions thereof, and criticism of *public address,* an old fashioned, conservative term that stresses the traditional role of rhetor-as-leader.

Although I shall make bits of what I may often mistakingly take as the whole, or close to it, harmonious, and you will, too, the result will be the clamor that we take for granted as the life force of active scholars. At best we shall enact the ongoing "conversation" that Richard Rorty[3] has taught us is the best we can expect of human intellect.

My speech has been personal. I hope not so personal as to be idiosyncratic. If it has been useful, it may be because as my father liked to say to me, "Robert, you will never be a complete failure. You can always be a negative example for someone."

I celebrate people, not theories in the sense that they are true or false or productive or unproductive in spite of their sources. The people I have celebrated today, and one in particular, are persons with whom I have had living contact in trying to thrash out the observations and problems that have motivated me. Of course what we are fond of calling rhetorical theory or theories have names attached; that is, our tradition is richly peopled. Let us grind their bones to make our bread, but let us not forget what we do.

What we do is embark on our many trips to Serendip. Is that a sensible destination? I think it is the only course to set. Besides, we can even tell ourselves that theory guides us. If we are lucky, like Odysseus, we may go astray, and while astray we may meet some extremely interesting people and stumble onto some answers that we'll take for a few minutes at least as the Indies.

The best we can do for a *vade mecum* is Cicero, heartening to Crassus' crazy advice about turning in every which direction to learn, to learn, to never cease learning. After all, that is the genesis of the liberal arts and should be the briar patch for any rhetorical critic.

Finally, in working with Donald K. Smith on confrontation, I came to recognize that his version of what we were trying to say

---

[3]Richard Rorty, *Philosophy and the Mirror of Nature* (Princeton: Princeton University Press: 1979), 389 ff.

was superior. His version was filled with colorful anecdotes culled from his misspent life in academic administration and honed by his restless imagination to fit the points he wanted to make. So I excised that sort of thing ruthlessly and sprinkled over the whole my own baleful brand of scholarly rectitude. That is ironic since we located *decorum* as a key to the strongest strain in modern rhetoric, as we were lighting the way into a postmodern rhetorical world.

I am afraid that the rhetoric of Miss Manners will have to await another day. What I am hoping for is that Smith will take the hint and cast all that I have been yammering about into a neat essay. I'll let him put his name first this time.

What I have been doing is what I think we all do, that is, inviting others to re-experience and casting that invitation in such a form that will not only arrest attention but constitute a matrix for further thought. I have tried to call to your minds the stuff of your own experience as scholarly workers in the vineyard of the rhetorical tradition. I wish all of us deep purple feet as we stamp around in our stuff, and I hope that at least occasionally we may help create a vintage we find heady.

I

CURRENT VIEWS
OF
PUBLIC ADDRESS

THE STATE OF THE ART IN PUBLIC ADDRESS SCHOLARSHIP

DAVID ZAREFSKY

The decision to publish a series of studies in public address is cause for celebration. Twenty years ago, such a venture might well have been derided as a last-ditch reactionary effort, on the part of scholars whom the field had passed by, to join in a misbegotten protest against "the tyranny of relevance." The story of the death, burial, and resurrection of public address scholarship over the past two decades is an oft-told tale.[1]

I

As the conventional wisdom would have it, public address was the dominant subject of study in the field of rhetorical scholarship during most of the 1930s, 1940s, and 1950s. Study after study accumulated, mostly biographical, mostly of dead orators. All were done in the same mold, the "cookie cutter" of neo-Aristotelianism. They appeared to lack justification save for the naive and often unexpressed belief that studying landmark orators would enable us to derive principles by which to improve our own rhetorical practice.[2] At their best, these studies were bad history and bad criticism both.

But, the story continues, all that was changed in the mid-1960s when Edwin Black exposed the pitfalls of neo-Aristotelianism.[3] In response to his clarion call, scholars abandoned public address, rushing instead to call themselves rhetorical critics or theorists. When Barnet Baskerville asked, "Must we all be 'rhetorical

---

[1]A succinct account was given, for example, by Bruce E. Gronbeck, in a paper, "The Birth, Death, and Rebirth of Public Address," presented at the Speech Communication Association convention, Denver, Colorado, November 1985.

[2]For an example in which this rationale was stated explicitly, see Warren C. Shaw, *History of American Oratory* (Indianapolis: Bobbs-Merrill, 1928), 672.

[3]Edwin Black, *Rhetorical Criticism: A Study in Method* (New York: Macmillan, 1965).

critics'?"[4] his inquiry seemed to many to be silly, because the answer was so obvious—"Of course we must." But now, in the 1980s, whether because of the oratorical success of Ronald Reagan or because our varied bicentennial celebrations have sensitized us anew to our heritage and tradition, public address studies once more have come into fashion and are enjoying a remarkable renaissance.

In fact, nothing of the sort happened. Public address studies never died. The very years which were supposedly the nadir of research in public address saw the appearance in our journals of extended controversy over the analysis of a specific text—Richard Nixon's "Vietnamization" speech of November 3, 1969. The exchange among Forbes Hill, Karlyn Campbell, and Robert Newman not only focused attention on the text but raised questions about the role of the scholar of public address which are with us still.[5] Those same years witnessed new attention to the public speaking of groups traditionally excluded from the public forum, chiefly blacks and women. And they witnessed the research leading to Stephen Lucas's *Portents of Rebellion*,[6] one of the first of a generation of book-length studies of important rhetorical acts.

What has happened, however, is that there has been a change both in the respectability of public address studies within the discipline and in the self-reflexive nature of the studies themselves. Both changes are related, and both bespeak the maturation of a field of study. They recognize that the earlier conception of public address studies was unduly rigid, in at least three respects. First, it presumed one object of study—the public oration—to the

---

[4]Barnet Baskerville, "Must We All Be 'Rhetorical Critics'?" *Quarterly Journal of Speech,* 63 (April, 1977): 107-116.

[5]See Forbes Hill, "Conventional Wisdom—Traditional Form: The President's Message of November 3, 1969," *Quarterly Journal of Speech,* 58 (December, 1972): 373-386; Karlyn Kohrs Campbell, "An Exercise in the Rhetoric of Mythical America," *Critiques of Contemporary Rhetoric* (Belmont, Cal.: Wadsworth, 1972), 50-58; Campbell, "'Conventional Wisdom—Traditional Form': A Rejoinder," *Quarterly Journal of Speech,* 58 (December,—1972): 451-454; Hill, "Reply to Professor Campbell," *Quarterly Journal of Speech,* 58, (December, 1972): 454-460; Robert P. Newman, "Under the Veneer: Nixon's Vietnam Speech of November 3, 1969," *Quarterly Journal of Speech,* 56 (April, 1970): 168-178.

[6]Stephen E. Lucas, *Portents of Rebellion: Rhetoric and Revolution in Philadelphia, 1765-76* (Philadelphia: Temple Univ. Press, 1976).

exclusion of other types of public rhetorical acts. Second, it presumed a perspective — the historical. The term "historical" was used in opposition both to "contemporary" and to "critical." Public address studies did not involve people or events that were of current interest or relevance; they therefore seemed antiquarian. Moreover, they represented the worst tradition of names-and-dates history, providing little more than chronology and certainly excluding interpretation or judgment. It was not hard to see why public address was regarded as the intellectual backwater of the discipline. Third, it presumed a method — neo-Aristotelianism, not as Artistotle himself probably would have done it but as a set of categories automatically applied to any speaker or speech. The resulting studies were not theoretically interesting and often had as their primary finding that the neo-Aristotelian categories could be made to fit virtually anything.

Throughout the academy, and particularly in the human sciences, the late 1960s and 1970s were marked by a self-reflexiveness about method and assumptions which called into question traditional models and paradigms. Public address studies were no exception. As scholars realized that rigidity as to the object, perspective, and method of study were constricting inquiry and producing studies that largely just replicated the assumptions, they began to probe in new directions. They examined other rhetorical forms besides the public speech, other units of study besides the individual orator, other perspectives besides the narrowly historical, and other methods besides neo-Aristotelianism. The resulting studies, now accumulating over a decade or more, make more substantial theoretical contributions, exhibit a richer array of approaches, demonstrate more methodological sophistica-tion and awareness of assumptions, and — at least in my opinion — are more interesting. Along with the growing recognition of rhetoric's centrality to culture, they help to explain the revival of interest in public address.

II

One could point to many signs of vitality in public address. To start with, we have enlarged the meaning of "public address" from a mode to a function of discourse. It seems self-evident that any rhetorical act is "addressed" and hence evokes a "public." What we study when we study public address, then, is really rhetorical practice in all its manifestations. (In a recent review essay, Lucas takes a similar position, concluding that the phrase "public address" really identifies all public discursive rhetorical acts.[7] Although discourse certainly is at the center of the rhetorical tradition, I am not sure why only discursive acts are addressed to a public.) By embracing a broader conception of public address and not reducing the term to formal oratory, our studies have enhanced the potential for understanding historical or rhetorical situations and for formulating theoretical generalizations.

Moreover, our research exhibits a healthy pluralism of methods and approaches. These range from the microscopic analysis of individual texts to the macroscopic study of movements and campaigns. The underlying metaphor or approach may be traditional neo-Aristotelianism enlarged beyond the "cookie cutter" mold, or it may be dramatism, formism, organicism, ideology, or who knows what. This pluralism serves several valuable purposes. It enables multiple perspectives to be brought to bear on a single work, as illustrated in the recent symposium on Lincoln's Second Inaugural Address.[8] It permits a more careful articulation of the relationship between text and context. And it permits us to see public address as a social process including, for instance, media in diffusing public messages among audiences.

Within the academy, public address courses are again fashionable, attracting healthy enrollments. My own university, Northwestern, may serve as a reasonable example. In 1970 the standard course in the history of American public address, which had been developed by Ernest Wrage, was scrapped in favor of one-quarter courses in the rhetoric of revivals, the rhetoric of demagogues, the rhetoric of social movements, and so on. In the mid-1970s the course was reintroduced, now retitled "Rhetorical history of the United States" to avoid the seemingly limiting term "public address," and it today exists alongside such generic courses as political communication, the rhetoric of war, and the rhetoric of

---

[7]Stephen E. Lucas, "The Renaissance of American Public Address: Text and Context in Rhetorical Criticism," *Quarterly Journal of Speech,* 74 (May, 1988): 243-262.

[8]The symposium appears in *Communication Reports,* 1 (Winter, 1988): 9-37.

social movements. Next fall 100 undergraduates will be reading
Puritan sermons and the debate between Webster and Hayne. This
experience is not atypical, and it has prompted authors and
publishers to issue appropriate textual and reference materials in
public address. Most of the standard anthologies are now out of
print, but Waveland Press has just issued Ron Reid's *Three
Centuries of American Rhetorical Discourse* and Longmans is soon
to publish a two-volume anthology edited by Jim Andrews and
me.[9] Under the editorship of Bernard Duffy and Halford Ross
Ryan Greenwood Press has published a valuable two-volume
reference work[10] and is undertaking an ambitious series of
rhetorical biographies. Such a healthy publishing program is both a
sign of and a stimulus for intensified scholarly activity.

   Another sign of health is that scholars in other fields are
discovering the role of public address. To be sure, they are not
citing our work as often as we would like, and they sometimes
remain oblivious to the discipline of Speech Communication.
Nevertheless, there is growing work in what we like to call the
cognate disciplines that reflects the importance of public address.
History is the field I know best. Perhaps reflecting the influence of
Charles Beard, many traditional historians seemed to assume that
the primary motives in history were economic, and that rhetorical
acts were at best transient and ephemeral, at worst attempts to
mask true motives. One searches in vain through standard histories
for extended treatments even of the Lincoln-Douglas debates as
historical acts, much less as texts which offer valuable historical
evidence about the culture or the time. But that is changing.
Twenty years ago Bernard Bailyn published *Ideological Origins of
the American Revolution,* in which he focuses on what the
colonists themselves said were the causes of the struggle, taking the

   [9]Ronald F. Reid, ed., *Three Centuries of American Rhetorical Discourse* (Prospect
Heights, Ill.: Waveland Press, 1987); James R. Andrews and David Zarefsky, ed.,
American Voices: Significant Speeches in United States History, 1630-1945 (New York:
Longmans, in press); David Zarefsky and James R. Andrews, ed., *Contemporary
American Voices: Significant Speeches in United States History, 1945-Present* (New
York: Longmans, in preparation).
   [10]Bernard K. Duffy and Halford Ross Ryan, ed., *American Orators of the Twentieth
Century* (Westport, Conn.: Greenwood Press, 1987); Duffy and Ryan, ed., *American
Orators Before 1900* (Westport, Conn.: Greenwood Press, 1987).

discourse of the revolutionary pamphlets seriously. Gordon Wood undertook a similar analysis of the early years of the republic.[11] More recently, historians have shown a strong interest in what they call "political culture," and—most importantly for our purposes— they maintain that the political culture of an age is constituted by its discourse. So, for example, Daniel Walker Howe, in his *The Political Culture of the American Whigs,* notes that the spirited debate between Whigs and Jacksonians was controlled by conventions of discourse.[12] Most recently, Jeffrey K. Tulis has published *The Rhetorical Presidency,* a particularly insightful analysis of how 19th and 20th century Presidents reflected radically different notions of the place of rhetoric in public affairs. Although the focus is limited to the Presidency, Tulis charts cultural attitudes and values about rhetoric in a manner not unlike Barnet Baskerville's *The People's Choice.*[13]

Although I emphasize the field of history, similar developments are taking place in other allied disciplines. Political scientists are focusing anew on political communication, and are examining rhetoric as a resource for power. Sociologists are finding symbolic structures as meaningful social units. Whole fields, of course, are becoming more aware of their own rhetorical practice, a phenomenon which has given rise to the Project on Rhetoric of Inquiry at the University of Iowa.[14]

There are dangers, of course, in the discovery of rhetoric by "outsiders." We could so rejoice at no longer being outcasts that we allow our own field of study to be defined by others; we could focus so much on disciplinary discourse that we forget that rhetorical practice traditionally has been associated with the public

---

[11]Bernard Bailyn, *Ideological Origins of the American Revolution* (Cambridge, Mass.: Harvard Univ. Press, 1967); Gordon S. Wood, *The Creation of the American Republic, 1776-1787* (Chapel Hill: Univ. of North Carolina Press, 1969).

[12]Daniel Walker Howe, *The Political Culture of the American Whigs* (Chicago: Univ. of Chicago Press, 1979), esp. 23-24.

[13]Jeffrey K. Tulis, *The Rhetorical Presidency* (Princeton: Princeton Univ. Press, 1987); Barnet Baskerville, *The People's Choice: The Orator in American Society* (Lexington, Ky.: Univ. Press of Kentucky, 1979).

[14]See especially John S. Nelson, Allan Megill, and Donald N. McCloskey, ed., *The Rhetoric of the Human Sciences: Language and Argument in Scholarship and Public Affairs* (Madison: Univ. of Wisconsin Press, 1987). A series of books on this theme is being published by the University of Wisconsin Press.

forum. But as signs of the vitality of public address, the rhetorical interests of scholars in other fields are valuable evidence.

Furthermore, our own studies have assumed greater depth and richness. With the exception of textbooks, for most of our history our discipline has been primarily a journal-article field. Whether that is because we undertook limited projects, or because publishers denied access to us for longer studies, is an unproductive question. The fact is that, particularly in the last decade, scholars in public address have produced a significant number of book-length manuscripts, with more on the way.[15] This is not self-evidently a sign of vitality—after all, much nonsense can be found between hard covers. But it does permit greater depth of research and exposition; it does permit scholars to undertake more ambitious inquiries which require more space in which to present the results; it does make our work more accessible to larger audiences, and it does increase the chances that it will be noticed and reviewed outside our own discipline. And, of course, the growing interest of respected university presses in publishing public address studies is itself a sign of vitality.

III

These types of evidence all point to health, intellectual ferment, and excitement about the study of public address. There is one theme which warrants discussion in more detail, however, because I believe it to be at the base of the recent renaissance. Our studies in public address are increasingly theory-driven, and cases are related directly to theories; this condition is a strength, but it

---

[15]Examples include Kathleen Hall Jamieson, *Packaging the Presidency: A History and Criticism of Presidential Campaign Advertising* (New York: Oxford Univ. Press, 1984); Ernest G. Bormann, *The Force of Fantasy: Restoring the American Dream* (Carbondale: Southern Ill. Univ. Press, 1985); Kathleen J. Turner, *Lyndon Johnson's Dual War: Vietnam and the Press* (Chicago: Univ. of Chicago Press, 1985); Frederick J. Antczak, *Thought and Character: The Rhetoric of Democratic Education* (Ames: Iowa State Univ. Press, 1985); J. Michael Hogan, *The Panama Canal in American Politics: Domestic Advocacy and the Evolution of Policy* (Carbondale: Southern Ill. Univ. Press, 1986); David Zarefsky, *President Johnson's War on Poverty: Rhetoric and History* (University, Ala: Univ. of Alabama Press, 1986); Roderick P. Hart, *The Sound of Leadership: Presidential Communication in the Modern Age* (Chicago: Univ. of Chicago Press, 1987); and Kathleen Hall Jamieson, *Eloquence in an Electronic Age: The Transformation of Political Speechmaking* (New York: Oxford Univ. Press, 1988).

also implies a possible weakness.

By "theory," I do not mean the rigor and rigidity of covering laws from which precise causal statements can be derived. Although originating in the philosophy of history, this approach sometimes characterizes theory construction in the social sciences. What I have in mind is a construct more like "explanation."[16] A study in public address is theory-driven if it is prompted by or suggestive of questions about processes or events which are broader than the given case and to whose answers the study can make a contribution. This is a justification for study quite different from the claim that it will be another study of a given type which is warranted because no one has done it before.

According to most models of the logic of inquiry, a researcher formulates a theoretically interesting question. When it is appropriate to test the question by controlled experimentation or a sample survey, the researcher does that. When it is appropriate to test the question by reference to a particular case—as, for example, in anthropology or history—that is what is done. Now, in fact, research often does not proceed in that way. I suspect that it is an intriguing aspect of the case which often is the initial motive for the study, and that only later does one's interest in the case lead to broader questions. But it does lead there, and in presenting the results of research, the scholar typically stresses the linkage between the specific case and the questions of broader significance. In this sense the most significant feature of much of our recent public address research is that it is guided and influenced by theory.

The theory which animates a given study might come from any of several places. Most obviously, it might come from rhetorical theory or the philosophy of communication. A particular precept is either developed or tested, as the case may be, by reference to specific rhetorical practice. An example from my own work is my attempt to explain Lyndon Johnson's advocacy of affirmative action by reference to Perelman and Olbrechts-Tyteca's theory of dissociation. More generally Ernest Bormann's history of

---

[16]On different approaches to the meaning of "theory," see Carl G. Hempel, "The Function of General Laws in History," *Journal of Philosophy,* 39 (1942): 35-48; William Dray, *Laws and Explanation in History* (London: Oxford Univ. Press, 1957).

early American public discourse flows from his own symbolic convergence theory of communication and his concept of fantasy themes and rhetorical visions.[17]

Another obvious source of theoretical underpinning for public address studies lies in the nature of the rhetorical object. Form and genre studies are the clearest example. Harrell, Ware, and Linkugel analyze Nixon's public defenses concerning the Watergate scandal by reference to the generic form of apologia which Nixon is assumed to exhibit. Likewise, Rod Hart's extended study, *The Political Pulpit,* proceeds from a theory of the inaugural address as a rhetorical genre.[18]

But rhetorical sources are not the only places where one might find theory which guides public address studies. Potent studies can relate to a theory of the situation or of the context; often such theories may derive from other disciplines. Theories of the rise and fall of Presidential power, the ebb and flow of liberalism and conservatism, the dialectic of reform and reaction, the power of metaphor, or the social basis of information processing—to name but a few—can provide firm grounding and linkages.

Whatever the source of theory in the particular case, public address studies are also guided by a more general if unarticulated theory of the process of public address itself—and from it, too, interesting questions may flow. It is a theory which blends elements of symbolic interactionism with Kenneth Burke's concept of identification. It holds that reality is not "given" but that we perceive it as we define it through symbols. Definitions of situations involve choices among symbols, and the choices are not neutral. The symbols then serve as the premises for argument and appeal to others. The exchange of symbols through discourse validates and modifies our views of the world, and likewise in exchanging symbols we modify others' views of the world, and in this way we influence and relate to them. This process of symbolic

---

[17]David Zarefsky, "Lyndon Johnson Redefines 'Equal Opportunity': The Beginnings of Affirmative Action," *Central States Speech Journal,* 31 (Summer, 1980): 85-94; Bormann, *The Force of Fantasy.*

[18]Jackson Harrell, B.L. Ware, and Wil A. Linkugel, "Failure of Apology in American Politics: Nixon on Watergate," *Speech Monographs,* 42 (November, 1975): 245-261; Roderick P. Hart, *The Political Pulpit* (West Lafayette, Ind.: Purdue Univ. Press, 1977).

exchange involves identification between speakers and audiences, and to study public address is to study how, within the frame of often unrecognized ideology, speakers' central values and proposals are connected with the ideas and predispositions of the audience, and how each modifies the other. The importance of such a study is that the creation and exchange of symbols is both the glue holding society together (through evoking common bonds) and also the force which moves people toward goals (by evoking a utopian symbolic vision).

The grounding of studies theoretically has obvious benefits. It permits generalization beyond the bounds of the particular case. It furnishes the criterion for evaluating research results, whether the particular inquiry "led" anywhere. It enables a discipline to develop a cumulative body of research, and in that sense to "get better." But there also are pitfalls to be avoided. Theories drawn from rhetoric and communication philosophy may develop the same cookie-cutter problem for which neo-Aristotelianism was reviled; the studies may say more about the all-encompassing nature of the theory than about the rhetorical act being examined. Theories which presume the constancy of a rhetorical form may be insensitive to the importance of context or the role of cultural change; the Tulis book, for example, in my opinion, casts serious doubt on the allegation that there are unchanging generic require-ments for the Presidential inaugural address. And theories drawn from context, situation, or other disciplines can become weak imitations of the real thing — the very charge that was invoked against earlier public address studies.

To my mind, though, there is an even greater pitfall in the assumption that theories must transcend particular cases. That assumption, of course, characterizes the perspective of the social sciences, according to which theory is a source of generalization. But we should also be sensitive to the perspective of the humanities, according to which a theory of the particular case may prompt useful study which enriches or deepens understanding of that case. This line of thinking begins with the premise that public address is an important phenomenon in its own right — not just for what a case study might contribute to rhetorical or scientific theories. It assumes that particular cases of discourse may present interesting questions, paradoxes, or anomalies, which a study of public address might answer by developing a "theory of the case."

Illustrative of excellent studies in this regard are Leff's analyses of space and time in Lincoln's "House Divided" speech and his Second Inaugural Address.[19] The result of each of those studies is to suggest a theory which more fully encompasses the case than do the alternatives. Leff's analysis of the "House Divided" speech responds to the accusations by some historians that the speech is inconsistent or that it develops farfetched charges which obviously were not believable. His study of the Second Inaugural Address speaks to the question of how Lincoln could fuse the secular and the sacred.

In summary, then, I believe the primary reason for the current greater strength of public address studies is that they are theory-driven, but we need to be clear about what that means. Theory permits drawing inferences which connect the study to something else — maybe to a broader generalization, maybe to an explanation of the specific case. Rhetorical studies need not always be driven by rhetorical theories, and in any case we need to be sure that our theories are sensitive to the richness of detail which is evident only in the study of particular cases.

IV

So far I have characterized the state of public address scholarship as mature and healthy. One sign of a mature and healthy field is that it can confront difficult issues about its own purpose and method. I should like to close by referring to several of these.

First, we need to settle the question of the relationship between history and criticism by reinventing, as it were, the "historical-critical method." Now, not all history is critical; not all criticism is historical. Granted. But any instance of public address consists of a text (using that term broadly) and hence is susceptible to critical examination. And any instance of public address occurs in some context and hence is susceptible to historical study. The emphasis between text and context will vary from one study to the next, but I find it hard to imagine a decent study of public address which does

---

[19]Michael C. Leff, "Rhetorical Timing in Lincoln's 'House Divided' Speech," *The Van Zelst Lecture in Communication* (Evanston, Ill.: Northwestern University, 1983); "Dimensions of Temporality in Lincoln's Second Inaugural," *Communication Reports,* 1 (Winter, 1988): 26-31.

not partake of both.

Perhaps another way to say this is that any public address study should be interpretive. It should say something that makes a difference about the work with which it is concerned. What it "says" is an argument, a statement containing an inference which goes beyond the text itself yet is supported by good reasons.[20] Excluded from this definition are such modes as simple narratives of what happened, restatement of the text, recitation of the factual conditions surrounding the delivery of the speech—pure history— or formulaic studies for which the context is irrelevant—pure criticism. The middle ground, what is both historical and critical, is where interpretive studies thrive. Yes, one can posit distinctions between rhetorical history and rhetorical criticism,[21] but for public address studies it does not seem to me to be useful to do so, since they embody both.

Second, having said that, it follows that public address scholars need to become more sophisticated with both historical and critical methods. I share Ronald Carpenter's concern[22] that we are not sufficiently meticulous about using the available primary sources to understand a historical situation, with the result that we may offer critical claims easily dismissed by reference to historical evidence— that we may offer, as it were, "a promising theory killed by a fact." As a discipline, we are not as skilled as we ought to be at knowing how to identify and locate the relevant primary sources, how to assess them, and how to use them as evidence for claims that we might advance. Likewise, our familiarity with theories of criticism needs to advance well beyond any of the formulaic approaches or any of the currently popular schools, such as structuralism and deconstruction, to a philosophical understanding of the act of criticism itself: What does it mean to make judgments? How can they be supported and tested? Especially in a world of critical

---

[20]This view of argument is obviously influenced by Wayne Brockriede, "Where Is Argument?" *Journal of the American Forensic Association,* 11 (Spring, 1975): 179-182.

[21]See, for example, Bruce Gronbeck, "Rhetorical History and Rhetorical Criticism: A Distinction," *Speech Teacher,* 24 (November, 1975): 309-320.

[22]See Ronald H. Carpenter, "Whatever Happened to the 'Historical' in Historical-Critical Method?" paper presented at the Southern Speech Communication Association convention, April, 1986.

pluralism, what distinguishes interpretation from misinterpretation?[23]

Third, we need to deal with all the same problems of canonization which confront our colleagues in literature. On the one hand, we do need to revisit what by common consent are a body of great speeches. Mohrmann is right in noting with surprise that many of these "great speeches" have never been subjected to careful rhetorical study.[24] Presumably, works acquire canonical status for some reason, and renewed attention to the "classic" texts might help us to understand those reasons. At the same time, the standard canon of public address is not neutral. Some groups of speakers are notoriously under-represented, and some topics are treated as taboo. We must be sure that our concept of a canon does not become a closed system and that we continually engage the question of what it means to say that any given instance of public address belongs in the canon.

Fourth, we need to clarify the stance from which the student of public address approaches the work. I have argued elsewhere that the analyst can be a commentator, explicating the rhetorical method in the text and making manifest what is latent in the work; or a partisan, entering the same discourse community as the rhetor and engaging his or her claims and arguments; or a judge who invokes and revises norms.[25] It is important to recognize the differences among these stances so that we do not slip from one to another. Although he does not use this language, that in effect is the charge Forbes Hill brings against Karlyn Campbell in their famous exchange: that is, that she is acting both as a partisan and as a judge, violating the ethical principle that one should not be a judge in one's own cause. It is also important to recognize that the function of commentary is primary; analysis which ignores questions such as "What is happening here?" and proceeds to refutation may be attacking a straw man, throwing volleys against a creation that might not be recognized by its own maker. Moreover, judgment

[23]This is the central theme of Wayne C. Booth, *Critical Understanding: The Powers and Limits of Pluralism* (Chicago: Univ. of Chicago Press, 1979).

[24]Cited in Michael Leff, "Textual Criticism: The Legacy of G.P. Mohrmann," *Quarterly Journal of Speech,* 72 (November, 1986): 377.

[25]David Zarefsky. "Argumentation and the Politics of Criticism," *Argument and Critical Practices: Proceedings of the Fifth SCA/AFA Summer Conference on Argumentation,* ed. Joseph W. Wenzel (Annandale, Va.: SCA, 1987), 53-59.

risks becoming self-sealing, calcifying into prejudice, because it does not open itself to confrontation with the thing judged.

Fifth, we need more comparative studies of the same rhetorical objects, exemplified by the symposium on Lincoln's Second Inaugural in the first issue of *Communication Reports*.[26] Comparative perspectives on the same text focus our attention on how the analyst's assumptions and methods shape the impressions one has of the object itself. They also invite attention to the need for standards of judgment and choice among competing interpretations. If one regards studies as making arguments, then the standards evolve from a notion of criticism as an argument field.

Sixth, we need to revisit the idea of rhetorical biography. Many of our earliest studies were biographical, and many were conceptually weak; we risk the *post hoc* fallacy if we assume that they were weak because biographical. A pattern of rhetorical choice that develops over time, significant changes in rhetorical practice, rhetorical method that is influenced by or responsive to important events in a speaker's life—all these are fruitful subjects for investigation. The biographical series planned by Greenwood Press affords scholars the opportunity to bring to rhetorical biography the maturity and theoretical grounding for the discipline that has been observed in other studies.

Seventh, we need to play our part in helping to explicate the fundamental construct of "public" on which public address scholarship is based. This need has several dimensions. Our studies implicitly presume a culture in which there is such a thing as a "public forum"; we need to explore how rhetorical practice is affected in cultures which lack such a construct. We also need to explore more carefully how the widening and narrowing of the public forum affect rhetorical practice; my colleague Tom Goodnight has initiated a productive line of work in this respect by focusing on the public, private, and technical as spheres of argument.[27] And we need to explore how discourse constructs and responds to crises in the nature of the public, such as the tangled nature of authority in the

---

[26]See note 8.

[27]G. Thomas Goodnight, "The Personal, Technical, and Public Spheres of Argument: A Speculative Inquiry into the Art of Public Deliberation," *Journal of the American Forensic Association,* 18 (Spring, 1982): 214-227.

late 1970s which my colleague Tom Farrell has explored through the discourse of President Carter.[28] The place where studies of rhetorical theory and practice join is precisely this elemental construct of "the public"; and it is at that place that case studies may make their most direct contribution to the advancement of theory.

And, finally, we need to keep discussions such as this one within their proper bounds. Assaying the state of the art is heady stuff, and the temptation to pontificate is sometimes great. Discourse such as this is useful if it helps to spot trends, focus issues, or stimulate scholarship. But it is parasitic if it fosters the extended "paradigm wars" which may substitute for the actual work of the discipline. Put simply, we do not need to spend time arguing about whether we follow a "rules" or "laws' perspective, whether we are historians or critics, whether we draw our inspiration from the humanities or the social sciences, or any of the other pseudo-issues which have plagued this and related disciplines. We should have a healthy tolerance for ambiguity about these matters, following Burke's admonition to use all that is there to use. Instead we should do what public address scholars do best: ground our theories in the data and not lose sight of the cases. Soundly conceived, skillfully executed studies of rhetorical practice are what will most assure the continued health of our field.

---

[28]See Thomas B. Farrell, "Knowledge in Time: Toward an Extension of Rhetorical Form," *Advances in Argumentation Theory and Research,* ed. J. Robert Cox and Charles Arthur Willard (Carbondale: Southern Ill. Univ. Press, 1982), esp. 138-151.

PUBLIC ADDRESS AND
SIGNIFICANT SCHOLARSHIP:
FOUR CHALLENGES
TO THE RHETORICAL RENAISSANCE

MARTIN J. MEDHURST

Surveying the state of rhetorical-critical scholarship in 1980, my late colleague G. P. Mohrmann noted: "On the surface it appears quite grand, and a reader might be inclined to believe that a lively mustang now is careening the range of criticism, but when the cosmic dust of the new terminology settles, what is really seen? Why, there is our litle hobby-horse rocking, rocking, rocking."[1] Mohrmann's comment was aimed primarily at the plethora of new methods that had burst upon the field over the preceding fifteen years, methods which, in his judgment, too often substituted jargon and specialized vocabulary for sustained, textual analysis.

Today, we still have our hobby horses, having added a few in the interim. But the state of rhetoric and public address at the end of the 1980s is no longer characterized by the search for method nor is it as staid, static, or artificial as the hobby-horse image implies. To the contrary, I shall argue that there are encouraging signs that rhetoric and public address studies may be in the initial stages of what Stephen Lucas has labelled a "renaissance."[2] Like all rebirths, this current renaissance (if that is what it is) both reacts against the recent past while simultaneously building upon it and breaks new ground while retaining elements from the old paradigm. If the late 1960s and 1970s were an era of experimentation, then the 1980s have been an era of consolidation leading, in the 1990s, perhaps, to a new flowering of the historical-critical-rhetorical impulse and the production of scholarship that makes a

---

[1]G. P. Mohrmann, "Elegy in a Critical Grave-Yard," *Western Journal of Speech Communication* 44 (1980): 269.

[2]Stephen E. Lucas, "The Renaissance of American Public Address: Text and Context in Rhetorical Criticism," *Quarterly Journal of Speech* 74 (1988): 241-260.

difference. And that, I shall argue, should be our goal—to make a
difference in the scholarly world at large.

I

Serving as Book Editor of the *Quarterly Journal of Speech*
over the course of the last several years, I have come to learn that
a standard *topos* of reviewers is this: the book is germane, the
research thorough, but no reference is made to scholarship in
Speech Communication even though such scholarship was available
and would have contributed to the goals of the study. So frequent
is this criticism—and it is almost always offered as a criticism—
that one must pause to ask: Why? What is it that other scholars
do not find our works important enough or germane enough to
cite? There are several possibilities.

Some suggest the argument from ignorance. They claim that
other scholars are simply not aware of our journals, books, or field.
We are not, they say, sufficiently indexed. If only others knew,
then surely they would cite our work. Some point to the insularity
of academic departments, the compartmentalization of all scholarship, implying that such oversight is unfortunate, but probably to
be expected in the hermetically sealed world of academia. Still
others blame the authors or publishers or the professional association for failing to publicize sufficiently the work done in our field.
What is needed, say these folks, is better public relations.

There may be some truth to all of these positions, but the
basic fact remains. The primary reason that we are not cited by
others, that our books are not academic best sellers, that our
leaders do not often appear in the popular media, that they are not
often called upon for expert commentary, that they do not serve
on the boards of many interdisciplinary organizations or journals,
is straightforward—that is, we have not produced much scholarship
that has made a difference. That, I am arguing, ought to be our
goal. To reach this goal, to push this rhetorical renaissance to
fruition, we need to pursue with vigor four trends that have
emerged in the 1980s: the sustained, book-length analyses of
rhetorical phenomena; the contribution to historical revisionism;
the close textual reading of individual artifacts; and the interpretation of rhetoric and public address as a cultural force that shaped
and continues to shape the American experiment.

As Robert L. Ivie notes in a recent review essay, "the pace of book publishing has quickened in recent years."[3] In the area of political rhetoric, alone, more books have been published in the period from 1984 to the present than in the previous fourteen years combined. Several of these works constitute substantial contributions to knowledge: Kathleen Jamieson on political campaign advertising; Kathleen Turner on LBJ's relations with the press; David Zarefsky on the Great Society as a rhetorical proposition; and Robert Ivie and Ronald Hatzenbuehler on the rhetoric of war, to name only a few.[4] But the characteristics which these books share (beyond the mere fact that they are books and not articles) is a key to understanding the nature of the renaissance in both its reactive and proactive dimensions.

Reacting against the norms of the past, each of these works is explicitly scholarly in orientation, making no pretense or claim to pedagogical value. The audience for such works must necessarily then transcend the orbit of the Speech Communication Association, an organization whose membership is heavily oriented toward pedagogy. Reacting against the impulse to address one's professional colleagues and students is a necessary prelude to engaging the proactive elements. Each of these books is based on primary source materials; each is written in an easily accessible style that eschews the jargon of years past; each is published by a university press; and each is explicitly addressed to the scholarly world at large rather than to communication professionals in particular. Each, in my judgment, makes a difference to a scholarly community, an intellectual dialogue, a historical era, or the ongoing cultural conversation. None of these several types of difference-making is to be despised or devalued. Each is important in its own way.

---

[3]Robert L. Ivie, "The Complete Criticism of Political Rhetoric," *Quarterly Journal of Speech* 73 (1987): 98.

[4]Kathleen H. Jamieson, *Packaging the Presidency: A History and Criticism of Presidential Campaign Advertising* (New York: Oxford University Press, 1984); Kathleen J. Turner, *Lyndon Johnson's Dual War: Vietnam and the Press* (Chicago: University of Chicago Press, 1985); David Zarefsky, *President Johnson's War on Poverty: Rhetoric and History* (University: University of Alabama Press, 1986); Ronald L. Hatzenbuehler and Robert L. Ivie, *Congress Declares War: Rhetoric, Leadership, and Partisanship in the Early Republic* (Kent: Kent State University Press, 1983).

Even so, one noted scholar of public address recently claimed that rhetorical analysts "must be concerned insistently and exclusively with the *conceptual record*."[5] The only proper function for public address scholars, according to this view, is to contribute to the building and refining of rhetorical or communication theory. Those who hold this view worry that some of us in public address are "becoming more interested in carrying on scholarly dialogue with American historians, with cultural analysts, or with students of theology than with...colleagues in the field of speech communication." Some such scholars hold that it "is delimiting and mildly insulting to describe David Zarefsky as a Johnson scholar or Michael McGee as a Wellington scholar."[6] Why?

If our scholarship really makes a difference is it not only natural that some people trained in our field will become known for their scholarship rather than for their training? Did Donald Cross Bryant find it insulting to be called a Burke scholar? Did Eugene E. White find it delimiting to be identified with Puritanism? Did Robert Gunderson hurt himself or the field of Speech Communication by consorting with American historians or editing the *Journal of American History?* Obviously not. These scholars and others like them were known for making a difference and they made that difference in large part by writing scholarly books — books that contributed to history, cultural analysis, and yes, even theology. We need to emulate the best of the past without regard to the particular kind of knowledge that is generated. To insist only on theory-based or theory-generative studies is to be playing Cardinal Barberini in the age of Galileo.

II

But continuing our sustained, book-length analyses is only the first step. If our renaissance is to occupy a place within the intellectual landscape, then a trend apparent in our journals must also continue: the contribution to historical revisionism. Whether it is Craig R. Smith revising our understanding of Webster's July 17th Address, Robert L. Ivie revising our view of cold war

---

[5]Roderick P. Hart, "Contemporary Scholarship in Public Address: A Research Editorial," *Western Journal of Speech Communication 50 (1986):* 284.
[6]Hart, 284.

idealism, or my own studies of Eisenhower's "Atoms for Peace" speech, in each case historical understanding is revised in ways that contribute to historical accuracy, the assessment of motives or the situated conceptualization of rhetorical artistry.[7]

If it is the case that such studies do not easily generalize to other speakers, speeches, or situations—if it is the case that they can be used neither to control nor to predict rhetorical behaviors and that their primary contributions arise, therefore, from their radical situatedness—then perhaps it is a mistake to insist on "the search for over-arching explanations of how public communication functions."[8] Perhaps it is the case that the explanation that accounts broadly for everything, accounts specifically for nothing. If that is so, then we advance our renaissance not by further generalization, but by narrower specialization.

One of the reasons that our scholarship has failed, to date, to make a difference is precisely because we have focused on general principles rather than specific applications. It is now time to take what we know (which is substantial) and apply it to problems, situations, texts, and artifacts that can be more fully understood, appreciated, interpreted, analyzed, or explained through application of rhetorical methodologies. In so doing, we shall often be playing the role of revisionists, a role that is both honest and honorable.

The revisionist operates by revealing that which is hidden, challenging that which is established, and questioning the interpretive paradigms that function as terministic screens in the ongoing search for truth. All three functions are demonstrated by the Smith, Medhurst, and Ivie essays.

Smith challenges established views when he argues that "analysis of [Webster's July 17, 1850] text and a careful reading of Webster's memos and letters of the time corrects a misconception advanced by historians such as David Potter, namely that Stephen

---

[7]Craig R. Smith, "Daniel Webster's July 17th Address: A Mediating Influence in the 1850 Compromise," *Quarterly Journal of Speech* 71 (1985): 349-261; Robert L. Ivie, "Metaphor and the Rhetorical Invention of Cold War 'Idealists'," *Communication Monographs* 54 (1987): 165-182; Martin J. Medhurst, "Eisenhower's 'Atoms for Peace' Speech: A Case Study in the Strategic Use of Language," *Communication Monographs* 54 (1987): 204-220; Martin J. Medhurst, "Rhetorical Dimensions in Eisenhower's 'Atoms for Peace' Campaign," a paper presented at the 1988 annual convention of the Western Speech Communication Association Convention, San Diego, California.

[8]Hart, 285.

Douglas was the real hero of the legislative struggle because he conceived of the idea of breaking Clay's omnibus bill into separate pieces of legislation. The fact is that Webster proposed that strategy in his July 17 speech and interrupted his speech to make sure that Douglas knew how that strategy would work." Smith concludes that "Webster's speech, his memos to Douglas, and the message he wrote for Fillmore give weight to the thesis that Webster was much more the innovator of strategy at this point in the proceedings than was Douglas."[9]

Medhurst questions an interpretive paradigm with respect to Eisenhower's 1953 "Atoms for Peace" speech. Both the speech itself and the public relations effort built around it located the interpretive framework in the realm of disarmament talks. By examining the speech and its aftermath through the terministic screen of "disarmament," scholars have generally viewed Eisenhower's atomic plan as a well meaning but wholly idealistic and ultimately unsuccessful step toward reduction of nuclear weapons. But by shifting the interpretive paradigm from "disarmament" to "propaganda," I tried to show how the speech accomplished three pragmatic goals with three distinct audiences. What has long been viewed as a disarmament failure can now be seen as a cold war, propaganda victory.[10] Changing the interpretive paradigm changes our understanding, both of rhetoric and of history.

Ivie reveals a heretofore hidden or unrealized set of motives in his study of metaphor and invention in cold war idealists, motives that would allow transcendence of both realist and idealist images of savagery. Ivie suggests the existence of a "replacement metaphor," one that would "take into account the evidence that both parties are rational and irrational, aggressive and pacific, competitive and cooperative, independent and interdependent."[11] In so doing, Ivie functions as the doctor of culture, envisioning a rhetoric that "seeks to perfect men by showing them better versions of themselves."[12] By revealing that which was previously hidden or unrealized, Ivie revises our vision of self and other and in so doing demonstrates the

[9]Smith, 349, 355-356.
[10]Medhurst, "Eisenhower's 'Atoms for Peace' Speech," 205.
[11]Ivie, "Metaphor and Rhetorical Invention," 180.
[12]Richard M. Weaver, *The Ethics of Rhetoric* (Davis, CA: Hermagoras Press, 1983), 25.

conceptual, world-creating power of rhetorical analysis.

Historical revisionism is an important trend precisely because it does make our scholarship significant. We are able to teach something to the scholarly world at large and that teaching function, as Edwin Black noted in 1965, is no small part of public address scholarship.[13] But because our journals are not standard reading for other scholars, it is crucial that we share our revisionism in the form of sustained, book-length analyses. It is an encouraging sign that many article writers, including the three I have used to illustrate my argument, are now producing such articles as preludes to larger, book-length projects. Thus one trend is literally growing out of the other — and that's all to the good. But there's a third trend that has also contributed to the renewal in public address: the close study of rhetorical texts.

III

It is important to recognize the intimate connections among close textual study, historical revisionism, and the production of book-length manuscripts. Interest in the functioning of texts is the *sine qua non* of making a difference, for it is in the explication of the rhetorical dynamics of the text that public address scholars are (or ought to be) most expert. And make no mistake about it, textual analysis that makes a difference does require expertise. Michael Leff writes, for example, about "the formidable number of elements involved in the enterpise: the close reading and rereading of the text, the analysis of the historical and biographical circumstances that generate and frame its composition, the recognition of basic conceptions that establish the co-ordinates of the text, and an appreciation of the way these conceptions interact within the text and help determine its temporal movement."[14] It is clear that textual analysis, like criticism generally, is "not an enterprise for triflers."[15]

The first step in pushing close textual analysis to the forefront of

---

[13]Edwin Black, *Rhetorical Criticism: A Study in Method* (New York: Macmillan, 1965), 6.

[14]Michael C. Leff, "Textual Criticism: The Legacy of G.P. Mohrmann," *Quarterly Journal of Speech* 72 (1986): 380.

[15]Edwin Black, "A Note on Theory and Practice in Rhetorical Criticism," *Western Journal of Speech Communication* 44 (1980): 336.

the agenda is to state unequivocally to ourselves, our colleagues, and our students that close examination of a text—speech, film, TV program, poem, novel, editorial, or other instance of symbolic inducement—is both intellectually respectable and potentially productive of various sorts of critical knowledge.[16] To those who cling to the notion that "enhancing the growth of rhetorical theory" is the *"raison d'etre"* of critical studies,[17] we must propose an enlarged vision of the scholarly world.

Not too long ago, a reader for *Quarterly Journal of Speech* sent me a critique: "Though masterfully written and professionally crafted, this essay amounts to little more than a commentary on a single speech. The speech seems to have been chosen because it was politically, historically, and journalistically important.... [But] there isn't a shred of newsworthy theoretical commentary here, no new conceptual problem being addressed, no hypotheses about rhetorical behavior being tested."[18] It is my view that when such a narrow standard of scholarly contribution and intellectual importance is employed, we must insist on an enlarged point of view.

But merely insisting is not enough. We must demonstrate by our critical practices the worth of sustained, textual analysis. An informal survey of the *Quarterly Journal of Speech* and *Communication Monographs* from 1980 to the present reveals a startling fact: We still produce very few close readings of texts. Indeed, if one eliminates the studies of individual filmic or televisual texts and examines only oratory and argumentative or didactic prose, one is hard pressed to identify more than twelve or thirteen textual analyses. In other words, we have produced an average of less than two close readings per year in our leading intellectual organs. Michael Leff and Stephen Lucas have provided brilliant theoretical

---

[16]See, for example, Richard B. Gregg, "The Criticism of Symbolic Inducement: A Critical-Theoretical Connection," in *Speech Communication in the 20th Century,* ed. Thomas W. Benson (Carbondale: Southern Illinois University Press, 1985), 41-62.

[17]The language is found in Lucas, but the sentiment comes from Samuel L. Becker, "Rhetorical Studies for the Contemporary World," in *The Prospect of Rhetoric,* ed. Lloyd F. Bitzer and Edwin Black (Englewood Cliffs: Prentice-Hall, 1971), 21-43. Becker says: "A major concern for every contemporary rhetorical theorist or public address scholar is to be confident that his work is contributing to the development of systems and theories." (22)

[18]Blind review. Copy in author's possession.

rationales for such studies,[19] and each has produced cogently argued close readings,[20] but one or two scholars does not a renaissance make. Neither does ten or twelve. If we really believe in close reading of texts, we must teach it, write it, and publish it. Most importantly, we must demonstrate its significance — historically, critically, conceptually, methodologically — to the scholarly world at large. We must show through our practice how we are making a difference and how that difference contributes to the ongoing scholarly dialogue.

To accomplish this goal, we need to bring to our analyses some of the insights, techniques, and, if appropriate, the terminologies of other, related fields. Does anyone doubt, for example, that the processes of language and cognition as described in the work of Richard B. Gregg hold promise for rhetorical analysts?[21] Does anyone doubt that the strategies of reading advanced by some of our literary friends may prove useful in the close reading of oratorical texts?[22] Does anyone doubt that ethnographic methods can be employed with profit by critics of oratory?[23] These insights and others, along with more traditional approaches based in metaphor, argument, style, or structure are the necessary correlates of advancing the art of close textual reading.

[19]Leff, "Textual Criticism;" Stephen E. Lucas, "The Schism in Rhetorical Scholarship," *Quarterly Journal of Speech* 67 (1981): 1-20.

[20]Stephen E. Lucas, "Justifying America: The Declaration of Independence as a Rhetorical Document," in *American Rhetoric: Context and Criticism,* ed. Thomas W. Benson (Carbondale: Southern Illinois University Press, 1989); Michael C. Leff and G.P. Mohrmann, "Lincoln at Cooper Union: A Rhetorical Analysis of the Text," *Quarterly Journal of Speech* 60 (1974): 346-358.

[21]Richard B. Gregg, *Symbolic Inducement and Knowing: A Study in the Foundations of Rhetoric* (Columbia: University of South Carolina Press, 1984).

[22]See, for example, Jane P. Tompkins, ed., *Reader-Response Criticism: From Formalism to Post-Structuralism* (Baltimore: Johns Hopkins University Press, 1980); Harold Bloom, et. al., *Deconstruction & Criticism* (New York: Continuum, 1979); Dilip Parameshwar Gaonkar, "Deconstruction and Rhetorical Analysis: The Case of Paul deMan," *Quarterly Journal of Speech* 73 (1987): 482-498.

[23]See Gerry Philipsen, "Mayor Daley's Council Speech: A Cultural Analysis," *Quarterly Journal of Speech* 72 (1986): 247-260.

IV

Finally, if the rhetorical renaissance is to be realized, we must both promote and study public address as a cultural force that shaped and continues to shape the American experiment. We must learn to articulate, on a sustained basis, the intellectual and cultural rationale for studying American oratory as Robert T. Oliver has recently articulated the case for public speaking as a culture-creating force in Great Britain.[24]

Given the great opportunities that are available in rhetorical-cultural studies, it is nothing short of appalling how few scholars of public address have sought to make the link between America's oratorical tradition and its cultural, educational, religious, political, civic, and economic heritage. In the 1980s, only three such studies stand out—and two of those were written by scholars trained outside of the speech communication field. I refer to Frederick Antczak's *Thought and Character: The Rhetoric of Democratic Education* (1985), Paul Erickson's *Reagan Speaks: The Making of An American Myth* (1985), and, most centrally, Ernest G. Bormann's *The Force of Fantasy: Restoring the American Dream* (1985). These works are about the place of oratory in society—oratory as a force that shaped American character, society, and social institutions. All are works of cultural, intellectual, and rhetorical history. All are published by university presses. All tell the scholarly world at large of the centrality of rhetorical discourse to the nature of American society, past and present. All bear eloquent testimony to the intellectual significance of public address as a liberal art. Here is an opportunity truly to make a difference and to advance the intellectual standing of the field at the same time. But time is short.

Other scholars have discovered the intellectual tradition of rhetorical studies and have begun to tell its story to the world at large. It should be a matter of some concern that most rhetorical-cultural history being written today is not being written by rhetoricians or people trained in public address. Consider these titles: *Rhetoric and History in Revolutionary New England* (1988); *The Art of Prophesying: New England Sermons and the Shaping of Belief*

---

[24]Robert T. Oliver, *Public Speaking in the Reshaping of Great Britain* (Newark: University of Delaware Press, 1987).

(1987); *The New England Soul: Preaching and Religious Culture in Colonial New England* (1986); *The Rhetorical Presidency* (1987); *Rhetoric and American Statesmanship* (1985).

These are precisely the sorts of studies that public address scholars could and should be writing. They are studies that contribute to a social, cultural, and historical understanding of the American experiment. They are broadly informed, aimed at articulating general truths to a broad-based, scholarly audience. They are the sorts of studies that our better graduates are perfectly capable of undertaking, yet so few do.

One might reasonably assume that if, in fact, we are in the midst of a true renaissance that there should be signs of renewal and reinvigoration at all levels. Lucas rightly points to some such signs—the Duffy/Ryan anthologies and forthcoming book series are, indeed, hopeful signs.[25] So, too, is the recent publication of Ronald F. Reid's *Three Centuries of American Rhetorical Discourse* (1988) and the appearance of the sixth edition of Johannesen, Allen, and Linkugel's *Contemporary American Speeches* (1988). Conferences such as the Wisconsin Symposium on Public Address are also signs—in all likelihood positive ones. But there are also some disturbing indicators on the horizon.

Not only do scholars in speech communication produce very little close textual analysis; and not only is most cultural-rhetorical history written by non-public address scholars, but an informal survey of our most recent dissertations—three hundred and fifty-six of them from mid-1986 to mid-1988—shows no trend whatsoever toward publication of future books, significant historical revisionism, close textual analysis, or contribution to the culture-creating role of public speech. Indeed, reading through the titles and brief descriptions gives, I would suggest, very little basis for optimism about the long-term future.

The commitment to close textual analysis—the movement I take to be at the heart of whatever renaissance may be in the offing—was represented in exactly one dissertation project during this

[25]See Bernard K. Duffy and Halford R. Ryan, eds., *American Orators Before 1900: Critical Studies and Sources* (Westport, CT: Greenwood Press, 1987); Bernard K. Duffy and Halford R. Ryan, eds., *American Orators of the Twentieth Century: Critical Studies and Sources* (Westport, CT: Greenwood Press, 1987).

period. By a generous count, one could add another fifteen to twenty that involved some attention to text, though not as the dominant focus. Even this liberal count, however, places textual study in the field of speech communication, as measured by dissertations completed, at only 5% of the whole. It is a fact that at the dissertation level, we are still a field dominated by pedagogical concerns, applied communication problems, metatheoretical explorations, and, of course, the various forms of social scientific study of communication.

CONCLUSION

The field of public address may, indeed, be on the verge of a renaissance, but if it is—if the renaissance is to come to fruition within the next decade—the four trends that I have identified must continue to grow. In addition, several other avenues, not much in evidence at present, need to be pursued with vigor. Let me touch briefly on some of the areas that I believe to be ripe for expansion.

First, we need to encourage more cross-fertilization between public address scholars and those in other fields. The Ivie/Hatzenbeuhler collaboration is a good model, but clearly not the only possible model. The point is that we must expand our reach beyond scholars of speech and rhetoric, and one way to do that is to engage in joint projects with people in history, political science, sociology, English, literature, anthropology, American studies, or with whomever else takes seriously the investigation of symbolic inducement. By doing so, we will increase the visibility of public address within the university structure and help to promote its acceptance and value in the academy at large.

Second, we need to take seriously the observations of Mohrmann and Lucas about the lack of a corpus of critical masterpieces. It has now been over thirty years since the final volume of *A History and Criticism of American Public Address* (1955) was published. It is time for a nationwide project to produce one or more volumes of criticism of universally recognized oratorical masterpieces. We have identified the problem; now it is time to work on the solution.

Third, there is a whole genre of oratorical communication that has been relatively untouched by rhetorical scholarship but which, in my judgment, constitutes the ideal unit of analysis for rhetorical and public address criticism. I refer to the persuasive public campaign. Michael Hogan has recently completed his *The Panama Canal in American Politics* (1986), a study that represents the type of work to which I refer. Christine Oravec has completed several articles on the conservation campaigns of the early twentieth century,[26] but where are the rhetorical studies of the Red Scare, Ban the Bomb, Civil Defense, War Bonds, Anti-Litter, and a host of other instances of intentionally structured public symbolic inducement? Herein lies a great opportunity for scholarship that makes a difference.

Fourth, contrary to popular opinion, we still need full-length rhetorical biographies, biographies that are built around the communicative abilities, strategies, and weaknesses of public figures. William Underhill's study of *The Truman Persuasions* (1981) is a good example as is Randall Bytwerk's *Julius Streicher: The Man Who Persuaded a Nation to Hate Jews* (1983). More recently, Martha Solomon has completed a study of *Emma Goldman* (1987) and Halford Ross Ryan has investigated *Franklin D. Roosevelt's Rhetorical Presidency* (1988), but four books in nearly ten years does not a renaissance make. We need good rhetorical biographies that illustrate the power of oratory to shape mind, self, and society.

Fifth, we need to recapture the truth that significant oratory does occur outside of the political realm. Important as political oratory is, there is also importance and signficance to rhetors such as Lee Iacocca, Donald Trump, Desmund Tutu, William Bennett, Ernest Boyer, Billy Graham, and yes, even Bruce Springsteen.[27] To the extent that we limit our interests to political topics and figures alone, to that extent will we always be subservient to the tyrannizing image of the age and to the academic supplicants who worship in the name of that image.

Finally, we need more studies of matters textual. Over the years there has been an on again/off again relationship between public

---

[26]Christine Oravec, "John Muir, Yosemite, and the Sublime Response: A Study in the Rhetoric of Preservationism," *Quarterly Journal of Speech* 67 (1981): 245-258; Christine Oravec, "Conservationism vs. Preservationism: The 'Public Interest' in the Hetch Hetchy Controversy," *Quarterly Journal of Speech* 70 (1984): 444-458.

[27]See, for example, Michael McGuire, "'Darkness on the Edge of Town': Bruce Springsteen's Rhetoric of Darkness and Despair," in *Rhetorical Dimensions in Media: A Critical Casebook,* ed. Martin J. Medhurst and Thomas W. Benson (Dubuque: Kendall/Hunt, 1986), 233-250.

address scholarship and textual studies. Over the course of the 1980s, the relationship has been mostly off. With the notable exception of Halford Ross Ryan's study of the evolution of FDR's Fourth Inaugural Address, and my own rather attenuated look at the eleven drafts of Eisenhower's "Atoms for Peace" speech, there seemingly has been little interest in the processes by which texts come into existence.[28] It seems to me to be an area in need of attention and one well worth the investment of scholarly time and energy.

Rhetoric and public address scholars can make a difference in the academic world at large. To do so, however, we must reclaim our inheritance, expand our horizons, modify our theologies, and revive the intimate relationship between thought and action. It is interesting to speculate about a possible rebirth; it will be more interesting to help make it a reality, to witness the day when the parts, having been named,[29] come together to form a significant whole, a whole that bears testimony to the import, power, and passion of public address. By focusing our efforts on sustained, book-length analyses, historical revisionisms, close textual reading, and the culture-creating role of rhetoric, we will produce the significant scholarship that characterizes a true renaissance.

---

[28]Halford Ross Ryan, "Roosevelt's Fourth Inaugural Address: A Study of Its Composition," *Quarterly Journal of Speech* 67 (1981): 157-166; Martin J. Medhurst, "Ghostwritten Speeches: Ethics Isn't the Only Lesson," *Communication Education* 36 (1987): 241-249.

[29]Mohrmann, "Elegy," 273-274.

PUBLIC ADDRESS AND RHETORICAL THEORY

JAMES ARNT AUNE

In preparing my paper, I came across these lines from Robert Frost's poem, "The Black Cottage." They seemed to illustrate the mood of this subject as we tentatively celebrate the resurrection of public address studies:

For dear me, why abandon a belief
Merely because it ceases to be true?
Cling to it long enough, and not a doubt
It will turn true again, for so it goes.
Most of the change we think we see in life
Is due to truths being in and out of favor.
As I sit here, and oftentimes, I wish
I could be monarch of a desert land
I could devote and dedicate forever
To the truths we keep coming back and back to.[1]

For rhetoricians, the truth we keep coming back and back to is that, regardless of our post-sixties adventures into theory and therapy, a certain kind of performance most compels our attention and even our love, from the sublimity of Burke's "On Conciliation" to the campy chicanery of Nixon's "Checkers Speech." If the mood, then, is one of celebration of a truth which has "come around again," it is also a mood of pragmatic humility: let us abandon the quest for a modern (or, even, post-modern) theory of rhetoric and instead concentrate on case studies, close readings, "middle-range" theories, or theories of context or situation. Or, as Professor Medhurst has put it so eloquently, "Just say 'No' to theory." While I do not wish to be read as condemning the practice of close reading, I do want to point out, from the perspective of a rhetorical theorist, what seem to be under-theorized aspects of current public address study. My main concerns are these: that the turn toward case studies may be

---

[1]Robert Frost, "The Black Cottage," *The Poetry of Robert Frost* (New York: Holt, Rinehart, and Winston, 1969), 58.

accompanied by an unnecessary turn toward theory-bashing, that
an uncritical commitment to symbolic interactionism may confuse
the moral and political thrust of the study of public address, and
that a restoration of the close connection between public address
and Western political philosophy may provide a better grounding
for our work than current alternatives seem to do.

Professor Zarefsky rightly distinguishes between theory and
method and argues that one major source of the recent revival of
scholarly interest in public address is a shift from method-driven
studies to theory-driven studies. At the same time, he suggests that
wrangling about theory or method seems to get in the way of
productive scholarship. It is unclear, however, precisely what
theory means for the student of public address. In recent usage, it
can mean inquiry into any of the following things: 1. The nature
of human beings as rhetorical or symbol-using animals; 2. The
nature of rhetoric as opposed to other modes of inquiry, with an
accompanying concern for the revival of rhetoric's historic place in
the liberal arts curriculum; 3. A prescriptive guide to rhetorical
practice; 4. The generation of insights into the nature and function
of rhetorical practice from the study of concrete instances of
rhetorical judgment; 5. The history and influence of technical and
philosophical ideas about rhetorical practice; 6. The nature of
"good speech" and the nature of the regime which would best
nurture such speech. A rhetorical theorist also might seek to
evaluate knowledge-claims emerging from rhetorical criticism,
which would make theory: 7. A field-specific branch of the
philosophy of science.

My concern here is largely with function 6—the nature of
"good speech" and the "best regime" and 7—the logic of
knowledge-claims advanced by rhetorical inquiry. The decline of
prescriptive theory (except, alas, in public speaking textbooks) is a
good thing, and these studies illustrate a salutary move towards
public address documents as instances of political judgment. A
useful analogy might be to the legal concept of the "theory of the
case," which provides a framework for argument and judgment in
a given forensic context, as opposed to a general theory of
jurisprudence. One wonders, however, how an attorney can ever
exhibit adequate legal judgment without an attention to the more
abstract problems of jurisprudence. So, too, a theory of the
rhetorical case is connected inevitably with larger questions of

rhetorical and interpretive theory.

As Professor Zarefsky points out, almost all recent work in public address is committed to one or another variant of symbolic interactionism and focuses on the power of discourse to create social reality by defining public life through particular symbolic choices. It is by no means obvious, however, what symbolic interactionism might mean. There are interesting tensions and competing perspectives within symbolic interactionism itself. I want to draw out some of these tensions in the hope of clarifying how an uncritical commitment to symbolic interactionism might go wrong philosophically.

Clifford Geertz suggests that recent concern with language and symbol in the "human sciences" is part of a larger turn towards interpretive explanation, which "trains its attention on what institutions, actions, images, utterances, events, customs, all the usual objects of social-scientific interest, mean to those whose institutions, actions, customs, and so on they are."[2] He then divides recent types of symbolic interpretation into a set of competing analogies which guide their inquiry: the game analogy, the ritual analogy, the drama analogy, and the text analogy. If you view social life as a game, you are likely to focus on things like rules, strategies, the self-rewarding character of competition, and the importance of outcomes. If you view social life as a ritual, you are likely to believe that social life is organized around the "re-enactment and thus the reexperiencing of known form."[3] The ritual theory is "pulled toward the affinities of theater and religion — drama as communion, the theater as stage." In contrast, if you view social life as a drama, you are more likely to trace affinities between theater and rhetoric—"drama as persuasion, the platform

[2]Clifford Geertz, "Blurred Genres: The Refiguration of Social Thought," in *Local Knowledge: Further Essays in Interpretive Anthropology* (New York: Basic Books, 1983), 22. There are other ways to tease out the instability of symbolic interactionism. For a quite different but, I think, complementary perspective, see Fred J. Kauffeld, "Rhetoric and Practical Necessity: A View from the Study of Speech Acts," in Joseph W. Wenzel, ed., *Argument and Critical Practices* (Annandale, VA: Speech Communication Association, 1987), 83-95. Kauffeld's indictment of "conventionalism" has affinities with my later indictment of "historicism" in this paper.

[3]Geertz, 28.

as stage."[4] Geertz's account of the text analogy is less satisfactory, but an enlarged version might suggest that if you view social life as a text, it is something to be decoded or translated. And, in a more radical version, the social text is to be de-constructed, its covert assumptions (often made in the service of existing power relations) laid bare.

The authors of the recent symposium on Lincoln's "Second Inaugural" in *Communication Reports* seem to illustrate these competing versions of symbolic interpretation.[5] Carpenter argues for more careful historiography in order to assess intention and evaluate strategy—suggesting a concern with the game-like quality of politics at the end of the Civil War. Carpenter sets his analysis against Ernest Bormann's characterization of the speech as having "helped rebuild and restore a sense of national community after its destruction during that conflict."[6] Aune tries to interpret the speech as a dramatic recognition scene in the long tragedy of American civil religion. Leff reads the speech in a ritual mode. Far less concerned with effect than the other critics, he shows how the speech "yields to the imperfections of the human condition, and by yielding, transcends them." Solomon, in a deconstructive mood, seeks to sever the speech from authorial intention and illustrate possibilities of aberrant decoding which reveal a text at war with itself.

Each of the four readings might reveal, on closer examination, a slightly different metaphorical characterization of the object of study. For Carpenter (and Bormann), the concern is with the speech as engine of change.[7] For Aune, the speech is a window

---

[4]Geertz. 27.

[5]See the studies in *Communication Reports* 1 (Winter 1988), 9-37: David Zarefsky, "Approaching Lincoln's Second Inaugural Address," 9-13; James Arnt Aune, "Lincoln and the American Sublime," 14-19; Ronald H. Carpenter, "In Not-So-Trivial Pursuit of Rhetorical Wedgies," 20-25; Michael Leff, "Dimensions of Temporality in Lincoln's Second Inaugural," 26-31; Martha Solomon, "With Firmness in the Right': The Creation of Moral Hegemony in Lincoln's Second Inaugural," 32-37.

[6]Ernest G. Bormann, "Fetching Good Out of Evil: A Rhetorical Use of Calamity," *Quarterly Journal of Speech,* 63 (April 1977): 139.

[7]My discussion of fundamental metaphors is influenced by Barnet Baskerville. "Must We All Be 'Rhetorical Critics'?" *Quarterly Journal of Speech,* 63 (April 1977): 113; and by Dudley Andrew, *Concepts in Film Theory* (New York: Oxford University Press, 1984), 12-13.

onto the past and, perhaps, a correcting vision for the present. For Leff, the speech is like a framed object of art appreciated within the framework of judgment and taste provided by the Western rhetorical tradition. For Solomon, the speech is a *mise en abime,* a vertiginous glimpse into the distorting mirror of ideology and textuality.

This exercise in tracing out the nuances of a recent critical controversy is intended simply to suggest that theory may have a role to play in explicating grounds of critical judgment. The difficult problem emerging from an examination of those grounds is the question of truth. Carpenter is interested in the truth of Lincoln's speech only from the standpoint of accurately assessing intention and historical effect. Aune asserts the truth of Lincoln's insight into political theology while using a method (Harold Bloom's tropology) which replaces truth with a doctrine of the inevitability of misreading. Leff concerns himself with the internal coherence of the speech's view of time, with an aim to explicating its strategy of "passive acceptance." Solomon comes closer to an evaluation of the speech's truthfulness but, like Aune, is committed to a theoretical perspective which reduces truth to the will to power.

All four critics, because they have been influenced by one or more of the varieties of symbolic interactionism, tend to focus on the speech as a strategy, suggesting an ultimate convergence with Geertz's game analogy or my engine metaphor, despite surface commitments to the other analogies or metaphors. Recent books by Ivie, Hogan, Zarefsky, and Turner reveal an obvious commitment to the notion of the public address document as a strategic move in a larger political game (despite differing degrees of theoretical self-consciousness). The problem, however, with a commitment to such a view is that it lays open problems of verification. Paradoxically, neither the Lincoln critics nor the other authors (with the possible exception of Hogan) provide much evidence about the way in which *audiences* had their perceptions of reality shaped by the documents in question. Nor do they demonstrate why rhetoric—as opposed to other, more "material," factors such as class interest—is a useful means of historical *explanation.* Moreover, they neglect *interpretation.* The traditional distinction between the sciences as providing "explanation-theory" *(Erklären)* and the humanities as providing "interpretation-theory" *(Verstehen)* seems to disappear, and as a result public address studies come to

occupy an uneasy middle-ground between Explanation and Interpretation.[8]

In order to develop a full explanation-theory, the advocates of
a game/engine view of public address need to confront directly the
advocates of a more materialist (not to be confused with economic
reductionist) view of social and political processes. They also need
to develop the resources provided by the new social history for
understanding how audiences actually respond to public address.
Bormann's work perhaps comes closest, but he seems reluctant to
address the problem of class-positioning in relation to audience
decoding or collective psychology. As Celeste Condit argued in her
review of Zarefsky's book, rhetoricians have thus far evaded the
opportunity to refute the Neo-Marxism so pervasive in the
historical profession and in the social sciences generally.[9] I wonder,
however, if rhetorical explanations will not always lose out to
more parsimonious economic explanations. An alternative is to
abandon the quest for explanation entirely (except as, say, an
explanation of the forces leading to specific strategic choices in a
speech). The recent turn to close reading, especially in Mohrmann's
and Leff's work, seems to do so. In their case (like Edwin Black's)
rhetorical criticism has an elective affinity with literary study
rather than with history or political science. I wonder, however,
what will happen when the important task of reading the canon is
complete. (Even though it hasn't been done, measured in academic
time this should not take very long.) How many speeches possess
the stylistic and conceptual richness of Cicero, Burke, Calhoun,
and Lincoln? From an aesthetic standpoint, does even the richest
speech measure up to Shakespeare or Tolstoy? It cannot, unless the
speech is viewed within the larger problematic of political
philosophy. The difference between a novel and a deliberative
oration is that the oration makes (at least a more direct) claim to
political truth. Curiously, however, a direct engagement with
political philosophy has not yet occurred in public address studies.
A symptom of this evasion is Robert Ivie's criticism of the recent

---

[8]The terms come from the German historiographer W.G. Droysen. See Roy J.
Howard, *Three Faces of Hermeneutics* (Berkeley: University of California Press, 1982),
14-17, for a useful discussion.

[9]Celeste Michelle Condit, Review of David Zarefsky, *President Johnson's War on
Poverty,* in *Quarterly Journal of Speech,* 72 (November 1986): 495-496.

collection by a group of Straussian political philosophers, *Rhetoric and American Statesmanship.* He criticizes them for subordinating rhetoric to "ideology" (a term which Straussians would avoid) and thus diverting "attention away from the rhetorical construction of ideology itself, thereby sustaining a naive conception of political motivation and inordinately reducing the circumference of the critic's domain."[10] Strauss himself effectively demolished such an argument in the first chapter of *Natural Right and History.* Ivie's argument, which I suspect would be an article of faith for almost every rhetorician in SCA, is a rhetorical version of what Strauss calls *historicism,* the doctrine that all speech, including philosophical speech, is limited to its historical world, culture, or *Weltanschauung.* A close cousin of positivism, historicism denies the possibility of timeless truths, except, that is, for the insight that all knowledge is historically (or rhetorically) determined. The paradox is, as Strauss points out, that "historicism thrives on the fact that it inconsistently exempts itself from its own verdict about all human thought."[11] My suggestion—and I think I am close here to Morhmann's reading of Calhoun and Leff's discussion of recent works on Aristotle—is that we abandon the positivist tinge of our commitment to the game-based notion of effect and strategy and that we abandon the historicist tinge of our commitment to drama and text-based symbolic interactionism, and instead view public address documents for what they really are: concrete instances of political judgment, embodiments of political philosophy.[12] Calhoun and Lincoln need to be read in our classes and in our studies more because they reveal competing political philosophies than because their speeches are more or less effective, or because they are masterpieces. The defense of reading rhetorical documents is itself

---

[10]Robert L. Ivie, "The Complete Criticism of Political Rhetoric," *Quarterly Journal of Speech,* 73 (February 1987): 100-101.

[11]Leo Strauss, *Natural Right and History* (Chicago: University of Chicago Press, 1953), 25. I am aware that citing Strauss, and especially his student Allan Bloom, may well get me into trouble with the academic left. I would simply note in passing that a thoroughgoing cultural conservatism hardly commits one to political and economic conservatism as well.

[12]See Michael Leff, "Recovering Aristotle: Rhetoric, Politics, and the Limits of Rationality," *Quarterly Journal of Speech,* 71 (August 1985): 362-373; G.P. Mohrmann, "Place and Space: Calhoun's Fatal Security," *Western Journal of Speech Communication,* 51 (Spring 1987): 143-158.

a political act which sets us apart from the positivist and historicist biases of modernity. The rhetorical tradition, at its best, is an enacted philosophy which is distinct both from sophistic relativism and post-Rousseauian liberationism. Joseph Cropsey notes that despite the very real differences among Plato, Aristotle, Cicero, Machiavelli, and Locke, all would agree that "political life rests upon the imperfection of man and continues to exist because human nature rules out the elevation of all men to the level of excellence."[13] In the utopias of modernity, all speech is fully transparent or simply playful conversation. What the new sophists of post-structuralism have in common, surprisingly, with Rousseau, Marx, and the positivists is this oddly unrealistic notion of communication. Leo Strauss was right: Socrates' arguments in the *Republic* were intended to show that the good city is attainable only in speech, an insight which commits us to a certain moderation and humility in matters political.[14] What Strauss (and his disciple, Allan Bloom) have given us from the standpoint of political philosophy, public address studies can give us from another direction. Public address studies declined in the 1960's because they could not compete with the positivist relevance of interpersonal and persuasion studies (and because they had chosen to argue on the positivist ground of effects). So, too, public address studies may decline into the historicism of "cultural studies," or "critical communication research," which, while affirming that everything is political, eliminate the possibility of rational politics by reducing speech to covert enactments of economic or patri-archal power.

I have tried, all too briefly, to describe a theoretical road not taken in public address criticism. To study public address must also mean to engage Plato, Aristotle, Hobbes, Locke, Rousseau, and — yes — Marx. The message is essentially correct: we will never have a grand theory of rhetoric. There is, however, a difference between theory and philosophy. Theory is ultimately the quest for a set of rules which ideally might guide practice. Philosophy is the inquiry

---

[13]Joseph Cropsey, "Karl Marx," in Leo Strauss and Joseph Cropsey, eds., *History of Political Philosophy,* second ed. (Chicago: Rand McNally, 1972), 777.

[14]Leo Strauss, "Plato," in Strauss and Cropsey, 7-63; see also Allan Bloom's translation and interpretive essay on the *Republic* (New York: Basic Books, 1966).

into the foundations and truths of a practice. In a time when our students are increasingly deprived of both history and philosophy —not only as courses but as resources for living—we need to think about the institutional implications of studying public address. Can we use our work to sever courses in public speaking from the agenda of the business administration major? Can we unite with William Bennett, Allan Bloom and E.D. Hirsch in the attempt to restore cultural literacy (while still pointing out their puzzlingly illiterate inattention to a central liberal arts discipline)? To return to the image from Frost with which I began this paper, the truth of our perspective, which is really the truth of the documents we study, *has* come back into favor, and we need to think about the dwelling, desert land or not, in which we house that truth.

II

SIX
CASE STUDIES

BURKE'S SPEECH ON CONCILIATION: THE PRAGMATIC BASIS OF RHETORICAL JUDGMENT

STEPHEN H. BROWNE

As is commonly the fate of Edmund Burke's art, the legacy of his *Speech on Conciliation* remains unfixed. Historians and critics unfailingly applaud the speech as a hallmark in the tradition of Western oratory, noting its wealth of imagery, its political insight, and its humanity. But aside from the uniform appreciation of its aesthetic qualities, consensus stops short of investing Burke's masterpiece with historical significance. This disjunction between rhetorical and political judgment finds its voice, ironically, in the appraisal of Burke's friend and patron, Lord Rockingham. The Marquis, after listening to Burke's address of 22 March, 1775, wrote:

> I never felt a more complete satisfaction on hearing any speech, than I did on yours this day; the matter and the manner were equally perfect, and in spite of envy and malice and in spite of all politics, I will venture to prognosticate that there will be but one opinion, in regard to the wonderful ability of the performance.[1]

Rockingham, as it turns out, was quite right: "in spite of all politics," Burke's speech has been ever since deemed an exemplary "performance." But can Burke's masterpiece ever be taken seriously as anything more than a "performance?"

If we review the verdicts of modern scholarship, the answer would seem to be no. Historians are inclined to judge the speech most harshly: while conceding its artistic achievement, they consistently have relegated the speech to the backwaters of hopeless causes and misplaced idealism. Ritcheson's study of Anglo-American politics during the age of colonial conflict, for instance, concludes: "Looking nostalgically to the past, Burke sought once more to ignore the ugly question of right, a question

---

[1]Rockingham to Burke, 22 March, 1775, *Correspondence of Edmund Burke* Thomas W. Copeland, gen. ed., (Chicago: University of Chicago Press, 1961) III, 139.

which, once raised, had made a return to the old system as
impossible as a return to childhood."[2] Whether in fact Burke was
guilty of such political nostalgia is certainly arguable; in any case,
Ritcheson's assessment is not isolated. Watson's analysis of the
reign of George III sounds the theme again by lamenting that
"Burke had, in the mysterious alchemy of his mind, turned this
practical compromise into a great living principle of a common-
wealth. He had done so, however, for the admiration of posterity
and not for use in 1775."[3] Even those traditionally more inclined
to symphathize with Burke's idealism stress its futility and
desperation. Guttridge is willing to grant Burke's appeal to be "a
noble one." But the argument was also "extremely convenient; for
the Whigs had nothing to suggest except to appeal to Time the
healer, and to leave the future to take care of itself."[4]

   The joint themes of futility and impracticality running throughout these observations are telling. Most important, they presume a
certain teleology, and judge the speech according to its failure to
achieve its alleged ends. The assumption is misleading and badly
stands in need of reexamination in the light of historical,
biographical, and textual evidence. Such evidence, we find,
supports a different understanding of the speech. Far more than a
hopeless but elegant appeal for imperial concord, the *Speech on
Conciliation* is a declaration and demonstration of Whig ideology
in its moment of crisis. I shall argue here that Burke's speech may
be understood in a more general sense as an act of exemplary
judgment. Its significance, accordingly, lies neither in its literary
qualities nor in its immediate persuasive effect (or lack thereof).
Rather, as an act of judgment, the oration instantiates Burke's
directives on political action.

---

   [2]James Ritcheson, *British Politics and the American Revolution* (Norman:
University of Oklahoma Press, 1954), 190.
   [3]J. Steven Watson, *The Reign of George III, 1760-1815* (Oxford: Clarendon Press,
1960), 201.
   [4]G.H. Guttridge, "The Whig Opposition in England During the Revolution,"
Journal of Modern History 6 (1934): 6.

I

Confronted with the fact of the proposal's overwhelming defeat, sympathetic students of Burke have located his achievement in the more rarefied realms of history, philosophy, and aesthetic appeal. There is much in the *Speech* which lends itself to this kind of analysis, but its immediate aims and context cannot be simply wished away. At its most elemental level, the *Speech* was delivered to secure Parliament's consent for Burke's conciliatory measures. It failed to do so, 70-278. Judged against a simple standard of effect, the speech must be regarded as failure. Thus Burke's oration may have been hopelessly idealistic, so the lore reads, but it was nevertheless a masterpiece of political reasoning and principle. In their effort to secure Burke's oration within the canon, his admirers have failed to appreciate its character as a public, pragmatic act. It will therefore be useful to focus upon the speech within its immediate context as a preface to formal analysis.

As a constant presence in the House debates on the colonies, Burke understood clearly the sentiments of Commons and the chances for appeasement.[5] Parliament was growing increasingly impatient with the refusal of the Americans to yield, and the Crown itself seemed intent upon breaking their rebellious spirit. Given this knowledge, Burke offered his plan of conciliation as much to display the principles of his party as to capture votes. But to do this he had to articulate those principles in the concrete terms of political deliberation. To do otherwise, in fact, would run counter to the very standards of utility and judgment which the speech announces and acts upon. Within a context of party ideology and a perceived threat to Whig principles, the speech may be seen as a composite of deliberative and epideictic conventions. As a celebration of Whig principle, the speech glories in a past sanctioned morally by human nature and the consent of the political community. But in order to reclaim that past, Burke not only had to ground party ideology in history, but also to expose Lord North's program as essentially a-historical — that is,

---

[5]Burke's relations with immediate audiences is examined in Donald C. Bryant, "The Contemporary Reception of Edmund Burke's Speeches," in *Historical Studies in Rhetoric and Rhetoricians,* ed., Raymond F. Howes (Ithaca: Cornell University Press, 1961), 271-293.

without precedent and hence without moral sanction. How Burke
achieves this end constitutes the rhetorical action and success of
the oration. Driving a wedge between his party and North's
administration, Burke locates the proper exercise of political
judgment in a stratum between abstract issues of right and
particular questions of expediency; he exposes, conversely, the
policy of the administration as the product of poor judgement:
over-rationalistic, detached, abstract, impractical. In this sense,
Burke's *Speech on Conciliation* may be deemed a success—not in
terms of final divisions, but as a political statement on the proper
grounds of political judgment.

At the same time, Burke's oration speaks to an audience more
distanced than the actors of 1775. Burke was a political thinker,
and his principles were meant to extend beyond the immediate
audiences and questions of the moment.[6] If he was not a
philosopher as such, he nevertheless explored the nature of politics
at a level higher than most, and he typically treated problems of
the state within the conventional forms of public discourse. At this
level, his audience expands to include those outside of Parliament
and, indeed, generations not yet born. In Burke's oration, as in
most of his other rhetoric, there are accordingly two audiences
being addressed: an immediate audience and a more remote
audience of ideal listeners, able by virtue of its distance to judge
with accuracy and insight. The respective appeals are not,
however, in contest or inconsistent. In keeping with his general
position—that the principles of his party represent a model of
proper political action—Burke displays to both audiences the
virtues of practical reason and prudence of action. These principles
are in turn established on the basis of experience and utility; they
are not, that is, abstract axioms or mere platitudes of statecraft. In
speaking to both audiences, Burke sought to provide a rationale
for action grounded in principle and expedience—principle as it
was generated from historical perspective, expedience as a question

---

[6]For Studies of Burke as a "philosopher in action," see Gerald W. Chapman,
Edmund Burke: The Practical Imagination (Cambridge, Mass.: Harvard University Press,
1967); John MacCunn, *The Political Philosophy of Edmund Burke* (New York: Russell
and Russell, 1965); Frank O'Gorman, *Edmund Burke: His Political Philosophy*
(Bloomington, Ind.: Indiana University Press, 1973); and Burleigh T. Wilkins, *The
Problem of Burke's Political Philosophy* (Oxford: Clarendon Press, 1967).

of propriety. So understood, this rationale offered to his audiences an exemplary standard of judgment. And in this way, Burke's oration was in fact a repudiation of his Parliamentary audience, but only in the sense that he confronted its momentary failure to exercise proper judgment. Burke appeals rather to the values and expectations of the audience in a different time, a moment in the past when it understood better than now the principles of right reason and action. Burke had therefore to reconfigure the historical understanding of his audience, and so to satisfy his "obligations to party and principle."

Within this historical and political context, we are in a position to understand Burke's *Speech on Conciliation* in a new light. The speech is not simply solicitous, and as such doomed to failure, but advisory as well. By all accounts the Rockingham Whigs were in a perilous state of disarray and *ennui.* Burke's oration was thus remedial and justificatory: it was in fact a performance, but a performance meant to illustrate the virtues of its own argument. Burke was seeking to resurrect an ideology failing badly, even as he announced and acted upon its avowed principles. The rhetorical action of the speech is therefore exemplary; and Burke, by repeatedly grounding these principles in particular historical circumstances, provides a vision of what his party may become. The speech works to create a particular kind of perspective; it asks the audience to recognize reconfigurations of the past in present circumstances, and thus to reaffirm its Whig legacy.

A careful reading of the structural and imagistic movements which control the speech bears out this alternative interpretation. The formal unity of Burke's oration is established on two levels, each reflecting the speaker's concern for the proper relationship between order and action. At one level, the speech is patterned on models of classical oratory; it thereby manifests an established order and its arguments are rationalized by relatively abstract considerations of form. At another level, however, the speech unfolds without clear divisions and without the aid of orthodox principles of structure. Here meaning is generated on the basis of certain psychological forces, made evident in the evolving structure of its appeals. In this sense, the speech may be understood as an instantiation of Burke's principle of judgment. For Burke, proper judgment involves the right ordering of rational principles and emotional warrants to action. He who would sustain a balance between these motive forces is the ideal practical politician, allowing neither sheer rationalism nor simple emotions to determine the course of political action. Hence the structures of the speech support Burke's ends: by showing himself to be rational, he endorses the role of principle in proper judgment; and by appealing to the emotionally-grounded patriotism of his audience, he complements rationalism with the power of experience and collective history.

The recognition of this structure should not, however, deflect attention from another equally important source of meaning. Burke seeks to induce a perspective ordered by experience — a perspective, that is, located in history, not outside of it. The essential action of the text cannot therefore be fully explained by the divisions and categories identified above, if only because they abstract from the particular requirements and motives of the occasion. In a very basic sense the movement of Burke's oration cannot be apprehended within classical forms. As it moves toward its end in action, the speech reflects an ever-widening perspective directing that action. Thus the enormous amount of detail which Burke provides is more than evidentiary support, conventionally understood: it represents as well a commitment to the particulars of political action. At the same time, the many axioms which characterize Burke's political perspective indicate his capacity for reasoning from principle. Together, the interplay of particular and principle direct the progress of the speech. As he moves forward, Burke employs this capacity for practical reason to order the particulars of historical experience into a rationale for action. The more his audience recognizes this history, the broader its perspective becomes, and the greater its capacity for right action. Burke must then present this history in all its variety, and yet order it as a form of moral sanction. In short, the action of the speech is cumulative, building principle upon fact and recognizing in fact the utility of principle.

More specifically, the progression of the text is directed through three phases: an ostensibly objective review of America and the facts of her condition; an argument for restoring colonial loyalty through self taxation; and a defense of the resolutions as the best course for future action. The oration advances in this way from the past through the present to the future. Each phase in turn demonstrates the proper constituents of political action, moving from fact (narration) to principle (argument) and culminating in action (resolutions). The meaning of the speech cannot then be captured within the classical form of the oration alone—it must, in addition, be identified as it progresses through these temporal and conceptual phases.

But the key to understanding the movement of the text is to see in these phases the repeated and relentless accommodation of immediate problems into a greater historical perspective. As the oration progresses, the accretion of examples works to identify Burke and his party with history itself, and to expose North and his administration as blind to its directives. The elemental action of the text is therefore a process of identification and division; it is a movement repeated throughout the oration in different contexts and different phases. But the lesson Burke would have his audience understand remains the same: right action is a function of practical reason, itself the result of historically-grounded judgment.

The oratorical genre serves Burke's purposes well. It had long been employed by opposition members as a means to challenge with relative freedom the policies of those in power, and had developed certain conventional traits of character and idiom. As an oral form the oration allowed for a degree of spontaneity not so easily produced in the political essay. Its adaptability to the moment, however, often meant that its effect was fleeting, especially in an era of limited parliamentary reporting. As a result, those who wished to have their sentiments recorded were compelled to print speeches in pamphlet form and have them distributed to area booksellers. The *Speech on Conciliation* was in this way offered to a greater and more distant public than could be found within Commons. Such a practice also helps to explain the speech's elevated tone and philosophic appeal. In Burke's hands, moreover, the oration represents an ideal rhetorical form, insofar as it is fixed by historical convention and is, at the same time, a response to immediate public issues. The form of the oration thus instantiates the very play of fixity and flux which shapes the *Speech on Conciliation*. This can best be seen by an analysis of the seven parts of the speech.

II

Introduction

The opening of the speech is at first glance unsurprising and seems to provide only a conventional access to the argument. As one of "many examples in the speech of humility assumed for the sake of oratorical effect," this facet of the Burke's oration is typically ignored.[7] If commented upon at all, it is seen as simply fulfilling a generic expectation. There would be some loss to the reader, however, in hurrying over the introduction, for here we find a precis of the speech as a whole. What appears to be a passing reference to the past, for example, can be taken as a telling account of circumstances leading up to the speech; and what may pass for affected humility may be viewed as an ironic assertion of character. This alignment of character and circumstances defines the rhetorical movement of the introduction, and so anticipates the tensive quality of the entire speech. In particular, Burke foreshadows what will become the major issue in this battle between the ancients and the moderns: the fixity which historical perspective brings to the flux of experience.

Burke's avowed surprise at the return of North's bill is tempered by a religious sensibility which sees in it an "omen," a "providential favor," possibly a "superior warning voice." Whatever its source, the return of the bill functions rhetorically as a synechdoche in the speech, as a moment in which the past, seemingly lost, is recalled to the present. As such, it provides a renewed opportunity to act, and, Burke says, "we are put once more in position of our deliberative capacity, upon a business so very questionable in its nature, so very uncertain in its issue." Against this uncertainty Burke counsels attention to "the whole of it together; and to review the subject with an unusual degree of care and calmness."[8] Though brief, the first paragraph suggests an intense concern for temporal relationships and indicates the

---

[7] Daniel V. Thompson, ed., *Burke's Speech on Conciliation with America* (New York: Henry Holt, 1923), 87.

[8] Burke, "Speech on Moving Resolutions for Conciliation With America," in *The Works of Edmund Burke* (Boston: Little, Brown, 1884), II, 101-102. All references to the speech come from this edition and hereafter are indicated parenthetically within the text.

grounds of proper judgment at the moment when past meets present.

As Burke recounts his role in the repeal of the Stamp Tax nine years earlier, his character accrues the benefits of past action, and we begin to witness the beginnings of a long process of character construction. Burke, newly elected to Commons, had then found himself "a partaker in a very high trust," and lacking natural talent, was "obliged to take more than common pains" to instruct himself on American affairs (p. 102). As a result of this self-education, Burke had developed some "fixed ideas concerning the general policy of the British Empire." "Something of this sort seemed to me indispensable," Burke concludes, "in order, amidst so vast a fluctuation of passion and opinions, to concentre my thoughts, to ballast my conduct, to preserve me from being blown about by every fashionable doctrine. I really did not think it safe or manly to have fresh principles to keep upon every fresh mail which should arrive from America" (p. 102). The nautical metaphor, a favorite resource of Burke's, here suggests a standard of judgment and action. Fixed by principle and steadied by his knowledge of American affairs, Burke was then able to act consistently and honorably while others yielded to the sirens of innovation and experiment. The metaphor, of course, has its quite literal reference, in that England and America are indeed separated by a vast and fluctuating ocean. It is a reality Burke will exploit with great effect later in the speech. The aim now is to set the speaker's past action in contrast to that of Parliament's and while Burke refrains from any direct indictment, the difference is clear enough. The following paragraphs thus recount the respective careers of Burke and of Commons since the repeal of the Stamp Tax.

The current state of affairs, we learn, is not the result of the Rockingham policy of conciliation, but of departing from that policy and from the principles which guided the administration generally. Distinguishing himself from the waffling and ineffective action of Commons, Burke says, "I have continued ever since, without the least deviation, in my original sentiments. Whether this be owing to an obstinate perseverance in error, or to a religious adherence to what appears to me truth and reason, it is in equity to judge" (p. 103). In the years since repeal, Parliament had made "more frequent changes in their sentiments and their conduct than could be justified in a particular person" (p. 103). Parliament's

failure, in short, was not in the past as such, but in its ability to
sustain that past. And so, Burke concludes, "by a variety of
experiments that important country has been brought to her
present situation—a situation which I will not miscall, which I
dare not name, which I scarcely know how to comprehend in the
terms of any description" (p. 103).

Far from being a posture of humility, then, the introduction
coordinates circumstances and character in such a manner as to
make the speaker a virtual embodiment of past virtue. The brief
narration, making up the first eight paragraphs, unfolds to reveal
the past as a rationale for action in the present; and even as the
introduction appears to diminish the achievements of the speaker,
it dramatizes the need for his leadership. The posture, moreover,
works to identify the proposition not so much with its author as
with forces more fixed and powerful than mere human agency.
Burke's maneuver thus grants to Commons the opportunity to
judge without embarrassment:

> I persuaded myself that you would not reject a reasonable
> proposition, because it had nothing but reason to recommend it.
> On the other hand, being totally destitute of all shadow of
> influence, natural or adventitious, I was very sure that if my
> proposition were futile or dangerous, if it were weakly conceived
> or improperly timed, there was nothing exterior to it, of power
> to awe, dazzle, or delude you. You will see it just as it is, and
> you will treat it just as it deserves (p. 105).

In this way, Burke sets up a key relationship between objective
fact and political judgment which informs the speech generally; he
will later indict North for his inability to see in the American
situation objective constraints on policy. At the same time, Burke
will attempt to demonstrate his own capacity to derive principles
of political action from material circumstances.

Thesis

"The proposition is peace." Burke's thesis could not be more
blunt: it follows no apparent transition and precedes a lengthy and
complex series of negative clauses. Its rhetorical effect, however, is
dramatic. Syntactically it mimics the oppositions Burke seeks to
establish, which in turn become the structural principles of the
speech. Action rooted in historical understanding is distinguished

by its natural simplicity; conduct initiated without precedent, without historical understanding, is marked by an artificial complexity and confusion. The following negative clauses thus become a bill of particulars against North's administration, and more generally against its very manner of reasoning. "The proposition is peace," Burke states, but not peace "through the medium of war; not peace to be hunted through the labyrinth of intricate and endless negotiations; not peace to arise out of universal discord fomented from principle in all parts of the empire; not peace to depend on the judicial determination of perplexing questions, or the peace marking the shadowy boundaries of a complex peace." Rather, Burke says, "it is simple peace, sought in its natural course, and its ordinary haunts" (pp. 105-6). As it is framed above by short, propositional statements, so the indictment is framed below. The false peace of North's plan is labyrinthine, intricate, endless, perplexing, shadowy, complex; Burke's is simple, natural, ordinary. Only a bill predicated on proven principles and historical perspective can return the past to the present, can, Burke concludes, restore the "former unsuspecting confidence of the colonies in the mother country" (p. 106).

As simple and ordinary as Burke's proposition avowedly may be, its appeal is grounded in principle. The maxims which begin paragraph ten indicate Burke's tendency to generalize from the particular, exercise the principle, and to thereby add force to his arguments as he returns again to particular issues. This interplay between the general and the particular informs the action of the later narration, but for now it works to further distance Burke's bill from North's. "Refined policy," Burke claims, "ever has been the parent of confusion." He would substitute instead "plain good intention," and a "genuine simplicity of heart." But precisely because, by his own admission, there is "nothing at all new and captivating" in Burke's proposal—because it has "nothing of the splendor of the project" of North's—the proposition commands assent. Unlike his own, North's project depends upon a "mode that is altogether new,—one that is, indeed, wholly alien from all the ancient methods and forms of Parliament" (pp. 107-8).

What those "ancient methods and forms of Parliament" are we come to understand as the speech progresses. As Burke undertakes and develops each phase we see that he is not only appealing to history as a form of proof, but that he is enacting it,

that the speech is a moment in the history it narrates. That
narrative itself is a lesson on how to read the past, and as the
audience follows the narrative movement of the text, it is induced
to assent to a vision of past which the orator both constructs and
embodies in his own discourse.

Narration

Burke's review of the Americans is throughout detailed,
systematic, and factual. But while he locates the problem in
phenomenal reality, Burke is careful to avoid mere litigiousness.
The narrative, rather, brings to light the meaning of material
circumstances. Facts provide the basis for judgment, and judgment
in turn orders the meaning of facts. The narrative thereby frames a
constant interplay between concrete reality and its interpretation.
As a result of this interplay the narrative generates an habitual
perspective in which the past is made proximic to the present. As
such, the past is exemplary and is embodied in one who exercises
its lessons.

Between the past and the present are forces which, if
recognized, give presence to history. The impetus of the past is
most evident in the imagery which dominates the narrative —
fecundity, familial attractions, and the inevitable progression of
events. In every case, the past is not simply an option. Whatever
the judgment which attends it, the past will unfailingly make itself
present. Such, for example, is the problem of America's burgeoning
population. While the House of Commons interminably debates
policy for a government of two million people, the number grows
at a formidable rate. In fact, Burke warns "your children do not
grow faster from infancy to manhood, than they spread from
families to communities, and from villages to nations." Given this
state of affairs, Burke is adamant to adjust our response to it. With
a thinly disguised attack on North's bill, Burke argues that "no
partial, narrow, contracted, pinched, occasional system will be at
all suitable to such an object." The failure of North's policy has
been exactly this — that it had failed to act according to observable
realities, had failed to understand the history of its own problem.
This being the case, the colonial problem had become greater than
the ministry's ability to handle it. North's government had lacked
perspective, and, unable to understand America's strength, had

trifled with it. However, Burke concludes, "you could at no time do so without guilt; and be assured you will not be able to do it long with impunity" (p. 110).

Nowhere in the speech is this sense of historical perspective so dramatically portrayed as in Burke's account of colonial commerce. After a relatively detailed review of Anglo-American trade, Burke slows the pace of the narrative, reflects upon the immediate occasion, and directs a contemplative gaze toward America. "It is good for us to be here," Burke explains "We stand where we have an immense view of what is, and what is past." This perspective has been required by the demands of the moment, but it reveals much: "Clouds, indeed, and darkness rest upon the future" (p. 114). The sublimity of the image intensifies as the passage develops; here it is notable for its temporal referent. Sublimity of experience is ultimately an expansion of one's capacity for experience, and it is this capacity Burke exercises as he surveys the Americans. To enhance that prospect, Burke takes his audience upon an unmistakably Virgilian journey.

Marvelling at the rapidity of English commercial growth, Burke employs the figure of one Lord Bathurst, whose life would have framed this development. At its beginning, Burke notes Bathurst would have been old enough "acta parentum jam legere, et quae sit poterit cognoscere virtus" (p. 114). Though misquoted, the allusion is telling, and portends a number of similar references. Burke sees in this particular scenario an opportunity to dramatize his general argument—that we must "study the example of the forefathers, to learn what virtue is." The Virgilian maxim thus directs our attention to the proximity of its moral claim, and shows Burke excavating texts of venerable wisdom. Developing the argument further, Burke asks us to suppose that "the angel of this auspicious youth [Bathurst]" had "drawn up the curtain and unfolded the rising glories of his country, and, whilst he was gazing with admiration to the then commercial grandeur of England, the genius should point out to him a little speck, scarcely visible in the mass of national interest, a small seminal principle rather than a formal body, and should tell him,—'Young man, there is America.'" It would take "all the sanguine credulity of youth," Burke continues, for Bathurst to believe that one day America would "show itself equal to the whole of that commerce which now attracts the envy of the world." In fact, Bathurst had lived to see the portentous growth of America, and Burke concludes, he would be "fortunate indeed if he lives to see nothing that shall vary the prospect and cloud the setting of his day" (pp. 114-115).[9]

There is no mistaking the occular imagery here: the passage is replete with references to "views," "vision," "foreseeing," "seeing," "scenes," "gazing," and "prospects." The aim is to portray the colonial problem in a particular fashion and to encourage a specific approach to its resolution. If the ministry could see with Burke's eyes, it would discover the problem to be located not in America, but in the English policy. Again, the insistent empiricism which marks so much of the speech here provides a standard for judgment. The perspective which Burke would have his audience assume, moreover, the historical sweep of circumstance. Unlike North's "contracted" vision, Burke's can discern the true nature of America's past. Only this expansive vision could finally recognize that "Whatever England has been growing into by a progressive increase of improvement, brought in by varieties of people, by a succession of civilizing conquests, and civilizing settlements in a series of seventeen hundred years, you shall see as much added to her by America in the course of a single life" (p. 115).

As if to focus the perspective he would induce, Burke insists upon unveiling the particular features and details of the colonial problem. Though perhaps taxing, the strategy is deliberate: Burke is relentless, because "generalities, which in all other cases are apt to heighten and raise the subject, have here a tendency to sink it. When we speak of commerce with our colonies, fiction lags behind truth, invention is unfruitful, and imagination cold and barren" (pp. 115-116). By implication, Burke's opponents, enamored as they are of "abstract ideas" and "general theories," are blind to the realities of the situation. The blindness prohibits the ministry from seeing a fundamental shift in the nature of Anglo-American relations. Attention to actual circumstances would have allowed the ministry to see what colonial wealth meant. Now, the commonplace image of parent child relations reverses its own terms. Once descriptive of English primacy, the familial metaphor has, in the face of material conditions, yielded to a greater reality. "For some time past," Burke explains, "the old world has been fed

---

[9] Virgil, *Fourth Ecologue.*

from the new. The scarcity which you have felt would have been a desolating famine, if this child of your old age, with a true filial piety, with a Roman charity, had not put the full breast of its youthful exuberance to the mouth of its exhausted parent" (p. 116). In addition to its striking reversal of a conventional image, the passage is important for its appeal to the Cymon and Xanthippe legend. Like Cymon, England had become virtually dependent upon its own child, and so can no longer act as she once did. This is a lesson generated from observation, not theory, and illustrated with recourse to an ancient legend. Once again, Burke has reconstituted from the past a rationale for judgment and action in the present.

Fixed within this exemplary perspective, Burke is able to better understand the prospects before him. He can, that is, articulate in principle his objection to specific proposals. These proposals are met with a series of maxims, but maxims rooted in experience, and not in "mere general theories." Properly grounded axioms are to be distinguished above all for their social utility; they are expedient precisely because they recognize the needs of the community and provide the principles of action necessary to meet them. Abstract theorizing, on the other hand, is marked by artifice and impracticality; it is overly rationalistic and hence cannot account for the variety of human experience and collective values. The effect of Burke's brief refutation is to trump North's self-avowed interest in the common good and to expose North's bill as faulty on both the level of principle and the level of expedience. Burke confesses that his opinion is "much more in favor of prudent management than of force,—considering force not as an odious, but a feeble, instrument for preserving a people so numerous, so active, so growing, so spirited as this" (p. 118).

A series of four objections make up Burke's challenge to North's bill. Though brief, each carries the weight of a principle achieved through experience. The use of force, which North's bill assumes, can only be temporary, for "a nation is not governed which perpetually is to be conquered." Force is also by nature uncertain, for "terror is not always the effect of force; and an armament is not always a victory." Again, force impairs the "object by your very endeavor to preserve it," and, Burke says, "I do not choose wholly to break the American spirit; because it is that spirit which has made the country" (pp. 118-9). Finally, and summarily, Burke objects to its lack of precedent. The English experience in America has in fact been pacific: "Our ancient indulgence has been said to be pursued to a fault. It may be so; but we know, if feeling is evidence, that our fault was more tolerable than our attempt to mend it, and our sin far more salutary than our penitence" (p. 119). The objections are then enclosed with an appeal to principle, simultaneously buttressed by material evidence and expedience. The accumulated effect of these maxims adds weight to Burke's argument generally, but they also enhance our view of Burke's reflective judgment. The maxims by which North's policy is refuted come at the end of a long series of factual observations—they do not precede those observations. Burke's argument thus negotiates a path between reductive theorizing and sheer facticity. The structure of the argument reveals Burke's domain of judgment between the general and the particular; and North's agenda, as a result, is more visibly impoverished for its failure to occupy similar ground. It is instructed by empty theory, is artificial, without precedent, ignorant of the past, and therefore cannot sustain its own claims to expediency. Burke's proposal, conversely, is revealed to be anchored in principle and experience and is therefore practical as well as virtuous. Burke's account of America's material wealth ends at the level of principle, and so forecasts the process and form of judgment he would have his audience assume. The factual and material basis of such judgment in turn provides a transition into Burke's subject, and his description of the American character and its resistance to arbitrary rule. This second narrative is in fact more interpretive and less detailed than the former, but borrows from it the standards and posture of empirical judgment. Burke can thereby exploit the yield from his first narrative to illustrate the dominant, yet ineffable, feature of the Americans—their "fierce spirit of liberty." Here too the account reveals a kind of judging about judgment, speech both referential and self-referential, which characterizes the oration as a whole. As such, the narration induces an historical perspective by showing the narrator to be infused with historical understanding.

Chief amongst the causes for the American spirit is its genesis in the English past. But the past in this sense is not to be taken as a distant object; it is, rather, close by and inevitable. "Abstract liberty," Burke explains, "like other mere abstraction, is not to be found." Instead, "liberty inheres in some sensible object," and America, like England, "locates its freedom in the issue of taxation" (p. 120). Like most such problems, the question of taxation is understandable only in terms of its historical placement and precedent and is resolvable only in those terms. In fact, Burke writes, "on this point of taxes the ablest pens and most eloquent tongues have been exercised, the greatest spirits have acted and suffered" (p. 121). Such experience, moreover, is made accessible and current by its presence in common law and lore. Their own right to grant monies—in effect to tax themselves—the colonists found sanctioned in the English Constitution and acknowledged in "ancient parchments." In addition to its genesis in the English past, and as a result of it, the very right to self-taxation had developed into a principle of immediate relevance. In much the same way as Burke's account of American circumstances progressed from fact to principle, so this account propels the American question from its basis in past experience toward its resolution in principle. Even as Burke attacks the ministry's appeal to abstractions and empty theories of right, he seeks to legitimize the colonial appeal to the principle of self-taxation. The Americans, Burke explains, understood as "a fundamental principle, that in all monarchies the people must in effect themselves, mediately or immediately, possess the power of granting their own money, or no shadow of liberty could exist" (p. 121). As opposed to North's reasoning, principle resulted from experience and was not ancillary to it.

A similar movement characterizes Burke's portrait of religion in America. The American character had been shaped by the flight from England; as a result Americans have a particular faith in the "dissidence of dissent and the Protestantism of the Protestant" (p. 123). Likewise, the American education system, by nature resists ill-suited government; its emphasis upon legal training ought to be warning enough to the current ministry: "Abeunt studia in mores." The Americans, as a necessary result, are well equipped to "augur misgovernment at a distance and snuff the approach of tyranny in every tainted breeze" (p. 125). Finally, the very physical character of Anglo-American relations thwarts arbitrary rule. The "disobedient spirit of the colonies," Burke explains, is due in part to the brute fact that they are separated from the mother country by an ocean. Simple as that fact is, it predicates an important principle of government: "In large bodies the circulation of power must be less

vigorous at the extremites. Nature has said it" (p. 126). Thus the
proximity of fact and principle, consonant with the relationship
between past and present, issues an unmistakable directive. Failing
to engage its policy with such standards, the ministry invites
disaster. The past, Burke concludes, will inevitably make itself felt;
and the American spirit of liberty "has grown with the growth of
the people in your colonies, and increases with the increase of their
wealth: a spirit that unhappily meeting with an exercise of power
in England, which however lawful, is not reconciled to any idea of
liberty, much less with theirs, has kindled this flame that is ready
to consume us" (p. 127).

Argument

Thus forewarned, the audience is now in a position, if not to
accept, at least to envision a new course of action. The ensuing
forty-seven paragraphs detail Burke's alternative. More than a
series of policy suggestions, however, this is a lesson in judgment.
Burke has heretofore exposed, and will again, the impotence of
theory to accommodate material problems. Here he demonstrates
the utility of historical understanding, and as he does so, reveals
the proper grounds for action and judgment. As the paragraphs
unfold, we see the past and its constraints laying a foundation for
Burke, directing his perspective as he would have it shape ours. It
is a pragmatic view, tending toward the general and the didactic.
This section of the speech accordingly summarizes and enacts the
principles previously introduced. As Burke establishes the conditions
of judgment, surveys possible courses of action, and finally arrives
at his proposition, we witness again discourse about judgment that
is itself exemplary.

As with all successful arguments-from-exclusion, Burke's concludes with a sense of inevitability. As such his position assumes
the strength of logical necessity. But in addition to this somewhat
transparent achievement, Burke's argument has advanced with a
subtle but irresistible progress. The speech has thus far ascribed to
experience and past fact a compelling, immediate force. Now,
coupling historical to logical necessity, Burke aligns rational and
moral imperatives in the service of his argument.

Careful to make clear what his proposal is not, Burke
introduces the bill with a now familiar insistence upon its practical

appeal. One fact, he begins, is clear: the source of America's complaint is its exclusion from British standards of liberty; that complaint, in turn, stems from the issue of taxation. The sheer reality of this fact sets in relief North's abstract approach to a concrete problem. Indeed, the fashionable tendency to locate the issue in questions of right is just such an abstraction. It therefore fails to meet the problem on its own terms and has rendered Anglo-American relations unnaturally complex. Burke promises to take the opposite course, and while admitting that "gentlemen of profound learning are fond of displaying" their concern for the question of right, he observes the baneful effects. Like Milton's vision of hell, Burke finds such idle speculation to be "the great Serbonian bog/Betwixt Damiata and Mount Cassius old/Where whole armies have sunk" (p. 140).[10]

In refusing to entertain the question of right, however, Burke does not so much ignore the problem as render it irrelevant. Over against this abstract, and therefore inappropriate, consideration, Burke's approach is unabashedly "narrow, confined, and wholly limited to the policy of the question" (p. 140). This insistence upon the practical ends of any given question allows Burke to engage the problem morally but not abstractly, concretely but not pedantically. Burke can now claim without inconsistency that it 'is now what a lawyer tells me I may do, but what humanity, reason, and justice tell me I ought to do" (pp. 140-141). Here the appeal to circumstances and principled response conflates honor and expedience, fusing particular facts within a general perspective. Although brief, this passage is propaedeutic to the remainder of the speech; and by establishing this calculus as the basis of judgment, Burke provides a standard by which to judge not only his resolutions, but those of his opponents. Unlike the North administration, Burke concludes, "I am not determining a point of law, I am restoring tranquility: and the general character and situation of a people must determine what sort of government is fitted for them. That point nothing else can or ought to determine" (p. 141).

Burke proposes first to "admit the people of our colonies into an interest in the constitution" (p. 141). The record of North's administration, and indeed all ministries since Rockingham's, had

---

[10]Milton, *Paradise Lost,* 592-594.

made clear the folly of excluding colonists from English privileges.
As Burke reviews that record, he again exposes North's administration not only as governing with impunity, but as failing even to
meet its avowed ends. The policy of the current ministry, in short,
was neither honorable nor expedient, "no more than suspicions,
conjectures, deviations, formed in defiance of fact and experience"
(p. 145). In lines which recall his introduction, Burke contrasts his
own perspective to that of North's, and thereby signals the progress
of the speech thus far. Burke claims to have assumed that "frame
of mind which was the most natural and the most reasonable,"
had sought a "total renunciation of every speculation of my own"
(p. 145). He had thereby come to realize that the only possible
solution was to allow the colonists into the ancient constitution —
that is, into the English past. As Burke concludes the paragraph,
he simultaneously summarizes the tenets of his speech and prepares
for their demonstration. Again, this section, like all preceding
divisions, eventuates in principles which unify the speech even as it
shifts direction and function. Its concluding lines are familiar
enough, and again show Burke to be acting "with a profound
reverence for the wisdom of our ancestors, who have left us the
inheritance of so happy a constitution and so flourishing an
empire, and, what is a thousand times more valuable, the treasury
of the maxims and principles which formed the one and obtained
the other" (p. 145).

Resolutions

We are not surprised, therefore, when Burke announces his
resolutions by first explaining how he arrived at them. It is this
process of discovery and insight which Burke would have others
follow and which functions synecdochally as a standard of Whig
political judgment. At this moment of crisis, then, Burke will not
seek answers in the fanciful and speculative texts of Plato, More,
or Harrington. His plan, far from utopian, is "before me; it is at
my feet,—'And the rude swain/Treads daily on it with his clouted
shoon'" (p. 154).[11] Like most of his allusions, this Miltonic image
serves to imbed Burke's argument historically and to convey a

---

[11]Milton, *Comus,* 634-635.

sense of homely, sublunar wisdom. And in fact Burke is willing to go no further in search of theoretical justification than "the ancient constitutional policy of this kingdom." Burke's argument, that is, mimes the character of the constitution, insofar as both are constrained by the historical development of principle. As to his resolutions generally, there can be no mistaking their source and legitimacy: "Return to that mode," Burke advises, "which a uniform experience has marked out to you as best, and in which you walked with security, advantage and honor, until the year 1763" (p. 154).

Taken together Burke's six primary resolutions are meant to grant colonists the right to self-taxation and to expose the poverty of North's program. But each resolution is so composed as to repeat under different guises the same rationale for action and adjudication. Each specific claim is anchored in historical fact, and together "these solid truths compose six fundamental propositions." As such, they are objective and compelling. "The propositions," Burke says, "are all mere matters of fact; and if they are such facts as draw irresistible conclusions even in the stating, this is the power of truth, and not any management of mine" (p. 154-155). Each resolution thereby assumes the moral and logical necessity of historical truth. Burke proposes first only that the colonists have not in the past had access to representation. This, Burke claims, "is a plain matter of fact, necessary to be laid down, and...it is laid down in the language of the constitution" (p. 155). The second resolution appeals to a similar facticity: the colonists have been unjustly taxed, thereby grieved, and ultimately incited to resistance. This conclusion, of course, is less certifiable in factual terms, but the historical appeal upon which it is based by now lends it credence. Burke will meet the problems of the past with constitutional measures generated from the past. Thus Burke exercises the historical force of the constitution, conceived as "the genuine produce of the ancient, rustic, manly, homebred sense of this country — I dare not rub off a particle of the venerable rust that rather adorns and preserves, than destroys, the metal" (p. 156). By participating in the construction of the past, Burke's resolutions evoke its authority and so claim an independent moral status. "Determining to fix articles of peace," Burke concludes, "I was resolved not to be wise beyond what was written." This, he says, "if it be not ingenious, I am sure is safe" (p. 156). Resolutions three and four—that no adequate system of representation has yet been devised for the colonies, and that the colonists themselves possess the means for such representation—Burke likewise asserts as facts. So too is the fifth a "resolution of fact," meant to point out the precedent for colonial grants in lieu of external taxation. The final resolution becomes an inevitable result of the preceding "facts." Burke asks his audience to recognize that in the past—that is, before the ascendency of North—grants from the colonies were beneficial to both America and England. "The conclusion," Burke insists, "is irresistible." Thus assent to historical fact becomes a basis for action and justification of Whig policy.

Burke's transition into the corollary resolutions repeats the controlling movement of the speech, now familiar as a progression from fact to principle to fact. Here again Burke exercises his irresistible conclusion to direct the terms of the following arguments. "The question now," Burke says, "on all the accumulated matter, is—whether you will choose to abide by a profitable experience, or a mischievous theory; whether you choose to build on imagination or fact; whether you prefer enjoyment of hope; satisfaction in your subjects or discontent (p. 162)?" These corollary resolutions call for repeal of George III's various and recent coercive bills, and so they would restore the tranquility Burke remembers in the days of Rockingham power. As with the primary resolutions, Burke appeals to historical sanction, principles which owe their authority not to abstract ideas of right, but to their proven utility. "Man acts from adequate motives relative to his interest," Burke concludes, "and not on metaphysical speculation. Aristotle, the great master of reasoning, tells us, and with great weight and propriety, to be wary against this species of delusive geometrical accuracy in moral arguments, as the most fallacious of all sophistry" (p. 170). This demand for English rights at the expense of English peace was precisely the problem with North's policy. The Rockingham Whigs, conversely, had employed a different and more effective calculus. During their ministries "everything was sweetly and harmoniously disposed," and Burke can only lament that the empire was then "more united than it is now, or that it is likely to be by the present methods" (p. 171).

Refutation

The speech enters now into a refutational phase, but the attack is only an extension of the principles generated thus far. Burke's refutation of North's plan is clustered around four points: (1) The plan is a "thing new, unheard of, supported by no experience, justified by no analogy, without example of our ancestors or root in the constitution" (p. 171); (2) It encourages court influence, and therefore imperils the constitution itself; (3) It cannot possibly achieve its avowed ends; and (4) The plan can only magnify logistical difficulties and so create greater discord. Given the nature of North's plan, Burke asks his audience to behold the differences. As he contrasts the two plans, we are provided a virtual summary of Burke's argument, employed to vanquish North's bill and to vindicate Rockingham policy. The contrast, moreover, articulates a rationale for action, in that Burke shapes ministerial policy into an immanent and insidious force, tolerated at the cost of imperial disaster. Burke's proposal is

> "plain and simple; the other full of perplexed and intricate mazes. This is mild, that harsh; this is found by experience effectual for its purposes; the other is a new project. This is universal—the other calculated for certain colonies only; this is immediate in its conciliatory operation; the other is remote, contingent, full of hazard. Mine is what becomes the dignity of a ruling people—gratuitous, unconditional, and not held out as a matter of bargain and sale. I have done my duty in proposing it to you" (p. 176).

Because the tone of the final sentence differs so markedly from its preceding lines, it is worth considering in greater detail. The sentence comes at the end of a series of antithetical constructions, and so lends closure to the argument. But the sentiment is more important for its moral implications: in declaring his obligations satisfied, Burke shifts attention from the issues specifically toward his character generally. In doing so, he establishes the terms of his conclusion. Burke now exercises fully the principles he has so far invoked and demonstrated, creating a vision of political order along notably Rockinghamite lines. Apologizing for the length of the speech, Burke nevertheless insists that "this is the misfortune of those to whose influence nothing will be conceded, and who must win every inch of their ground by argument." Here a thinly

disguised attack on privilege and court influence tells us more than
what the passage reveals on its surface. It is, of course, consistent
with Burke's long-standing suspicion of the "King's friends." But
the lines also indicate something about the Rockingham Whigs and
indeed about Burke himself. Long divested of its ties to the court,
the party, since the ascension of George III had been forced upon
its own resources. Burke's party, when it had failed, did so through
a failure to act decisively. As its representative, Burke undertakes
through his speech to correct the party's malaise, to give it voice
and direction, and ultimately to vindicate its principles. What
Burke says of himself, therefore, may be understood as a reflection
upon the Rockingham legacy. "I have this comfort," Burke
concludes, "that in every stage of the American affairs I have
steadily opposed the measures that have produced the confusion,
and may bring on the destruction, of this empire. I now go so far
as to risk a proposal of my own. If I cannot give peace to my
country, I give it to my conscience."

Peroration

The conclusion of speech is no mere summary, but a
consummation of its rhetorical action which elevated historical
action to the status of principle. Arguments have been interwoven
with appeals to both honor and expedience, themselves now
indistinguishable. This conflation has been achieved through a long
series of structural permutations, wherein facts blur into truths, and
circumstances into maxims. Once established, the principles direct
our apprehension of history. In this fashion, Burke exploits the
evidentiary force of material circumstances and the moral force of
historically-grounded truths to create a rhetorically compelling
vision. "As long as you have the wisdom to keep the sovereign
authority of this country as the sanctuary of liberty, the sacred
principle consecrated to our common faith, wherever the chosen
race and sons of England worship freedom, they will turn their
faces toward you." Burke thus vanquishes North's program, placing
in its stead a plan principled but not impractical and expedient but
not unjust. He has demonstrated exemplary judgment, creating a
perspective capable of taking in historical truth as well as current
expedients. It is within this perspective that Burke fashions his
advisory appeal. The speech has been a lesson in reading history,

and if it is a decidedly Rockingham history, nevertheless it articulates its ideals at a moment of crisis. Burke's history, like the form and character of his oration, is a composite of carefully designed images, allusions, and progressions. As such it may well be nostalgic, but it is nevertheless available for those who would learn and act upon its truths. Burke's history, moreover, is an appealing one, peopled by the likes of Horace and Milton, Aristotle, Ovid, and Virgil. From such luminaries Burke sought to enlighten a people seemingly blind to their own past. The rhetorical accomplishment of Burke's speech is thus its identification of history with Whig history and the lessons of the past with the advisory function of his argument. Most important perhaps, Burke understands that to represent history is not enough — that to make history present one must embody history. The *Speech on Conciliation* is ultimately an act of exemplary understanding, a process in which venerable truths are situated within immediate political contexts. There will be those who, like the current ministry, neglect the truths of history. But "to men truly initiated and rightly taught, these ruling and master principles, which in the opinion of such men as I have mentioned have no substantial existence, are in truth everything and all in all" (p. 181).

III

This movement of Burke's oration has been conducted along several levels of progression. Clearly the ostensible form of the speech is indebted to classical models; as such, the speech may be seen as an example of conventional form in the service of an argument from history. At this level the speech suggests a rational consistency and structure in keeping with Burke's purposes. The meaning of the oration cannot be fully apprehended, however, unless we attend to its more subtle progression through temporal and conceptual phases. Here Burke charts a movement from past to present to future as a means of grounding principles of judgment in human experience. These temporal phases thus embody conditions of past fact — the axiomatic basis of political decision — and a rationale for deliberative action. So ordered, Burke's oration offers to both immediate and historical audiences a standard for rhetorical judgment.

The *Speech,* finally, may be seen as a practical extension of the principles Burke would celebrate. Certainly the *Speech* is notable for its wealth of imagery and aesthetic appeal. More significantly, its meaning is constituted as a form of discursive action and requires for its completion the exercise of rhetorical judgment. Burke's audience, however expansive and however distant, is nevertheless obligated to understand the oration in its capacity as an audience, to apprehend its meaning according to the standards of human community and practical reason. As an exemplary exercise in rhetorical judgment, moreover, Burke's oration is able to reconfigure human experience free from the constraints of the moment and the burdens of speculative principle. From the perspective it induces, we are thus led to see in the *Speech* an example of what it means to deliberate wisely.

BURKE'S SPEECH ON CONCILIATION
AS OPPOSITIONAL DISCOURSE
JOHN LOUIS LUCAITES

Edmund Burke's speech on "Moving His Resolutions For Conciliation With The Colonies" must surely be considered one of the most important speeches he ever delivered in the Halls of Parliament. Or at least so it must be considered by those of us living on this side of the Atlantic Ocean. Although it was delivered several weeks prior to the "shot heard 'round the world," it did not reach the colonies in pamphlet form until well after that fateful event. Nevertheless, it was to play an important role in the rhetoric of the American revolution, indicating to the revolutionaries that they had at least one sympathetic voice in the Parliament in which their representation had been negligible at best. Moreover, as is often the case with oratory that is designated as "great," Burke's "Speech On Conciliation" outlived its original historical context. So, for example, in the nineteenth century it was institutionalized in McGuffey's readers as a model for teaching high school students the fundamentals of good writing, its selection prompted as much, no doubt, by its vivid and laudatory depiction of the American frontier character, as by its compelling use of tropes and figures. And indeed, until the 1950s it was virtually impossible to graduate from an American high school without having studied the speech in one context or another. Finally, it should not pass our notice that the only eighteenth-century British statesman honored with both a statue and a park in our national capital is Edmund Burke, and that the sentiment inscribed on the base of the statue is drawn from the conclusion of this very speech: "Magnanimity in politics is not seldom the truest wisdom; and a great empire and little minds go ill together."[1] It is thus

---

[1] The monument and park are at Massachusetts Avenue and 11 St. NW. See Gerald Chapman, "Burke's American Tragedy," in *Jackson and His Age,* ed. James Engell (Cambridge: Harvard University Press, 1984), 386-8.

altogether appropriate that as students of American Public Address we consider this speech with greater care and attention
than has heretofore been forthcoming, for it is of America and
America's history every bit as much as if it had been spoken by
George Washington, Thomas Jefferson, or Abraham Lincoln. It
might not have been written specifically for or delivered specifically to an American audience with any of these purposes in
mind, but its effects, both in the eighteenth century and today—
however unintended—have made it an integral part of our
national culture and ideology.

   The relationship between rhetoric and ideology provides the
starting point for the response that I want to make to Professor
Browne's excellent essay. The intellectual and political traditions
out of which the terms "rhetoric" and "ideology" emerge have
seldom been comfortable bedfellows: the sophistical and Aris-
totelian traditions out of which rhetoric originally emerged have
typically been concerned with the positive and reconstructive
uses of language and public discourse in a contingent universe,
while the social theoretical traditions out of which ideology
emerged have been more frequently concerned with stripping
away the imaginary and illusory distortions of language and
public discourse that promote a false consciousness. In recent
years, however, there has been a concerted effort by rhetoricians
and social theorists alike to probe the relationship between
rhetoric and ideology as a conceptual foundation for more
emancipatory theories of public consciousness and social and
political change. As I will suggest a bit later, when understood
in its own context as part of a specific rhetorical process of
opposition, Burke's "Speech On Conciliation" provides an excellent resource which one might use as the grounding for such a
project.

   Before I turn to that task, however, I must make a confession. Like Professor Browne, I too have wrestled with the
problem of how to understand and to report on the unique and
dynamic weaving of text and context, of argument and image,
and of theory and practice in Edmund Burke's speaking and
writing without altogether distorting the meaning or disrupting
the integrity of the particular document under consideration. My
suspicion is that the problem is in some large measure a
function of the conventions of our own scholarly discourse

which demand that we proceed in a deductive and linear manner of presentation, even though we are trying to come to terms with discourses that are altogether organic in their construction and performance. In my own case, the document that has given me so much trouble has been Burke's *Reflections On The Revolution in France,* a volume-length public letter that is at once easier and more difficult to deal with than the "Speech on Conciliation." It is an easier document to handle because it is so much longer and thus provides more room to chart the interacting structures that constitute its organic meaning and power; it is more difficult, however, because it takes account of virtually every public argument made for and against the Whig interpretation of the English Constitution from 1680 to 1789, and thus it is more difficult to isolate and identify Burke's *specific* motivations.[2] I mention the difficulty in dealing with Burke, because studying Browne's effort to understand the "Speech on Conciliation" has been enlightening for me—not simply because he does an excellent job of charting the internal tensions that inform the action of the text, but because the lacuna that I will attempt to identify in his essay has helped me to identify a similar omission in my own study of Burke's *Reflections.* My critique, then, should be understood as a kind of self-therapy: what I have to say about Professor Browne's reading of Burke applies in almost every particular to my own readings of Burke.

Browne begins his essay by commenting on the unfixed legacy of Burke's "Speech on Conciliation," a problem predicated on the fact that while the speech has received the highest of accolades offered an oration in the Western tradition, it was nevertheless an abysmal failure in influencing the course of the Parliamentary debates over the American question to which it was presumably addressed. Thus, while the principles proposed in the speech are frequently praised for their high ideals and humanity, they are just as frequently dismissed for their futility and impracticality. Browne is of course correct when he indicates that the *telos* of "immediate effect" is altogether misleading. In

---

[2]John Louis Lucaites, "Flexibility and Consistency in Eighteenth-Century Anglo-Whiggism: A Case Study in The Rhetorical Dimensions of Legitimacy" (Ph.D. diss., University of Iowa, 1984), 121-235.

its stead, he argues that a better understanding of the speech
can be had if we think of it as a declarative and demonstrative
performance of the Whig ideology at a moment of crisis. "Its
significance," he notes, "lies in neither its literary qualities nor
in its immediate persuasive effect (or lack thereof). Rather, as
an act of [exemplary] judgment, the oration instantiates Burke's
directives on political action." We have here, then, not Burke
the politician, promoting a particular cause, but Burke the
philosopher-in-action, speaking didactically as the Whig conscience of the British Empire.

The historical and textual analysis that is provided for us in
support of this argument is compelling. Historically there does
not seem to be much evidence to indicate that Burke's speech
would or could have had much *immediate* effect on the intentions
of the North ministry to be more belligerent in its treatment of
the colonists. As Browne indicates, one month prior to Burke's
resolutions for conciliation, Lord Chatham had offered similar
resolutions for conciliation, and they were soundly defeated in the
House of Lords by a margin of 2-1. Shortly following that vote,
North proposed his resolution, which Burke was to take to task
in his speech as a policy of "ransom by auction," and it passed
in the House of Commons by a margin of 3-1. It is highly unlikely that one as astute as Burke would have missed or ignored
the virtual inevitability of North's policy becoming law, and so
one must look elsewhere for Burke's motivation for speaking.

Browne takes us to the text of the speech itself, where, with
both clarity and elegance, he painstakingly identifies the manner
in which Burke integrates the classical, deliberative structure of
the speech with the "psychological forces, made evident in the
evolving structure of its appeals," and at the same time, induces
his audience to participate in the Whig myth, a perspective
ordered by cultural experience and actively located in the history
of which the speech is the present moment. By charting Burke's
weaving of historical facts, cultural maxims, and ideological
principles in the context of a particular problem, Browne demonstrates for us the force behind Burke's commitment to grounded
principles of judgment in human experience, just as he demonstrates that the action of the text is a function of this rhetorical
judgment. The speech is thus directed not so much at North
and his ministry with respect to the American question, as it

designed to take advantage of the American question as a vehicle for establishing a standard of rhetorical judgment.

As I indicate above, the analysis here is compelling, and, if for no other reason than that, it helps us to understand the organic unity of the speech text itself. I cannot help believing, however, that just as it is misleading to assume that "immediate effect" defines the *telos* of the speech, it is also hazardous to isolate the speech text, which is only one element in the rhetorical process, from the larger context. The risk here is that we may misjudge the meaning and power of the rhetorical transaction. Put in other words, I am not sure that Browne's analysis provides a complete answer to the compelling question with which he began: "Why does Burke take the trouble to speak at all?" I raise this issue because I think that Browne is absolutely correct when he says that the speech is a performance, and equally correct when he indicates that it is grounded in a pragmatic function of rhetorical judgment. A fuller understanding of the power and historical significance of that speech requires us to consider the specific nature of that performance, as well as the character of the judgment to be made.

I do not want to be misunderstood here. I agree with Browne's conclusion that the "Speech on Conciliation" reveals the application of a philosophy of history to a theory of society and that it enacts a rhetorical judgment. It seems altogether reasonable, therefore, to assume that at least *one* of Burke's purposes here *might* have been to display a prudential model of rhetorical and political action. Indeed, one can find a similar interaction of fact and principle, of character and convention, of theory and practice, in virtually every one of Burke's major rhetorical efforts promoting the Whig myth of society, including his *Thoughts on The Causes of The Present Discontents,* his *Letter To The Sheriffs at Bristol,* his speeches "On Economic Reform" and "The Nabob of Arcot's Debt," his *Appeal From The Old to The New Whigs,* and his *Reflections on The Revolution in France.* The point to be made here is that with each of these efforts, it was not simply the particular exigence which provided the ground for displaying and promoting the Whig ideology—although in each instance it was displayed and promoted. Rather, each effort represented an attempt to integrate the historical experience of Whiggism with the particular exigence at hand, towards the end of producing both

right reason and at the same time a particular action. And in order
to understand the force of any of these efforts, one must not only
isolate the right reason, but also the particular action. To this end,
one must do more than simply read the text and identify its formal
action, but must also examine the way(s) in which it functions in
the larger context(s) in which it is made to do work. And, I might
add here that both the function and the context are subject to
variation throughout the life of the text, such that its significance
(and perhaps even its internal action) change as it functions
differently in different contexts.

In brief, let me give an indication of the kind of analysis I
have in mind by recalling for you that the Parliamentary rhetorical
context in which Burke operated was vastly different from the
Congressional system that operates in contemporary times. Although
the Reagan Presidency might incline us to think otherwise at
times, we live today in a relatively open society where public
policy is generally shaped and formed in committees and then
publicly debated on the floors of the Houses of Congress. Except
when the President's party is in full majority, one can never know
in advance with any confidence what the outcome of a particular
vote might be. Such was not typically the case in eighteenth-
century England, where the political system reflected a relatively
closed and insular power structure. As Michael McGee has
demonstrated, the political power necessary for the day-to-day
conduct of the state resided in the Crown and his or her ministers.
Deliberations in Parliament were seldom and formulary, almost
always acceding to the desires of the Crown, except under those
limited circumstances in which a popular outcry gave those in
opposition the opportunity to demand more careful justifications of
ministry policies. Under such circumstances it was possible for the
opposition to persuade the "independents" who held the balance of
power in Parliament to vote against a particular policy, thus
indicating to the Crown that his ministers held no authority in
Parliament, or to embarrass a particular minister for his incompetence and/or corruption into resigning, lest he embarrass the
monarch. On more than one occasion the King's ministers were
known to have begged for the opportunity to resign. The primary
rhetorical process in Parliament in eighteenth-century England,
then, was one in which the role of the political opposition was to
force ministerial justifications for uses of political power that were

minimally consistent with the dominant ideology. And if they could restrict the terms of such justifications, either through direct refutations that gradually and eventually exhausted the ministry rationale, or through alteration of the range of meaning for various ideological commitments, thus limiting the terms of the debate, they might even be able to control the specific actions and policies that the Crown promoted.[3]

Except for a very short period of his life, Edmund Burke sat in Parliament as a member of His Majesty's "loyal opposition," and the vast majority of his speeches and pamphlets reflect the refutative strategies peculiar to the rhetorical process in eighteenth-century England. In this context it might make sense to examine Burke's "Speech on Conciliation" for its specific functions as an oppositional discourse, designed not simply to promote and herald Lord Rockingham's version of the Whig ideology or to establish the appropriate philosophical standards of rhetorical judgment, but to restrict the propriety of using "force" as an instrument for maintaining the Empire by persuading Lord North (and future ministers) to justify particular usages in terms of the Whig ideology. As such, Burke's masterful weaving of historical experience and cultural principles serves as much to undermine the ground for North's justification for his resolutions as it does to provide a model of exemplary rhetorical judgment. And to ignore that function (and its possible effects) is to ignore the real genius of Burke's rhetoric which produced the slim possibility of influencing the immediate question before Parliament, and the more likely possibility of establishing the terms in which future deliberations might take place.

In the end, I think that my proposed reading of Burke's "Speech on Conciliation" operates in the same vicinity as Browne's reading, although we seem to be moving in different directions. Each of us maintains that Burke was a philosopher-in-action. The difference between us is that Browne's focus on the "formal"

---

[3]The analysis in this paragraph is abstracted from Michael McGee, "The Rhetorical Process in Eighteenth-Century England," *Rhetoric: A Tradition In Transition,* ed. Walter R. Fisher (East Lansing: Michigan State University Press, 1974), 99-121. See also Archibald S. Foord, *His Majesty's Loyal Opposition, 1714-1830* (Oxford: Clarendon Press, 1964).

action of the speech text leads him to underscore the word
"philosopher," while my emphasis on the *function* of the speech
text in the context of the eighteenth-century rhetorical process
leads me to underscore the word "action." And it is precisely this
tension between philosophy and action, between theory and
practice, that leads me back to my introduction and the suggestion
that to consider Burke's "Speech On Conciliation" as an oppositional discourse might provide a means to probe the relationship
between rhetoric and ideology as they serve to create public
consciousness and promote or restrict social and political change.

Until recently, attempts to theorize the relationship between
rhetoric and ideology have been hampered by the reductionist
tendencies of the materialist and symbolist theories of social
change in which they operated, making it difficult to chart the
recursive interaction of material and symbolic environments that
we now believe to be so important in understanding the construction and maintenance of social and political consciousness. More
recent attempts to theorize this relationship in American rhetorical
studies, in British cultural studies, and in Continental social theory
in general, have helped us to overcome this problem through the
development of materialist theories of rhetoric, as well as theories
of articulation, structuration, symbolic capital, etc.[4] In the wake of
such work we are far less likely to encounter rhetorical studies that
cling to antiquated notions about the nature of social and political
change. This makes it all the more curious that those of us
operating in the area of rhetorical studies have been so inclined to
cling to antiquated notions of rhetorical effect.

The problem here is not that we simply privilege immediate
effect as the primary criterion for judging a discourse; Edwin Black
dealt that notion a timely death-blow in 1965.[5] The problem is the

---

[4]For example, see Michael McGee, "A Materialist's Conception of Rhetoric,"
Explorations In Rhetoric: Studies in Honor of Douglas Ehninger, ed. Ray E. McKerrow
(Glenview, IL: Scott, Foresman, 1982), 23-48; Stuart Hall, "Signification, Representation,
Ideology: Althusser and the Post-Structuralist Debates," *Critical Studies in Mass
Communication* 2 (1985): 91-114; Anthony Giddens, *Central Problems in Social Theory:
Action, Structure and Contradiction in Social Analysis* (Berkeley: University of Cali-
fornia, 1979), 49-103; and Pierre Bourdieu, *Outline of A Theory of Practice,* trans.
Richard Nice (Cambridge: University Press, 1977), 159-97.

[5]Edwin Black, *Rhetorical Criticism: A Study In Method* (New York: Macmillan,
1965; Madison: University of Wisconsin Press, 1978).

boomerang effect that has seemingly developed in response to Black's critique of neo-Aristotelianism. Rather than to work to develop our understanding of the range of effects which rhetoric can produce, our tendency has been either to ignore the question of rhetorical effect altogether, as if immediate and intentional effects were the only kinds worthy of being studied, or to treat the issue of effect with a tired nod as we turn our vision ever inward to the text itself and to increasingly formalistic analyses. And in the end, we seem only to distance ourselves from our disciplinary heritage, for rhetoric has always been the discourse of power and effect — it was its power and effect that led the likes of Aristotle and Isocrates to embrace it, and it was the same power and effect that led the likes of Plato to excoriate it.

If rhetoric is to regain its position in the academy as the capstone of a liberal education, we need to direct our attention more specifically and directly to the problem of rhetorical effect, considering with some care the range of possible effects produced by a given rhetoric, both immediate and protracted, and both intended and unintended. And it is precisely in this context that I believe that Burke's "Speech On Conciliation" can be of most use to us, for it represents the genius of a man who was caught in a closed political system that made it almost impossible for him to have the kind of direct impact on his audiences that we have identified as an immediate effect. Nevertheless, it was a rhetoric that was effective in interpolating the ideology and the culture in which it operated. We no longer live in the closed political system of eighteenth-century England, but it may well be that the analogous dominance of the mass media over contemporary conceptions of ourselves as a homogeneous national public make the need to consider the forms and functions of oppositional discourses immediate and present today. And in that context, I can certainly think of no better place to start than with Edmund Burke's "Speech On Conciliation."

LA PUCELLE D'ORLEANS
BECOMES AN AMERICAN GIRL:
ANNA DICKINSON'S "JEANNE D'ARC"

KARLYN KOHRS CAMPBELL

The story of the woman who came to be called Jeanne d'Arc has been a cultural and philosophical Rorschach test. She has been presented as the flower of chivalry,[1] debunked as a witch and strumpet[2] or an impostor,[3] mocked in a bitingly satirical poem,[4] and presented as a romantic heroine by English,[5] German,[6] and French writers.[7] She has been claimed as Italian and German (she was born in Lorraine, after all), and a body of Jewish literature has identified her with the suffering and persecuted through the centuries.[8] A Confederate writer claimed her as the symbol of *la guerre à outrance*.[9] The Petainists of Vichy exploited her story to stir up anti-British sentiment; the Gaullists made her a symbol of

---

[1]Christine De Pisan, *Ditié de Jehanne d'Arc,* ed. Angus J. Kennedy and Kenneth Varty (1429; reprint ed., London: Oxford University Press, 1977).

[2]William Shakespeare, *Henry VI, Part I.*

[3]Margaret Alice Murray, *Witch-Cult in Western Europe, a Study in Anthropology* (Oxford: Clarendon Press, 1921).

[4]Voltaire, François Marie Arouet, *The Virgin of Orleans or Joan of Arc,* trans. Howard Nelson (Denver: Alan Swallow, 1965).

[5]Robert Southey, *Joan of Arc in Poems, Ballads and Lyrics* (Boston: Manning & Loring, 1796); Thomas De Quincey, *Joan of Arc and Other Selections from Thomas De Quincey* (Boston: Leach, Shewell & Sanborn, 1847).

[6]Friedrich von Schiller, *Die Jungfrau von Orleans: Eine Romantische Tragödie* (New York, Holt, 1801).

[7]Alphonse de Lamartine, *Joan of Arc: A Biography,* trans. Sarah Moore Grimké (Boston: Adams & Co, 1852); Jules Michelet, *Vie de Jeanne d'Arc* (Paris: Gustave Rundler, 1865).

[8]Charles Lightbody, *Judgements of Joan* (London: Harvard University Press, 1961), 163-165.

[9]John Fentonville, *Joan of Arc: an Opinion of her Life and Character Derived from Ancient Chronicles* (Richmond, 1864).

French independence;[10] Mark Twain's Joan was a Victorian lady,[11] in the words of George Bernard Shaw, "skirted to the ground,... an unimpeachable American school teacher in armor."[12] More recently, her story has been retold in plays by Shaw,[13] Maxwell Anderson[14] and Jean Anouilh.[15] When she was canonized in 1920, over 12,000 works had been published about her in France alone.[16]

The continuing creation of narratives is occasioned by the mysterious and unsatisfactory nature of her story and the troubling fact that Joan was a woman warrior. American versions of her life appeared in the nineteenth century, encouraged by the publication of the historical record in the 1840s,[17] by the rise of the lyceum or national system of adult education,[18] and the inception of the woman's rights movement, which challenged the prevailing social mythology embodied in the cult of true womanhood and, in its search for role models, saw Joan as an obvious choice.[19] Women

------

[10]Lightbody. Also see: Marina Warner, *Joan of Arc: The Image of Female Heroism* (New York: Alfred A. Knopf, 1981).

[11]Mark Twain, *Personal Recollections of Joan of Arc by the Sieur Louis de Conte (her Page and Secretary) Freely Translated out of the Ancient French into Modern English from the Original Unpublished Manuscript in the National Archives of France by Jean François Alden* (1886; reprint ed., Hartford, CT: The Stowe-Day Foundation, 1980).

[12]Bernard Shaw, *Saint Joan: A Chronicle Play in Six Scenes and an Epilogue* (New York: Brentano's, 1924), xxxix - xl.

[13]*St. Joan* was originally performed in 1920.

[14]Maxwell Anderson, *Joan of Lorraine: A Play in Two Acts* (Washington, D.C.: Anderson House, 1946).

[15]Jean Anouilh, *The Lark,* trans. Christopher Frye (New York: Oxford University Press, 1953).

[16]Edward Lucie-Smith, *Joan of Arc* (London: Allen Lane, 1976), xi.

[17]Jules Quicherat, *Procès de condamnation et de réhabilitation de Jeanne d'Arc dite La Pucelle publié pour la première fois d'après les manuscrites de la Bibliotheque royale, suivis de tous les documents historiques qo'on a pu réunir, et accompagnés de notes et d'éclaircissements* (Paris: J. Renouard, 1841-49).

[18]David Mead, *Yankee Eloquence in the Middle West: The Ohio Lyceum, 1850-1870* (1951; reprint ed., Westport, CT: Greenwood Press, 1977); Anna L. Curtis, "A Brief History of the Lyceum," *Who's Who in the Lyceum,* ed. A. Augustus Wright (Philadelphia, PA: Pearson Brothers, 1906), 15-34.

[19]Lamartine. Also see: Elizabeth Cady Stanton, "Convention Address," *Proceedings of the Woman's Rights Conventions Held at Seneca Falls and Rochester, New York, July and August 1848* (New York: Robert T. Johnston, 1870), 19. And Joan continues to serve this purpose, see: Andrea Dworkin, "Virginity," *Intercourse* (New York: Free Press, 1987), 83-105.

reformers of the nineteenth century were often called Joan of Arcs, an epithet frequently applied to Anna Dickinson herself.[20]

Dickinson's lecture is of interest because Dickinson was a famous, highly successful, early woman speaker, because the lecture was among the earliest if not the earliest American version of Joan's story,[21] as well as being one of the most popular of its time,[22] delivered on over a thousand occasions between 1870 and 1884,[23] and because its popularity attests to the impact of social mythology on public discourse. On the one hand, Dickinson's lecturing career opened doors for other women reformers and activists; moreover, she made her first speech in support of woman's rights and continued her support subsequently, although she remained apart from the organized movement.[24] However, despite her sympathy for these causes and Joan's suitability as a "feminist" model, Dickinson not only transformed her into a democratic, Protestant populist, but also into a "true woman." In what follows I argue that the lecture's popularity is attributable primarily to Dickinson's assimilation of Joan into U.S. culture,

---

[20]Giraud Chester, *Embattled Maiden: The Life of Anna Dickinson* (New York: G.P. Putnam's Sons, 1951), 30, 35, 49, 51, 59; Charles F. Horner, *The Life of James Redpath and the Development of the Modern Lyceum* (New York: Barse and Hopkins, 1926), 145; and James Harvey Young, "Anna Elizabeth Dickinson," *Notable American Women, 1607-1950,* 3 vols., ed. Edward T. James (Cambridge, MA: Belknap Press, Harvard University, 1971), 475. They were also attacked as Amazons. "Among the excrescences upon the body politic is one which may be best described by its Greek name Gynaekokracy, which manifests itself in the absurd endeavors of women to usurp the places and execute the functions of the male sex. ... We find in the early Greek writers the first mention of this social deformity under the name of the *Amazons*—an appellation given to a community of female warriors, because, it is said, 'they *burned off their right breast,* in order to handle the bow more expeditiously.' ... The last development of the kind is in the person whose name stands at the head of this article .... Of her more ardent admirers, some compare her to the Maid of Orleans, others to Phryne or Lais of the olden time," ("Anna E. Dickinson and the Gynaekokracy," *The Geneva* [NY] *Gazette,* 12 March, 1866; Anna E. Dickinson Papers, Library of Congress, Reel 25, cont. 26, 217).

[21]Francis Cabot Lowell III, *Joan of Arc* (Boston: Houghton Mifflin, 1896), and Twain.

[22]Considering its popularity and its subject, one wonders why, unlike Russell H. Conwell's "Acres of Diamonds," it has never been anthologized or analyzed.

[23]Anna E. Dickinson Papers, Library of Congress, Mss. 17,984, container 14, 471-507.

[24]Young, 475.

buttressed by the lecture's style and Dickinson's personal link to
her story.[25]

JOAN'S STORY

The historical record cannot resolve the contradictions among
versions of Joan's life. While it is true that "primary sources are
abundant and diverse, unique for a medieval personage and rare
for a historical figure of any pre-modern period,"[26] the conflicts
between the record of her original trial in 1431 and that from the
proceedings of 1456 that exonerated her of charges of heresy are
insuperable obstacles.[27] Charles Lightbody notes political reasons
for discrepancies: "If Henry VI [of England, who was attempting
to become King of France] financed the trial from interested
motives, so equally did Charles VII [of France, whose coronation
Joan arranged] finance the Rehabilitation from motives at least
equally interested".[28] Put simply, Henry wished to prove and
Charles to disprove that Charles had been crowned due to the
efforts of a heretic. Historical evaluations of these conflicting
versions are affected by ideology. Lightbody comments that one's
"attitude to the Rehabilitation and to the trial is likely to furnish
... a master key to any writer's general philosophy as well as to his
[sic] attitude twoard Joan of Arc, in particular."[29] In other words,
there is no definitive record for much of this; what one takes to be
the truth about Joan depends on one's predispositions. Moreover,
the contradictions in the record are an invitation to recast her story
in some more consistent and satisfactory form.

Consider, for a moment, Joan's amazing achievements. She
was a teenage, runaway girl who convinced a king and his court to
give her horses and armor and put her in charge of a final effort to

---

[25]One can never know precisely how her audiences understood her lecture. I have
used what is known of prevailing social mythology of the period—the cult of true
womanhood—as a framework for interpreting the meaning of the lecture. Critically, the
meaning of a text is what the most illuminating and encompassing critical argument says
that it is.

[26]Frances Gies, *Joan of Arc: The Legend and the Reality* (New York: Harper &
Row, 1981), 2.

[27]Lightbody, 118-53.

[28]Lightbody, 147.

[29]Lightbody, 143.

raise the siege of Orleans; she was a pious but illiterate peasant who defended herself against the learning of the theologians of the University of Paris and the casuistries of the Inquisition; she was a fifteenth-century woman who wore male dress and played male roles and who gained acceptance as such while insisting on her womanhood and virginity.

There are endless mysteries. Just what were her "voices?" What force of character made this illiterate, teenage, peasant girl so persuasive to the people of Chinon (who paid to have male garments tailored for her), to the King, his courtiers, the churchmen of Poitiers, and the soldiers? How did a peasant girl learn to ride, handle a sword, and fight a battle? Why did the fortunes of the Armagnacs (supporters of Charles VII) change so dramatically with her appearance? Finally, how is it that, condemned by the Church as a heretic in 1431, she was rehabilitated by the Church in 1456?[30]

The unsatisfactory and mysterious character of her story is attested to by what writers have done to it.[31] Some, incredulous at the exploits of an illiterate peasant, made her into a bastard princess;[32] some, outraged that she was abandoned by King and Church, denied that she was burned;[33] some, dismayed by her defeats, rewrote her story as if she had fulfilled her mission with the coronation of the Dauphin at Rheims;[34] and some male historians,

---

[30]Her rehabilitation was initiated in 1450 by the King; on July 7, 1456, a Church-conducted investigation concluded: "We say, pronounce, decree, and declare the said trial and sentence to be contaminated with fraud, calumny, wickedness, contradictions, and manifest errors of fact and law, and together with the abjuration, the execution, and all their consequences, to have been and to be null, without value or effect, and to be quashed .... We proclaim that Joan ... did not contract any taint of infamy and that she shall be and is washed clean of such ... " (Gies, 236) The issue of Joan's voices was left unsettled, and remains unsettled. Interest in her was revived by the events leading up to the French Revolution. In 1869, Felix Dupanloup, the Bishop of Orleans, appropriately enough, initiated the process that eventuated in sainthood. She was beatified in 1909 and canonized in 1920.

[31]Lucie-Smith, 3.

[32]Victoria Sackville-West, *Saint Joan of Arc* (London: Michael Josephy, 1936), 326-7.

[33]Gies, 257-58.

[34]Gies, 258; Andrew Lang, *The Maid of France, Being the Story of the Life and Death of Jeanne d'Arc* (London: Longmans, Green, 1908).

embarrassed by the role a woman played in forging a French nation, belittled what she did.[35] Frances Gies concludes: "[E]very biographer and historian who has written about Joan has in one way or another expressed dissatisfaction with her real story."[36]

The prejudices of some male historians aside, Joan's story is particularly troubling because she was female. Marina Warner notes that she "eludes the categories in which women have normally achieved ... immortality."[37] She was not a queen, a courtesan, a beauty, a mother, an artist of some kind, nor, until much later, a saint. "She is anomalous in our culture, a woman renowned for doing something on her own, not by birthright. She has extended the taxonomy of female types; she makes evident the dimension of women's dynamism."[38] It is her bravery, her stamina, her fighting ability, and her daring that are celebrated. Joan's achievements were those associated with males, as was her dress, and reaction to her dress—the subject of five charges at her trial,—is a clue to the disturbing quality of her sexuality.[39] Warner argues that Joan dressed herself in two intertwined uniforms of positive *vir*tue (from the Latin *vir,* man),[40] maleness and knighthood, and concludes:

> Through her transvestism, she abrogated the destiny of womankind. She could thereby transcend her sex; she could set herself apart and usurp the privileges of the male and his claim to superiority. At the same time, by never pretending to be other than a woman and a maid, she was usurping a man's function but shaking off the trammels of his sex altogether to occupy a different, third order, neither male nor female, but unearthly, like the angels whose company she adored.[41]

---

[35]Gies, 259; Anatole France, *Vie de Jeanne D'Arc* (Paris: Calmann-Levy, 1908).

[36]Gies, 258. Evidence of a distortion made for dramatic purposes appears in a program note Jean Anouilh wrote for the original French production of *L'Alouette,* where he refers to the trial judges "who spent long months harassing that weary, undernourished little girl, haggard and thin (yes, I know she was a big healthy girl, but I couldn't care less)."

[37]Warner, 6.

[38]Warner, 9.

[39]Warner, 143.

[40]For links between gender and virtue in the United States, see: Ruth H. Bloch, "The Gendered Meanings of Virtue in Revolutionary America." *Signs,* 13 (1987): 37-58.

[41]Warner, 145.

The name I shall give to this gender-synthesizing role is androgyne.[42]

The link between Joan's unusual gender role and her relationship to feminism was discussed in an article in the *Catholic World* following Joan's beatification in 1909.

> There is scarcely a figure in all history who embodies, in so exceptional and quintessential a degree, the ideals toward which modern womanhood is striving. For the modern ideal, so far as it is sound, so far as it is in anywise sane, is fain not to destroy but to fulfill. It would leave to woman all the hereditary virtues of her mother — adding, so far as might be, the latent but not less hereditary virtues of her father.[43]

Reaction to Joan as a woman warrior is complicated by her name. *Jeanne d'Arc* is an invention. Joan never used it.

> Joan's name was written *Darc;* but until the early seventeenth century, this surname was pronounced to end either with an open vowel or with a voiced *r*. The particle *de* is an invention … The grant of the du Lys arms in 1430 to Joan's family spells her name *Day.… Jane Day* presumably transcribes phonetically the way Montaigne pronounced her name [in 1580].[44]

In the late sixteenth and early seventeenth centuries, when Joan began to be written about by classicists, her name was Latinized, required that the *c* be pronounced, and once the *c* was sounded in Latin, it began to be sounded in French.[45] Thus, d'Arc came into being, and *Arc,* meaning "bow," "arch," and "curve," linked Joan to a body of imagery associated with women since antiquity and made familiar by Homer and Virgil and Ovid and other texts in which appear Diana, the hunter, and Penthesilea and Hippolyta, queens of the Amazons.[46] The Amazons worshipped Diana and lived by her example, spurning men, hunting game, and rejoicing in battle, and as such, the Amazon "dramatizes sexual difference."[47] Moreover, despite appearances, "amazon" is an image symbolizing

---

[42]Warner's chapter 7, 139-58, is entitled "Ideal Androgyne."
[43]Katherine Brégy, "Jeanne d'Arc," *Catholic World,* 94 (February): 657.
[44]Warner, 199.
[45]Warner, 200.
[46]Warner, 202.
[47]Warner, 215.

male supremacy. The Amazon was praised for her male qualities, her physical skills, courage, accuracy of aim, speed of foot, endurance in battle, not for her choice of role. That "amazon" is a symbol of rejection of the feminine is clearest in one detail of the myth, that Amazons severed a breast by burning in order to improve their hunting and fighting skills. Such self-mortification symbolizes murder, specifically self-murder; it is a violent rejection of femininity.[48] Joan was, then, a troubling figure; she was at the same time outside traditional gender categories—an androgyne— and, yet, linked to symbols of sexual difference and conflict—the Amazons.[49]

DICKINSON'S "JEANNE D'ARC"

As part of the lyceum movement and as a supporter of early woman's rights efforts, Dickinson was in an ideal position to Americanize Joan's story. Dickinson began her public career in 1860 at age 17 when she spoke extemporaneously on woman's rights and on anti-slavery. In 1861, introduced by Lucretia Coffin Mott, she made her first full-length speech on "The Rights and Wrongs of Women" in Concert Hall in Philadelphia before an audience of some 800 people. In 1862, she made speeches on the war, including a lyceum lecture delivered in Boston. She became a national celebrity when in 1863 she was hired by the Republican Party to canvass in political campaigns in Connecticut, New Hampshire, New York, and Pennsylvania; her speechmaking was recognized as the major factor in Republican victories in those states, victories vital to the Union cause. On January 16, 1864, by invitation of President Lincoln and Republican members of

---

[48]"The self-slaughter of the Amazons' warrior ways and their terrible engagements with their destroyers [Amazonomachies] represent a ritual combat between feminine and masculine elements, reduced to a confining apartheid, in which the male is shown ultimately to prevail. The analogy of this in Joan's case is her martyrdom" (Warner, 216). See also: William Blake Tyrrell, *Amazons: A Study in Athenian Mythmaking* (Baltimore: Johns Hopkins University Press, 1984).

[49]In that regard, relying on Freudian concepts, Joan's historic role has been attributed to problems of sexual identity, father fixation, latent homosexual tendencies, and penis envy by psychohistorians (Roger Money-Kyrile, "A Psychoanalytic Study of the Voices of Joan of Arc," *British Journal of Medical Psychology* 13 (1933); Lucie-Smith, esp. 24-26, 219).

Congress, she addressed the nation's political establishment and became the first woman to speak in the House of Representatives.[50] She was introduced by Vice President Hannibal Hamlin who said that, like Joan of Arc, she seemed to have been sent by Providence to save the nation.[51] At that moment she was the most famous and adored woman in the country.

Dickinson formally entered the world of the commercial lyceum in 1866 and immediately was recognized as one of its most successful lecturers, rivaled only by one or two men. By 1872, she was delivering some 150 lectures per year and grossing over $20,000 annually. Although under different titles, her lectures consistently treated some aspect of "universal freedom, universal suffrage, universal justice,"[52] and explored fundamental social and political principles and their application in contemporary life. Her audiences came to expect "highly informative, if strongly opinionated, discussions of important social and political questions of the day," rendered entertaining by her style, described as "an overpowering array of facts, examples, and testimony interlarded with a graphic sense of the dramatic, a vividness of expression, a sense of climax, and a richness of voice that could respond with infinite variations to the emotional demands of her subject."[53] Although a popular lecturer, her success did not result from pandering to audience attitudes. Her biographer, Giraud Chester, sums up her career in the commercial lyceum this way:

> She was blatantly and self-consciously nonconformist and seemed to take delight in asserting her individuality and refusing to accept without question or protest the code of behavior that shaped the lives of her contemporaries. She dressed as she desired; she traveled where and how she willed; she delivered lectures on subjects [prostitution] many people felt should not even be mentioned in the presence of unmarried young ladies. As a result, she antagonized many of her former ... supporters.[54]

---

[50]Young, 475.

[51]Chester, 5-6.

[52]Chester, 92. "Jeanne d'Arc" bears more resemblance to Dickenson's plays than to her other lectures.

[53]Chester, 89 and 24.

[54]Chester, 86.

In fact, Dickinson defied hostile audiences, as, for example, when she championed the rights of Chinese immigrants to Californians!

In 1870, for the first time, Dickinson offered a lecture outside the realm of current political and social controversy—"Jeanne d'Arc."[55] Her lecture on Joan was a resounding popular success for several reasons. First, it capitalized on the link between the speaker and Joan of Arc evident in Vice President Hamlin's speech of introduction. As one reporter commented: "Miss Dickenson [sic] *knows* Jeanne Darc [sic]. The history of the girl has become so a part of herself that she follows the heroine through sad triumphs and suffers with her.... The subject is eminently fitted to Miss Dickenson—or she to the subject."[56] Dickinson's role in saving the Union would have piqued general interest in this lecture.

In addition, the lecture was highly dramatic in style. Dickinson did not merely speak; she declaimed. Reading her words, one can easily hear the full-throated tones and see the sweeping gestures of an earlier time. Dickinson both confronted and involved the audience by presenting her material in dialogue form, e.g. "Need of a miracle, here?" "'How,' say you, 'unmolested?'" "Let us see if that statement will hold water." And in terms of diction, the language was archaic, suggesting historical authenticity, e.g., "as the old chronicles tell us," or "this testimony, sworn and proven, lies tonight among the State Papers of France, for whoso to examine that has need or desire." Finally, in addition to being stylistically dramatic, Dickinson offered her audience a structured drama: a hero emerged, her mission was fulfilled, she faced reverses but, ultimately, died in triumph.

However, these factors, although significant, played only a minor role in the lecture's success. More important was Joan's transformation into a woman with whom nineteenth-century Americans could identify.

In her lecture, Dickinson emphatically distinguished her version of Joan's story from those of others. She dismissed the versions of Hume, Schiller, and Shakespeare, and rejected the representations of Jules Michelet and Alphonse de Lamartine as

---

[55]Apparently it was last presented in 1895 in Asbury Park, NY (Chester, 274).

[56]"Jeanne Darc," *The New Brunswick Daily Times,* n. d., c. 1874; AED Papers, Library of Congress, Reel 23, cont. 22, 230.

typical French treatments of women—"outward courtesy that veils inward contempt"—as well as the American Catharine Beecher's hypothesis that Joan's "voices and visions ... were the results of a disease; a distempered condition of the body, affecting the organs of sight and sound."[57]

By contrast, Dickinson's Joan was a real and ordinary person, not a legend, a saint, or a creature of blind fate. She was a patriot who worshipped at the altar of a civil religion; and, despite her mission to see a king crowned, she became a democratic populist. Spiritually, Catholic Joan was shown to be Protestant. Finally, Dickinson's Joan triumphed in death, giving her life for her country; she was not a threatening, troubling "amazon," but a "true woman," that is, pure, pious, domestic, and submissive.[58]

Most fundamentally, Dickinson had to struggle against past views of Joan as a "larger-than-life" figure. As presented in the lecture, Joan was a real person whose life was fully documented. In telling her story, Dickinson said, "one does not speak of a myth, of a legend, of a tale that is told. One does not say, 'Perhaps it was thus'.... One simply says, so it was." Joan herself was described in terms reflecting rural, agrarian, frontier values: "[S]he lived a life chiefly out of doors, that was simple, strong, vigorous, active, wholesome." Dickinson systematically debunked any suggestion that her call was unique or her powers unearthly. She said: "I believe she was called to her work. —Not by voices. By signs, by wonders in the air. No. I believe *she* was called, just as you and I are called, since I know full well that every soul that ever yet was sent into the world, had its work appointed of God, and the voice of conscience, to drive it on."

She denied that Joan performed miracles. Dickinson explained that Joan recognized the King among his courtiers at Chinon castle, not by revelation, but as anyone would who had been in Chinon for three days. The King and Court accepted this illiterate peasant girl because "they saw of what stuff she was made and for

---

[57]Beecher was the first to attempt a systematic study of U.S. women's health, which she found deplorable. However, I am unable to locate the essay to which Dickinson referred.

[58]Barbara Welter, *Dimity Convictions: The American Woman in the Nineteenth Century* (Athens: Ohio University Press, 1976), 21.

what work she was ready." She brought no miracles to the siege of Orleans, only "two hundred men-at-arms, ... some food for starving mouths. She brought herself." What Joan meant was reinterpreted through the words of Isaiah. Chapter 61 begins: "The Spirit of the Lord God is upon me; because the Lord hath ... sent me to ... proclaim liberty to the captives ...." " Verse 3 contains the words Dickinson used: "to give them beauty for ashes, the oil of joy for mourning, the garment of praise for the spirit of heaviness ...." " In other words, Joan contributed morale. Her plan of campaign to break the siege was simple and commonsensical, "what Napoleon put into practice centuries later." Her power and her leadership came from her resolve, her good sense, and her stamina, not from some divine power. She had a "quickness of thought that pertains to genius," but hers was "that rarest of all genius, the genius of Common Sense." She was a person like the Americans in Dickinson's audience or like Americans as they would wish to be in times of national crisis. "She had goodness in a generation of infidelity,—she had genius in a time of commonplace—above all she had faith. ... this goodness, this genius, above all this faith, made her the fit leader of a faithless King, a shattered army, a dispirited and heartbroken people." Even on her day of triumph, the coronation at Rheims, Dickinson claimed that she retained a sense of her common roots:

> 'Twas a dizzy height. Did she lose balance, there? Was it necessary to place behind her, as behind Caesar, (in his triumphs,) a slave, to whisper, 'remember, thou too, art but human'? She was a peasant. She was a girl of 18. She had all France at her feet and was the marvel of Europe. What was her ambition?

Dickinson answered that she asked the King's leave to return home: "Let me return, ... under my mother's roof, ... go out as in times past, in the open fields, to tend my father's sheep." In contrast to other versions of her story, this Joan was a person with whom ordinary Americans could identify.

As a monarchist, Joan was also a problematic figure for Americans, but Dickinson transformed her politics. She said: "Her parents were peasants,—poor—but, with the independence that always comes from actual ownership of the soil." Her political skills came from her ability to reflect the thoughts and feelings of the French people. "A child of the people, understood what would touch the hearts of the people. A soldier, knew what would rouse the courage of soldiers." She was consistently presented as struggling against the generals and the King's advisors, described as "dissolute young courtiers." No character similar to Shaw's Dunois, Joan's trusted friend and advisor, appeared. Joan was loved by the ordinary soldiers she commanded and by the people, but despised by the aristocrats and betrayed by the generals. After her defeat at Saint Denis, Dickinson said: "The courtiers, in too many cases, hated her for her power, and were envious of her success, and they made the most of the opportunity, to reveal their bad feelings. The people, the common soldiers, loved her, as of old." Joan knew, even before it happened, that "her King would prove faithless." As a result, Charles VII became merely the tool through which Joan worked to save her country; she represented the will of the people.

Joan's extreme religious piety was another challenge, but Dickinson made Joan religious in an American sort of way. A religious framework explained the meaning of her life. Early the audience was told that Joan was the fulfillment of prophecy — a wrong against a woman had to be righted by a woman, just as Mary's child erased Eve's curse:[59] "A war, that began by denying — right — to a woman, was ended, by a woman. A war, the onset of which was the sacrifice of legitimacy in the person of a young girl, was closed, victory gained, peace established by another young girl." "Thus," said Dickinson, secularizing the principle by quoting Shakespeare, "the 'Whirligig of Time brings in his revenges.'" Joan had been called; she announced that she was "come from God." Recall, however, Dickinson's statement that Joan was called as each of us is called. She summed up Joan's mission by saying, "Manifestly they made her lose her life to find it again," a distortion of Matthew 10:39, which reads: "He ... that loseth his life *for my sake* shall find it" (italics added). Rather than impelled by God, France's needs "made her lose her life to find it." Joan's story was of this world. At the end, the significance of Joan's life was summed up in a paraphrase of the words of St. Paul, but the words, "She had fought the good fight. She had finished her

---

[59]Gal. 3: 13.

course. She had kept the faith," were a remarkably secular tribute to sticking to one's principles in the face of opposition.

Because Joan was tried on charges of heresy, Dickinson exploited the opportunity to present her as a Protestant:

> I pray you, who care to estimate this girl, and her character aright, to remember that before the word "Protestant" was spoken in Europe, before Luther was dreamt of, this child, this peasant, this Catholic, facing prelates of her own church, life and death hanging on the balance, answered them after this wise: "As to my work, my battles, my signs, they were the toils of human hands. I am content to submit them to the judgment of the Pope and his Council, men great in power, yet, human beings like myself. But for mine inspiration — it came of Heaven. I yield it, to Heaven, alone. I refuse to recognize the right of any man to interfere between the soul, and its God."

Dickinson's account turned Joan's religion into simple patriotism. "Her patriotism was her religion. Her religion was her life." The struggle that engaged Joan was not unlike the American Revolution, a struggle for independence, to forge a nation. The villains of this tale were British. Bedford, the English regent, hoped to destroy "France as an independent power," to "reduce it, as a vassal, to our [the English] crown." William Glasdale, the English commander at Orleans, was a soldier who violated the laws of war; the Earl of Warwick, renowned as the very flower of chivalry, flaunted its most fundamental rules; England's allies, the Burgundians, were venal, abusive, treacherous, and unjust. Joan's victory over the besieging British at Orleans echoed Andrew Jackson's victory over the British at New Orleans in 1815. Dickinson said: "She so loved France [not God]; she so sorrowed in its sorrow; she so longed to live for it, to suffer for it, to die for it at need, that by and by this one supreme thought took absolute possession of her being." Given Anna Dickinson's personal relationship to the Civil War, it would have been easy to hear such words as a celebration of the Union and of those who were willing to fight and die to see it preserved, a reading that would have heightened American appreciation of Joan's story.

There were two dimensions to Joan's heroism, one related to her as an ordinary person, the other related to her as a woman. On one level, she was heroic in ways that recall the ordinary American heroes of Ronald Reagan's rhetoric — she rose to meet a crisis, to break the siege of Orleans and enable the Dauphin to be crowned at Rheims. Dickinson detailed the process by which Joan finally reached the King at Chinon, and it was a story of courage, obstinacy, and physical endurance. She was heroic because she fearlessly hurled herself into the fight, battle axe in hand. She risked her life to lead her men and to protect them in retreat. She endured the pain of a severe wound to fight on. She remained steadfast even in imprisonment; Dickinson called her "helpless, yet, heroic." Alone, with her soul and her God, she faced "ninety judges on the bench," and her soul and her God "sufficed."

The heroism of the ordinary person who rises to meet a crisis is related to the one point at which Dickinson hinted at overt sexism in Joan's treatment by others. After describing Joan's military strategy at Orleans and comparing it to that of Napoleon, she commented: "Of the man, the world says, 'What august power! What commanding genius!' Of the woman, under precisely similar conditions, it cries, 'Why what a lucky accident it was, she should happen to hit upon that plan.'" Dickinson rejected narratives that belittled Joan and demanded that she receive credit for what she had done.

As noted earlier, Joan as a woman warrior was a troubling sexual figure. Dickinson's transformation of Joan into a Protestant democratic patriot pales in comparison to her assimilation of Joan into the cult of true womanhood. Just how greatly she was transformed can be demonstrated by three undisputed facts from Joan's life.[60] First, Joan was not submissive. She actively rejected marriage, successfully defending herself against a breach of promise suit brought by a young man from Toul, presumably over a betrothal arranged by Joan's parents. Joan left home without parental permission, and during her struggle to reach the King at Chinon, they did not know where she had gone or what she was doing. Second, she reveled in her male roles. She inspired by leading her troops in battle. She enjoyed fighting, usually urging — not always wisely — that the attack be pressed. She was confident,

---

[60]These "facts" are agreed to in both the trial and rehabilitation or can be verified from outside sources and are accepted in most accounts pretending to accuracy. On these specific points, see, respectively, the hostile, psychohistorical biography of Lucie-Smith, 23, 32-35, 103, 106, 215, 217, 219-21, and the analyses of Joan narratives by Lightbody, 18, 71, 73, 150, and Warner, 45, 113-114, 153-54, 170-73, 179.

opinionated, and persistent; the King and Dunois, among others, found her difficult to control. She gloried in her special armor and the elegant trappings of nobility, dress that symbolized her mission and her commitment to it. Third, she had no desire for martyrdom. Twice she attempted escape, once by jumping from the tower of Beaurevoir castle into a dry moat and almost killing herself. She was kept in shackles thereafter because she would not promise to forego another attempt. In fact, confronted with the scaffold on which she was later burned, Joan signed an abjuration, but abjured it in turn when its implications — life imprisonment and denial of her mission and the authenticity of her voices — became clear. In effect, she "sacrificed" her life to preserve her identity.[61]

In transforming Joan into a "true woman," establishing Joan's purity and piety posed little challenge. They have been accepted generally, except by psychohistorians and those who have followed the so-called "English theory" that she was a witch and harlot or merely an imposter. However, as reported by Dickinson, Joan put on male dress for reasons of practicality, not because she was putting off the limitations of femininity: "Nothing should stand betwixt her and her work. The woman's dress would expose her to difficulty, danger, insult, perchance, death itself." After her recantation, she put on male clothing only under duress: "[S]he cried again and again for her peasant garments and they were withheld, till, to save herself from insult, from danger, nay, from absolute violation she put it on." Joan's piety was noted, first in childhood, when Joan attended mass daily. To the end, she kept her eyes fixed on the cross and "prayed for these her enemies."

Establishing her domesticity and submissiveness presented a greater challenge, as indicated by the facts noted above. Joan's disobedience of her parents was rationalized as duty overwhelming affection, a subtle way of suggesting that hers was a higher obedience. After the coronation, presented in the lecture as the completion of Joan's mission, Dickinson told her audiences: "The soldier's work, was done. The patriot's labor, was ended. The

---

[61]In support of this, Warner writes: "In 1888, the devil's advocate, whose task in canonization proceedings is to argue the case against the candidate, compared her to Christopher Columbus, someone who had achieved great things, but not altogether for the glory of God" (264).

woman's heart cried for home." Like a wife/mother, Joan was compassionate, even toward her enemies; she pitied those who fell and prayed for their souls. When Joan's request to return home was rejected, she submitted: "She prayed,—she entreated,—as a good, a loyal subject, she yielded to the commands of the king." Her femininity was stereotypical: "This voice, that brought comfort to the fainting hearts of men, was a woman's voice:—that of a girl, young and beautiful, and unselfish, and wise with that wisdom which, through all ages, entering into holy souls, has made them prophetic, and friends of God."

A nineteenth-century American Joan probably had to be a true woman; surely no other image could have been the centerpiece of a popular lecture of this period. But how could this woman warrior have been absorbed into the cult of domesticity? By the tactic of treating her death as martyrdom,[62] a move that transformed Joan into a "true woman" whose life was sacrificed for France.

Joan's story as told in the lecture was not a tragedy, at least not in the classical sense. It included the story of a hero with an overarching conviction of personal mission, who triumphs, then faces reversals, the destruction of hope, and extinction. But the moral message of Joan's story followed the pattern of the Adam-Christ myth. There was no *hubris* in the classical sense, because what impelled Joan to her death was obedience to divine will, which made her a hero-victim, a paschal lamb, in effect. There was no defiance of the gods, no *hamartia,* and the death of such a hero is a victory, not a defeat. In this form, her story is "intended ... to exhort and to indoctrinate others to revere her high example ... she does not inspire cautionary pity and fear, but incites us to

---

[62]Warner explores the ideological and aesthetic complexity of viewing Joan's death as martyrdom, but not necessarily in the form developed by Dickinson (267-73). She writes: "At one level [when Joan's death results from her adjuring the abjuration], her martyrdom is a consummation of her unbending trueness to herself, a concept that underlies the essence of heroism .... But at another level, her death in the fire is the only triumph in an ideological climate [of moral absolutism] where change means deterioration, a gradual haemorrhage of grace from the state of first innocence, the pure child" (266-67). Later, linking martyrdom to attitudes toward women who violate traditional roles, she add: "If the central presence of sexual pleasure-in-pain in the Christian concept of martyrdom is recognized, martyrdom can at least be understood in its psychological place without being trivialized .... We are back with the Amasonoma-chies, the defloration of the unattached female in death ..."

imitation. She is admonitory, not minatory."[63] Her story becomes a
moral exemplar peculiarly suited to rhetorical ends, and shaped in
this fashion, her life can be appropriated to serve many ideological
purposes.

When framed this way, Joan's transvestism, her skill in battle,
her physical strength and endurance, her love of action, and her
inviolability — all the qualities that might be claimed as feminist —
are transmuted because, in the final conclusion, they are offered on
the altar of male supremacy. Like an idealized true woman, Joan
became a ministering angel unselfishly devoted to king and
country, which here substitute for husband and family. This
perspective on Joan was suggested early in the lecture. In
describing Joan's childhood, for instance, Dickinson emphasized
her unselfishness and foreshadowed her martyrdom: "Things small,
things petty, things base, things that are for self and self alone ...
by and by such matters as these were crushed to death in her."
Later, she said, Joan abjured, not in despair and confusion, but
only to gain time to complete her sacrifice. Dickinson suggested
that she "said to herself, '... if I sign it [the abjuration], I gain
freedom thereby. I can finish the battles of the King, they are
nearly done! After that, what matter!'" However, according to
Dickinson, once she had signed, she discovered that her sentence
was life imprisonment. How, then, did Joan come to die? In the
words of the lecture:

> And on the eighth morning, as she would rise from her bed, she
> found — lying beside it, not the peasant gown she had sworn to
> resume, and on which hung her life, — but the steel links of the
> armor, she had promised never to wear again.
>
> She knew that to clothe herself in that armor would be to
> dress herself in her shroud; — to enter those steel links, would be
> to enter the open door of her tomb, and so standing, she cried
> again and again for her peasant garments and they were
> withheld, till, to save herself from insult, from danger, nay, from
> absolute violation, she put it on.
>
> 'Twas but a trap in which to catch her. Spies had been
> watching. They ran with hasty steps to tell the Bishop of
> Beauvais. And she, where she stood in the gloom of her

---

[63]Warner, 268.

dungeon, could hear the Bishop's feet sounding on the flagstones of the courtyard outside, could hear his voice, jarring the solemn stillness of the Sabbath morning as he cried to the Earl of Warwick, where he hung from an upper window, "Aha! We have caught her!"

And the next day she was carried out to her death.[64]

Here Dickinson has reduced Joan to nothingness. Joan has become a pawn moved by others, a creature without choice, a scapegoat and victim. In the story told by Dickinson, Joan did not die to affirm her mission or the authenticity of her voices; she was a casualty of political conflict, crushed by the machinations of the English abetted by their Burgundian allies. Pure, pious, and passive, she was murdered. In such circumstances, was there anything a true woman could do? She could die well, and in dying, according to this plot line, she triumphs.[65] "And here," said Dickinson, "at the selfsame moment of her life, she manifested herself, supreme. Dying, she conquered the living."

The lecture's long conclusion tells the story of Joan's execution, described in terms that echo Christ's crucifixion: She was spat upon, she was lifted up on a high scaffold, she prayed for her enemies, and at the final moment, the soldiers "cry out, 'Ah, look at her! Listen to her! See her! See a Saint of God we are about to burn!'"

The period in which this lecture was delivered coincided with the rise of what has been called social feminism,[66] a time when

---

[64]Based on the dramatic form of the lecture, I take this passage to be the key in establishing Dickinson's view of Joan's character.

[65]In his essay on Joan, Thomas De Quincey made martyrdom one of the few achievements available to Women: "Yet, sister woman, though I cannot consent to find a Mozart or a Michel Angelo (sic) in your sex, cheerfully and with the love that burns in depths of admiration, I acknowledge that your can do one thing as well as the best of us men ... — you can die grandly, and as goddesses would die, were goddesses mortal" (21).

[66]William O'Neill used this label to refer to the views that, after 1875, dominated the U.S. women's movement. Those he calls "social feminists" "justif[ied] their activities on the grounds that society was an extension of the home and woman's work in it merely an enlargement of her maternal powers ... (*Everyone Was Brave: History of Feminism in America* (New York: Quadrangle, 1971), 353). As O'Neill indicates, the conception of woman's nature central to the cult of domesticity was the foundation for the arguments characterizing social feminism. Such arguments were present in woman's rights rhetoric from the beginning, but achieved dominance only in the 1870s, see: Steve Buechler, "Elizabeth Boynton Harbert and the Woman Suffrage Movement," *Signs* 13(1987): 78-79.

woman's rights, particularly suffrage, were justified in terms of the benefits woman's influence would bring. Social feminism did not attempt to alter the image of woman enshrined in the cult of domesticity, but to broaden the sphere in which her influence would be felt. Suffragist rhetoric shifted from arguments based on natural rights to arguments based on expediency — women's votes were the means to moral ends. As presented by Dickinson, Joan was woven into the fabric of social feminism, which explains the lecture's ongoing national popularity during the rise of the Woman's Christian Temperance Union under its great president, Frances Willard, the pre-eminent social feminist.[67] Joan's violation of the female role was made acceptable because she died a sacrifice to traditional, even male, ends — placing a French King on the throne of France.

Analyzing Anna Dickinson's "Jeanne d'Arc" is an occasion to study the link between a powerful symbol of great antiquity, the biography of an extraordinary personage, and the social mythology defining woman's role. The ancient, powerful symbol of the androgyne — Amazon is its misogynist version — unifies the powers of the female with the actions and roles typically identified with the male. In her life, Joan embodied that symbolic convergence; that is, she was a female who always insisted on her femaleness (she never pretended to be male), who played male roles (as warrior, initiator, actor) while remaining independent of and untainted by any male (a virgin). Symbolically, this androgyne incarnated the range of human potential. As such, her life story invited exploitation, i.e. efforts to link her symbolic power to whatever cause. However, because she embodied a gender role that violated cultural assumptions about womanhood, her story also invited distortions, retellings that would alter her life to make it fit

---

[67]The relative appeal of arguments based on natural rights and on expediency can be suggested by the size of the competing organizations. In 1876, the WCTU had some 13,000 dues-paying members; by 1890, under Willard's leadership, it had grown to 250,000 with branches in every state and territory, all cities and most local communities. By contrast, in 1890, the membership of the combined suffrage organizations, the NAWSA, was approximately 13,000 (Ruth Bordin, *Woman and Temperance: The Quest for Power and Liberty, 1873-1900* (Philadelphia: Temple University Press, 1981) and Karlyn Kohrs Campbell, *Man Cannot Speak for Her*, 2 Vols. (Westport, CT: Greenwood/Praeger, in press).

the prevailing social mythology, retellings that, in effect, would acculturate the androgyne. That a nonconformist and woman's rights/woman suffrage advocate such as Anna Dickinson should have connived in that process merely demonstrates the power of socialization.

In Dickinson's lecture, Joan became a character in the plot that decreed that a true woman had to die if she violated her culturally determined role, a plot that confined a woman's power to dying as a sacrifice to male ends. As a result, Joan, the independent woman warrior, became a symbol reinforcing the sexist values of nineteenth-century America. In similar narratives, writes Warner, Joan has been made into "a suitably versatile talisman for a host of causes conducted by men, military and political."[68] A feminist reading not only illuminates this lecture but, more generally, makes intelligible how Joan could have been apotheosized by so many non-feminist authors and how she could have become the symbol for so many male supremacist causes.

---

[68]Warner, 217.

RESPONSE TO KARLYN KOHRS CAMPBELL'S ANNA E. DICKINSON'S JEANNE D'ARC: DIVERGENT VIEWS

WIL LINKUGEL
ROBERT ROWLAND

In a truly excellent essay, Karlyn Kohrs Campbell has brought to our attention an immensely popular lecture of the nineteenth century, Anna Dickinson's "Jeanne D'Arc," a lecture that in all senses is worthy of rhetorical study. In the interest of dialogue we will view Campbell's essay and Dickinson's lecture from two divergent perspectives. First, we will treat the lecture from the "true woman" perspective used by Campbell, and then in the spirit of critical pluralism will suggest that another interpretation of the essay may be possible, the assumption being that no single critical method can exhaust the study of such an important work. The second part of our critical response will be labeled the "mythic perspective."

THE "TRUE WOMAN" PERSPECTIVE

Perhaps the most important task of the nineteenth century woman's movement—when taken as a whole—was to generate a new image of "woman" in the popular mind. Anna Howard Shaw, one of the most prominent orators of the movement, referred to this prototype as a "New Woman." The existing and approved image of woman was that of a "ministering angel" or a "clinging vine"—a woman who was, as Campbell tells us in her paper, "pure, pious, submissive, and domestic." This "true woman" was to leave the "hard knocks" activities of politics and the business world to the "stronger and more intellectual" male, and at all times occupy herself with the gentler and more refined activities of hearth and home. Feminist rhetors wished to replace this stereotype in the minds of people with a new woman who sexually was feminine, but in all other matters, be it politics, business or public speaking, was neither male nor female, but a human dealing with life's problems and conducting life's business.

Rhetors could use three channels in their efforts to advance feminism. The first was enactment. For example, Anna Howard Shaw's tremendous rhetorical success can be explained partially by the fact that she herself manifested the traits characteristic of a citizen-voter. To some extent at least, Anna Dickinson likewise can be seen as enacting the "new woman": She was extremely effective on the platform, displayed a keen mind, and demonstrated good linguistic skills.

The second channel was argument. Rhetors might attempt to convince the public that there were fundamental reasons for women's rights, including the right to suffrage, that women were capable of practicing the franchise meaningfully, and that they would not turn into sexual monstrosities if they assumed roles that previously had been regarded as sheerly masculine. Anna Dickinson initially used this route also. As Campbell has mentioned, by 1872, she delivered "some 150 lectures per year" on aspects of "universal freedom, universal suffrage, universal justice." But as Campbell has noted, she never participated directly in the woman suffrage movement and was never a member of any woman suffrage organization. She may have been more of a performer than a reformer; she traveled on the lecture circuit, not on the campaign trail. And, as Campbell has pointed out, when the lyceum shifted toward entertainment, Dickinson turned to an entertainment medium, play writing.

The third channel open to feminist rhetors was the generation of a new image of woman in the popular mind through the use of a prototype. Dickinson's Joan of Arc lecture contains the elements that might have entered into the construction of such a prototype. In this respect, the lecture emerges as one of the most intriguing and significant works in the corpus of nineteenth century woman's rhetoric. And Campbell has made an important contribution by bringing to our attention a lecture that attracted a great many hearers in its time, but which, since it never appeared in published form, has largely escaped contemporary notice. In this instance, as in much of her other work, Campbell demonstrates that archival research is crucially important to the study of public address.

Campbell gives three reasons for the popular success of the lecture: (1) Dickinson capitalized on the link between speaker and subject, for Dickinson, like Joan, "had violated the limits of traditional womanhood," faced "jeers and revilings," and had taken positions unpopular with the establishment; (2) Dickinson spoke in "high style" in order to achieve historical authenticity; and (3) Dickinson transformed Joan "into a woman with whom nineteenth-century Americans could identify." Here we have the basis for the persona of the "new woman." Joan's story is grounded in "courage, obstinacy, and physical endurance"; her herosim is characterized by "persistence, determination, and stamina."

Campbell, however, finds that there were two dimensions to Joan's heroism, "one related to her as a real, ordinary person, the other related to her as a woman." Quite rightly, it is the second dimension of Joan's heroism that chiefly interests Campbell, and she perceptively observes: "Joan as a warrior was a troubling sexual figure." She proceeds: "Dickinson's transormation of Joan into a Protestant democratic patriot pales in comparison to her accultura-tion of Joan as a 'true woman'." Unfortunately, "all the qualities that might be claimed as feminist are transmuted because, in the final conclusion, they are offered on the altar of male supremacy."

Campbell laments that as "nineteenth century American Joan had to be a true woman; no other image could have been the center-piece of a popular lecture of the time." She then relates Dickinson's portrayal of Joan to the rise of social feminism, which occurred at "a time when woman's rights, particularly suffrage, were justified in terms of the benefits woman's influence would bring. Social feminism did not attempt to alter woman's image, but to broaden the sphere in which her influence would be felt." This, Campbell tells us, "explains the lecture's ongoing national popularity."

It is possible that Campbell is kinder to Anna Dickinson than a critic ought to be. As she has so ably demonstrated, Dickinson failed to transform Joan into the "new woman" archetype, but instead returned her to the "true woman." The feminist conception of the "new woman" was to be somewhere between "the true woman" and the "Amazon"—she was to be a woman who did not deny or mortify her femininity; neither was she to be submissive and subservient to the male and bound to stereotypical sexual roles. Rather she was men's equal, his complement or counterpart, a person who utilized her talents, whether they were the deftness of hand and fingers for sewing or surgery, the mental acuity for teaching or research, or the practical sense for running a family or a business.

Why did Dickinson fail to establish the "new woman" with

the Joan of Arc story? One explanation is that she herself was so thoroughly acculturated that she could not embrace the image of the "new woman"; the other, more cynical explanation is that she sacrificed that ideal for commercial gain. After all Dickinson lectured for profit, and she stood to gain by adapting her message to the widest possible audience. Especially in the South, where the lecture proved very popular, this consideration required assimilating Joan into the image of the "true woman" rather than of the "new woman."

When hard core woman suffragists went to work in the 1870's for equal suffrage, Dickinson, opinionated and aloof, did not join in but instead became a playwright, whose public appearances were limited to this highly profitable lecture. According to Campbell, the popularity of Dickinson's lecture was related to the rise of social feminism, which did not attempt to alter woman's image, but to broaden the sphere in which her influence would be felt. Yet at that time Susan B. Anthony, Anna Howard Shaw, and Elizabeth Cady Stanton—whom no one would call social feminists—were stumping the country representing the feminist position, and they were gaining audiences also. Campbell's essay makes us aware of Dickinson's skill as a speaker and of the appeal of a lecture transforming Joan of Arc into American terms. But she fails to demonstrate that the transformation of Joan into a "true woman" was essential to the power of the lecture. It is not clear whether a different depiction of Joan might not have been equally compelling and powerful. It is not clear that "no other image could have been the centerpiece of a popular lecture of the time."

Dickinson in her lecture engaged in a good deal of casuistic stretching of the Joan of Arc legend in order to Americanize it. If that casuistic stretching was justified, Joan could have been depicted as "the new woman" just as easily as the "true woman." The qualities of courage, persistence, determination, physical endurance, and related characteristics which Joan represented were indeed those of a new woman. Throughout history there have been speeches that have transformed society, but there also have been instances when rhetors failed to take advantage of golden opportunities to achieve significant rhetorical impact. Anna Dickinson, perhaps the most adored American woman of her day, failed to establish a role model consistent with the feminist aspiration for a "new woman" prototype, and her rhetoric may have impeded rather than advanced the cause of women's rights.

In summary, we highly commend Campbell's power of descriptive analysis but suggest that a somewhat harsher critical judgment of Anna Dickinson could be rendered.

A MYTHIC PERSPECTIVE

Now, in the interest of critical pluralism, we want to take a somewhat different perspective on the Dickinson lecture. After reading the lecture, it occurred to us that a mythological analysis might prove productive and might yield a somewhat different result. What follows is such an analysis.

In her study of Dickinson's lecture Campbell argues that Dickinson had to "struggle against past views of Joan as a legendary, mythical, 'larger-than-life' figure." According to Campbell, Dickinson's Joan "was a real person, not a legend." Campbell is clearly correct that Dickinson struggled against views of Joan of Arc as a crazied mystic, but the conclusion that Dickinson's Joan was not a mythic hero may be problematic. Perhaps Dickinson did not so much transform Joan into an American girl as transform her into a mythic hero appropriate for American women.[1]

Dickinson's problem was to purge the "false" elements from the story of Joan of Arc, in order to recast Joan as a mythic model. The mythic elements in Dickinson's lecture are obvious, and Campbell identifies a number of them. For example, she notes that Dickinson treated Joan as bringing to an end the cycle that began the Hundred Years War. While Dickinson treated Joan as a real person, she also depicted her as possessing qualities that go far beyond those of ordinary people. Even as a child, she possessed perfect piety, goodness, kindness, charity, and seriousness. She was a better soldier than any man and, centuries before Napoleon,

---

[1]For discussions of the role of myth, see Joseph Campbell, *Myths to Live By* (New York: Bantam, 1972); William G. Doty, *Mythograph: The Study of Myths and Rituals* (University of Alabama Press, 1986); Mircea Eliade, *Myth and Reality,* trans. Willard R. Trask (New York: Harper 1963); Northrop Frye, "Literature and Myth," *Relations of Literary Study,* ed. James B. Thorpe (New York: Modern Language Association, 1967). Howard Garner, *The Quest for Mind: Piaget, Levi-Strauss and the Structuralist Movement* (Chicago: University of Chicago Press 1981); Claude Levi-Strauss, "The Structural Study of Myth," *The Structuralists from Marx to Levi-Strauss,* ed. Richard and Fernande DeGeorge (Garden City, N.Y.: Doubleday, 1972).

invented the military strategy that would be associated with his name. And while Dickinson treated Joan as more Protestant than Catholic, she did not deny her special relationship with God. People saw in her "what men always have and always will recognize to the end of time — the eye and the voice of the Master soul, where it blazes and when it speaks." Later Dickinson described a scene in which Joan tells an assembled council of war that their decision is wrong: " 'Believe me, the councils of men shall come to naught, but that of my God shall stand'." Still later Dickinson quoted Joan during her trial, " 'I am come from God. I have naught to do here. Dismiss me to God from whence I came'." Dickinson, it seems, may not have been concerned with de-mythologizing Joan, but only with eliminating those elements of the myth that would tarnish its credibility for the American audience. Perhaps she did not reject the mythic, but redefined it.

Campbell is quite right to emphasize the adaptation in Dickinson's lecture, but that adaptation may have been so effective precisely because it was part of a mythic narrative. Dickinson perhaps attempted to transform Joan into a mythic hero, who could serve as a model for American women. For, like Joan of Arc after the crowning of the king at Rheims, "everyone of us, you and I, my friend, have had or will have our day from which we date." By emulating her strength, her common sense, her will, and her independence American women could become like Joan of Arc. They might not defeat the English, but they too could have a "day from which we date." In this reading, Dickinson's narrative, really did not transform Joan into an American girl. To be sure, Dickinson downplays Joan's Catholicism and her supernatural visions and voices because those events were not acceptable to her audience. But in Dickinson's narrative, Joan remains a messenger from God. She is a mythic hero who came from God to save France, and now, in Dickinson's transformed story, offers the solution to the problem facing woman.

We tell myths to solve problems that cannot be solved through other means. In the mythic narrative, a social problem may be confronted and solved through the actions of the hero. Thus, myths provide the heroes who define a society and solve contradictions. Perhaps Dickinson sought to present Joan as such a hero. A lecture defining the proper role for women might have confronted head-on all of the negative social attitudes toward feminism. But in a story those attitudes at least partially could be side-stepped. A good story operates aesthetically and enthymematically. The power of the story pulls the audience in, and the theme of the story then acts as an enthymeme, which the audience completes on its own.

Campbell's analysis of the plight of social feminism is surely on target, but it is possible at least that Dickinson's Joan offered a way out of this trap. It is the function of myths to resolve social contradictions, and in her description of Joan, Dickinson may have sought to solve the contradiction between true womanhood and feminism. According to Dickinson, after the victory at the siege of Orlean and the crowning of the king at Rheims, Joan of Arc wanted to go home: "The soldiers's work was done. The patriot's work was ended. The woman's heart cried for home." But the king would not let her go. And consequently she stayed and met her destiny. This passage might be interpreted as establishing the extent to which Dicksinson's story serves a traditional masculine ethic. After winning her battles, Joan of Arc wanted to return to her home, but the masculine ego wins out, and she must fight on. That may not have been, however, what Dickinson was saying. For immediately after receiving her orders from the Crown, something happened to Joan: "But it was noted that from this time a great sadness fell upon her and that she no longer originated plans. She was content to execute the orders of others." And as soon as she gave up her independence, she became vulnerable. The next paragraph describes a battle outside Paris, which she had "not planned" and "against which she had protested." The result was that "she and her men were driven back."

Thus, the key to understanding Dickinson's response to the cult of true womanhood may be revealed not in Joan's expression of her desire to return home, but in the immediately succeeding passage, where she yields to masculine authority. Viewed in this way, Dickinson's text deploys the strategy of myth to overcome a dilemma confronting feminism as it existed in her time. As mythic hero, Joan's power and well-being arise from her independence, from her capacity to act as her own conscience dictates. But when she compromises her independence, she loses her own integrity and her awesome prowess as a soldier and leader.

If this interpretation is plausible, then it might seem that Dickinson embeds a message in her lecture that goes well beyond the pieties of social feminism. Her narrative presents Joan as a model of feminine strength and achievement, and the model depends upon a quality denied other women—independence. Thus, Joan's story suggests that independence offers the only avenue for overcoming the plight of women. So long as Joan listens to and obeys her inner voice, she remains feminine and potent. As she acquiesces to external, male authority, she becomes an instrument of other, inferior wills, ineffective even for the purposes of those who control her.

Presented as straight-forward argument, Dickinson's message would have violated entrenched social values; she likely would not have won a hearing. Dickinson, therefore, might have masked this radical message both by adapting to conventional values and by placing the message in a mythic context. The lecture, then, might have subtly implied a perspective that so exceeded the norms of the day that it could not have been articulated in propositional form.

This reading, of course, is largely speculative, but our objective is not to determine the meaning of the text, but to open possiblities. Surely, Campbell's reading offers a plausible account of Dickinson's rhetoric and its placement in the nineteenth-century context. Yet, a text of this complexity resists explanation through any single interpretative frame. Where one reading finds in the text a consistent representation of "true womanhood"—a model of pious submission to the masculine world—another reading may attend to the twists in the narrative line and find a subtle but powerful protest against the repression of feminine independence.

METAPHOR AND MOTIVE
IN THE JOHNSON ADMINISTRATION'S
VIETNAM WAR RHETORIC
ROBERT L. IVIE

The Johnson administration's unsuccessful campaign to rally public support for the Vietnam war is a revealing moment in the rhetoric of the Cold War.[1] No other event demonstrates so clearly the reach as well as the limits of the containment doctrine. Although the motive to contain the spread of international communism led almost inevitably to American military engagement in Southeast Asia, it proved unable to sustain the national will long enough to prevail in Vietnam.[2]

Lyndon Johnson, as Herbert Schandler notes, realized from the beginning "that solid support at home was a prerequisite for the success of his policy in Vietnam." Although Johnson struggled throughout his presidency to secure public support for the war, America remained skeptical that its interests were sufficiently at risk to warrant the costs incurred. "To the American people," Schandler observes "the danger to the national interests of the United States posed by the Communist threat to South Vietnam had not been made evident, and the cost of meeting that threat had become too high."[3]

The President and his advisors, painfully aware of their rhetorical plight, attempted repeatedly to devise a strategy that would remedy the problem. Their collective struggle to articulate a compelling motive for the war, however, became hopelessly entangled in a self-neutralizing cluster of images that emphasized "containment" of communist aggression over giving "birth" to a free Vietnam — a hierarchy of terms that weakened recurrent

[1]Wayne Brockriede and Robert L. Scott, *Moments in the Rhetoric of the Cold War* (New York: Random House, 1970).

[2]George C. Herring, *America's Longest War: The United States and Vietnam, 1950-1975* (New York: John Wiley & Sons, 1979), x.

[3]Herbert Y. Schandler, *Lyndon Johnson and Vietnam: The Unmaking of a President* (Princeton, New Jersey: Princeton University Press, 1977), 326, 346.

appeals to standing "firm," taking "risks," and defeating a "savage" opponent. The counter-forces at work among these five key images, I shall argue, prevented the Johnson administration from developing the metaphor of containment into a sufficiently persuasive definition of the Vietnamese situation and, more importantly, kept the President and his advisors from reconsidering the presumed necessity of escalating American involvement in the war.

KENNETH BURKE ON METAPHOR AND MOTIVE

As a case study in the rhetoric of motives and rhetorical invention, the Johnson administration's failed strategy for articulating America's vital interests in Vietnam underscores the importance of attending to what Kenneth Burke says about metaphorical development as well as reduction. Burke's bi-directional model of metaphor's relationship to motives highlights the impact of terministic incongruities on the organizing principle of a rhetor's master image, a potentially disruptive effect that became especially problematic for LBJ's rhetorical strategists.

Burke links metaphor to motive through the term "perspective." That is, a perspective, or general framework of interpretation, is a systematic extension of a master metaphor, and a motive is a shorthand term for interpreting a particular situation.[4] "Cold War," for instance, is a shorthand term for depicting U.S.-Soviet relations in the post-World War II era. It constitutes "a rounded statement" about the two adversaries' motives vis-a-vis one another to the extent that it integrates a grammar of terms for act, scene, agent, agency, and purpose.[5] Its meaning, in turn, devolves from a broader perspective on America's historic mission and the character of its adversaries, a perspective that itself is rooted in a master image of America's special covenant with God.

In his essay on the "four master tropes," Burke observes that we typically refer to a metaphor as a perspective (instead of as a figure or trope) when it is used literally or realistically. Just as "metaphor is a device for seeing something *in terms of* something else," it is also the case that "to consider A from the point of view

---

[4]Kenneth Burke, *Permanence and Change: An Anatomy of Purpose,* 2d ed. (Indianapolis: Bobbs-Merrill Co., 1965), 25, 31.

[5]Kenneth Burke, *A Grammar of Motives* (Berkeley: University of California Press, 1969), xv.

of B is...to use B as a *perspective* upon A."⁶ Thus, in Burke's view, "every perspective requires a metaphor, implicit or explicit, for its organizational base."⁷ Philosophies and scientific theories "are hardly more than the patient repetition, in all its ramifications, of a fertile metaphor" which serves "as the cue for an unending line of data and generalizations"; the line of development is continuous from figurative-metaphorical-analogical forms of thought to literal-rational-logical constructions of reality.⁸

Whereas a perspective, or orientation, emerges from realizing the heuristic potential of a master metaphor, a motive in Burke's system is a subset of a perspective.⁹ One's perspective is a general orientation or point of view, a broad framework of interpretation that includes "a bundle of judgments as to how things were, how they are, and how they must be," i.e., a view of "how the world is put together."¹⁰ Motives are subdivisions of these larger frameworks of meaning, interpretations of specific situations, "molded to fit our general orientation as to purposes, instrumentalities, the 'good life,' etc.'¹¹ A vocabulary of motives contains "a program of action" for responding to a situation.¹² Thus, from a master metaphor emerges a general perspective that consists of motives or shorthand terms for interpreting situations. The interconnectedness of these linguistic phenomena underscores the essential simplicity of Burke's otherwise complex system: symbolic action amounts to naming one thing in terms of another, to treating a trope as a realistic perspective and acting as if it applies literally to a particular situation. The Burkeian critic interested in tracking down motives therefore looks for the "God term," or the "'Rome' term to which all roads lead."¹³ Motivational complexities can be reduced to metaphorical simplicities by discovering the term that organizes the speaker's perspective

---

⁶Burke, *Grammar,* 503-504.

⁷Kenneth Burke, *The Philosphy of Literary Form: Studies in Symbolic Action,* 3d ed. (Berkeley: University of California Press, 1973), 152.

⁸Burke, *Permanence and Change,* 95, 100.

⁹Jane Blankenship, Edward Murphy, and Marie Rosenwasser, "Pivotal Terms in the Early Works of Kenneth Burke," *Philosophy and Rhetoric* 7 (1974): 6-9.

¹⁰Burke, *Permanence and Change,* 14, 81.

¹¹*Permanence and Change,* 25, 29.

¹²Kenneth Burke, *Attitudes Toward History* (1959; reprint, Boston: Beacon Press, 1961), 92.

¹³Burke, *Grammar,* 105.

and provides corresponding terminologies for defining situations.

In the Johnson administration's Vietnam war rhetoric, however, we encounter a motivational complexity that resists mere reduction to a metaphorical simplicity. LBJ's master metaphor of containment exercised less than complete authority over his administration's terminology of war motives. His various key terms interacted upon and neutralized one another to an extent that undermined their ability to sustain a national incentive for war. No shorthand term for the situation in Vietnam seemed sufficient by itself to summarize a complex motivational cluster.

The complexities of LBJ's mixed terminology of war motives underscores the importance of Burke's observations about motivational diversity, i.e., about attending to the line of development as well as the point of departure. In his words, "As soon as we encounter, verbally or thematically, a motivational simplicity, we must assume as a matter of course that it contains a diversity."[14] This is a dimension of motivation easily overlooked in the search for a master metaphor or generative principle.

Burke captures the ironic relationship between metaphorical reduction and development when he observes that "if you *start* with your Rome term, the process of tracking down the roads that lead *to* it will in effect take you *from* it."[15] Reduction (following pathways to a master metaphor) and development (taking the same paths in the opposite direction) simultaneously simplify and complicate motives. As Burke writes:

> In any term we can posit a world, in the sense that we can treat the world *in terms of* it, seeing all as emanations, near or far, of its light. Such reduction to a simplicity being technically reduction to a summarizing title or "God term," when we confront a simplicity we must forthwith ask ourselves what complexities are subsumed beneath it. For a simplicity of motive being a perfection or purity of motive, the paradox of the absolute would admonish us that it cannot prevail in the "imperfect world" of everyday experience.[16]

The irony of complicating matters by simplifying them obtains

[14]Burke, *Grammar,* 101.
[15]Burke, *Grammar,* 105.
[16]Burke, *Grammar,* 105.

whenever we attempt to link a summarizing term to various contributing terms in a single line of dialectical or rhetorical development. Each contributing term in the line of development contains its own perspective or "sub-certainty," and all such terms "integrally affect one another" despite the effort to subsume them under a single "perspective of perspectiveness." Each "sub-perspective" is "needed to produce the total development," but any of them can be viewed in terms of any of the others; they are all simultaneously "adjectival" and "substantial"—a collection of incongruities, or potentially competing perspectives, mustered into a more or less coherent whole by the organizing principle of a master metaphor, the authority of which depends upon its ability to accommodate varying degrees of incompatibility among the terms upon which it depends for its own development.[17]

The potential for "perspective by incongruity,"—i.e., for wrenching a word loose from its customary or correct category and applying it metaphorically, or oxymoronically, to another category in order to gauge a situation differently, perhaps even more usefully—is a function of each word's limited validity as the representative anecdote for all the terms encompassed in a given framework of interpretation.[18] The several key terms in a definition of a situation are related to one another by the principle of synecdoche, or representation, rather than through metonymy, or reduction. Metonymy itself, Burke argues, "may be treated as a special application of synecdoche." Terms are connected by a road that can be travelled in either direction, from whole to part and part to whole, not just in a single, irreversible direction. Their identification with one another is compensatory to their division from one another.[19]

Thus, it is important to examine "the interaction of terms upon one another," to determine how their various "degrees of being" mingle as a system (i.e., where they clash as well as where they blend) in order to explain the motivational force of a

---

[17]Burke, *Grammar,* 512, 513, 516.

[18]Burke, *Attitudes,* 308-309; Burke, *Permanence and Change,* 92.

[19]Burke, *Grammar,* 508-510; Michael Leff, "Burke's Ciceronianism," in *The Legacy of Kenneth Burke,* ed. T. Melia and H. Simons (Madison: University of Wisconsin Press, in press).

summarizing term.[20] Metaphor understood as a process of representation rather than simple reduction takes into account the incongruities that are endemic to any rhetoric of motives. It leads a critic to consider not only which term provides the speaker's generative principle but also the extent to which that master metaphor, or God term, integrates and diverges from the perspectives implicit in the speaker's other key terms. Such an approach to LBJ's Vietnam war rhetoric reveals the compromises necessitated by maintaining containment's mastery over contributing images of birth, risk-taking, strength, and savagery.

METAPHORICAL DEVELOPMENT OF THE CONTAINMENT MOTIVE

The Johnson administration's master metaphor of containment was expressed negatively as anti-communism in McGeorge Bundy's earliest advice to the President.[21] It took the form of standing firm against the pressure and terror of the communist advance, of avoiding retreat and reducing the risk of a chain reaction that would start with a "collapse of anti-communist forces" in South Vietnam and then Laos, neutralization of Thailand, "heavy pressure on Malaya and Malaysia," "neutrality in Japan and the Philippines," damage to U.S. prestige in Korea and Taiwan, and then "further retreat." Bundy warned against betraying Saigon's "new regime" of "anti-Communists" in order to keep a vulnerable barrier from collapsing under the pressure of a communist onslaught.[22] America was fighting against communism, not for freedom, in Southeast Asian.

This negative image of anti-communism was poorly aligned with the metaphor of risk-taking to the extent that it required peril

---

[20]Burke, *Grammar,* 512, 504.

[21]As a study in rhetorical invention, this paper focuses primarily on declassified memoranda, reports, speech drafts, and other documents written by and for the president and his advisors and reflecting upon the administration's perception of the available means of persuasion. Many of the documents were originally classifed secret and top secret, indicating their sensitive nature and suggesting their conformity with the administration's actual beliefs about the war.

[22]McGeorge Bundy, Memorandum for the President, 6 January 1964, NSF. Aides Files: McGeorge Bundy, Box 1, Lyndon B. Johnson Presidential Library (hereafter LBJ Library).

and sacrifice for something less than the immediate cause of freedom and democracy. A related complication was the dependence of the administration's containment rhetoric on the problematic assumption of South Vietnam's status as an independent nation victimized by communist aggression. The President told his audience at Syracuse University on August 5, 1964 that "aggression unchallenged is aggression unleashed."[23] Standing firm against aggression in a test of the free world's manhood and will was a metaphorically consistent line of development, except that it required the public to take for granted South Vietnam's otherwise disputed status as a sovereign nation.

Nevertheless, Douglass Cater advised Bundy that the President should reconfirm America's commitment not to "shrink from what is necessary" because "the communists base their strategy on the premise that the free nations are soft and irresolute." The United States' responsibility was to support nations like Vietnam whose "independence has been guaranteed by international agreements," for to do otherwise, as President Eisenhower had warned five years earlier, "would 'set in motion a crumbling process that could, as it progressed, have grave consequences for us and for freedom.'"[24]

South Vietnam's nebulous status as an independent nation on freedom's embattled frontier became increasingly problematic as the administration prepared to escalate America's military involvement in the war. On the one hand, Johnson's advisors stressed the language of communist encroachment, implying an attack on the free world by the savage forces of terror and subversion. On the other hand, they neither claimed explicitly that South Vietnam was an established member of the free world nor called for the defeat of the communist aggressor, settling instead for a relatively tame and gradual military response to what was purportedly a mortal threat. Thus, they assumed the metaphorically anomalous position of being less than completely firm (i.e., sort of soft) toward communist savagery.

---

[23]"Remarks at Syracuse University on the Communist Challenge in Southeast Asia," August 5, 1965, in *Public Papers of the Presidents of the United States: Lyndon B. Johnson, 1963-1964* (Washington, D.C.: United States Government Printing Office, 1965) 928. [Hereafter *Public Papers*]

[24]Douglass Cater to McGeorge Bundy, 23 May 1964, NSF Aides File: McGeorge Bundy, Box 18, LBJ Library.

In May of 1964, for instance, Bundy recommended a Presidential decision to "use selected and carefully graduated military force
against North Vietnam" on the grounds that the U.S. could not
"tolerate the loss of Southeast Asia to Communism." He argued
that "all separate elements of the problem...should be treated as
parts of a single problem: the protection of Southeast Asia from
further Communist encroachment." America did not "intend or
desire the destruction of the Hanoi regime," Bundy continued, only
that "terror and subversion" end.[25] By June 10, he had drafted a
top secret memorandum recommending a Presidential message and
a series of "public statements of high officials or by such devices as
a White Paper" to communicate the "increasing firmness of the
Administration's position."[26]

Bundy's commitment to the vehicle of firmness continued to
work its will upon his attempt to articulate United States' interests
in Vietnam. By July 1, the image of being firm had been extended
to a vision of risk-taking and passing a test in Vietnam, but the
image was again blurred by Bundy's characterization of the South
Vietnamese as anti-communists. In a memorandum to Johnson,
Bundy argued that South Vietnam was "a test of U.S. firmness" and
that "the stakes in preserving an anti-Communist South Vietnam
are so high...we must go on bending every effort to win." He was
"confident that the American people are by and large in favor of a
policy of firmness and strength in such situations."[27]

By early January, 1965, as work continued on the State of the
Union address, Secretary of Defense Robert McNamara had begun
to sense the imbalance that was emerging between the administration's strong rhetoric and its more restrained   policy. Bundy
assured Johnson, however, that "without firm U.S. language, the
danger of further erosion in Saigon is bound to grow."[28] Bundy's
continuing commitment to the language of strength evolved by the

[25]McGeorge Bundy, Memorandum to the President, 25 May 1964, NSF Aides Files:
McGeorge Bundy, Box 1, LBJ Library.
[26]Memorandum for Discussion, 10 June 1964, 5:30 p.m. Draft, NSF Aides File:
McGeorge Bundy, Box 2, LBJ Library.
[27]McGeorge Bundy, Memorandum for the President, 1 July 1964, Draft 2, NSF
Aides Files: McGeorge Bundy, Box 1, LBJ Library.
[28]McGeorge Bundy, Memorandum for the President, 4 January 1965, NSF Aides
File: McGeorge Bundy, Box 2, LBJ Library.

end of January into a joint recommendation (with McNamara) to abandon the President's "middle course" in order to pursue a policy of "escalation." In effect, they wanted the administration's policy to catch up to its rhetoric, but their position was hampered by a still-problematic image of the South Vietnamese.

As Bundy put it, "What we are doing now, essentially, is to wait and hope for a stable government" while there is a "spreading conviction [in Saigon] that the future is without hope for anti-Communists." He argued further that the U.S. should make every effort "to prop up the authorities in South Vietnam as best we can," but also pointed out that current policy kept the U.S. from increasing its commitment to Vietnam "until there is a stable government, and no one has much hope that there is going to be a stable government while we sit still. The result is that we are pinned into a policy of first aid to squabbling politicos and passive reaction to events we do not try to contol." Bundy and McNamara called for "harder choices" that would give a "sense of firm and active U.S. policy" and demonstrate America's willingness "to take serious risks."[29]

The Vietnamese for whom the U.S. was being asked to fight were portrayed in Bundy's memorandum as anti-communists who needed to be propped up and as squabbling politicos who required first aid. They were neither stable nor democratic, but the administration had gotten caught in a rhetoric of containment the vitality of which depended upon defending the frontiers of freedom against communist aggression. The metaphorical concept of firmness extended to risk-taking was not well aligned with the administration's vague and problematic image of the South Vietnamese as an established nation of anti-communists.

Understandably, Bill Moyers sensed the need for "a *different* kind of Presidential speech," which he discussed with Bundy and reported to the President in early February of 1965. He proposed a "kind of 'White Paper' speech in which in some detail you discuss the history of our commitment, the motives behind our commitment, the nature of the Communist aggression, and the relations of our responsibilities to our interests around the world—as well as the

---

[29]Memorandum for the President, 27 January 1965, NSF Aides Files: McGeorge Bundy, Box 2, LBJ Library.

protection of freedom elsewhere."[30] In short, Moyers was saying
that the administration had failed to link its actions in Vietnam to
the public's perception of America's vital interests, specifically the
commitment to defend freedom where it is imperiled.

Moyers' rhetorical solution, however, missed the mark by
failing to address directly South Vietnam's nebulous image. Instead,
he recommended an emphasis on communist savagery as a way to
demonstrate freedom's peril: "Two or three paragraphs" on the
subject of "Viet Cong terrorism" would reinforce the President's
hand and would be "a source of renewed energy to freedom-loving
peoples around the world." It would "give the American people a
rare glimpse into the *real* nature of the struggle in which we are
involved in Southeast Asia." Once the American people were told
"some of the facts concerning the atrocities of the Viet Cong," they
would be able to "relate our presence in Vietnam to the defense of
liberty in West Berlin."

Having secured the President's approval of this strategy for
justifying the war, Moyers drafted a plan for an address featuring a
bevy of decivilizing vehicles such as "criminal acts," "kidnapping,"
"murder," "terror," "treachery," "sabotage," "torn apart," and
"gutted."[31] At the same time, Bundy was informing Johnson that
"the propensity of the American people to punch the Communists
in the nose over Vietnam seems considerably less than it was six
months ago."[32]

The administration was aware of its difficulties but seemingly
blind to the rhetorical limits of trying to identify the South
Vietnamese with freedom's cause indirectly. James Greenfield
informed the Secretary of State that "the public problem on Viet-
Nam" required a "public statement, either on a Presidential or
Secretarial level, that reiterates the United States' stake in this
country," including "the consequences for both the U.S. and the free
world that would occur if the United States did not carry out its

[30]Memorandum for the President, 9 February 1965, NSF—Speech File, Box 3,
LBJ Library.

[31]"Ideas for a Speech," NSF Aides File: McGeorge Bundy, Box 3, LBJ Library.

[32]Memorandum for the President, 9 February 1965. NSF: NSC History, Box 40,
LBJ Library.

commitment in Asia."[33] His solution was to take the public "back through the accords, back through our mounting involvement as this new kind of warfare unfolded, back through our countless statements that we want no bases or no territory for ourselves. We should remind the public that a free Viet-Nam is worth the risks, both because of our obligations to the Vietnamese and to ourselves."

Having a stake in Vietnam and taking risks for a free Vietnam required more than a long and laborious recital of America's gradual involvement in the war. Thus, James Thomson of the National Security Council wrote Bundy, on February 19, a "Dove's lament," indicating that he continued "to believe that a policy of sustained reprisals against the North entails greater risks than we have any right to take in terms of our world-wide interests."[34]

By the end of June a potentially powerful remedy to the rhetorical problem of identifying Vietnam directly with freedom's cause emerged in Bundy's analysis of the differences between French and American involvements in Southeast Asia. He informed the President that whereas "France in 1954 was a colonial power seeking to reimpose its overseas rule [and therefore] out of tune with Vietnamese nationalism," the United States "in 1965 is responding to the call of a people under Communist assault, a people undergoing a non-Communist national revolution."[35] Yet, Bundy stopped short of referring to a democratic revolution in South Vietnam. America, instead, was fostering a "non-Communist national revolution." Even at this point of near insight, the negative doctrine of containment blocked Bundy's ability to draw on a positive image of nation-building that encompassed the birth of Vietnamese freedom. Although the President's advisors continued to talk about the "grave stakes" and a "crucial test" in Vietnam, their negative doctrine of containment returned them once again to the pessimistic position that "it was not useful to talk about 'victory' [because] what was really involved was preventing the expansion of

---

[33]James L. Greenfield to the Secretary, 16 February 1965, NSF: NSC History, Box 40, LBJ Library.

[34]James C. Thomson, Jr. to McGeorge Bundy, 19 February 1965, NSF: NSC History, Box 40, LBJ Library.

[35]Memorandum for the President, 30 June 1965, NSF Aides Files: McGeorge Bundy, Box 3, LBJ Library.

Communism by force; in a sense, avoiding defeat."[36]

While Douglas Cater was advising Bundy of the urgency of getting ahead "with planning for public support," including the distribution of "speech materials to friendly Senators and Congressmen" and the establishment of a Citizens Committee, the President was holding a series of Cabinet Room meetings on July 21, 1965, to discuss and debate McNamara's recommendations for escalating further the commitment of American military forces in Vietnam.[37] NSC staff member Chester Cooper reported the next day, in a top secret memorandum for the record, an exchange between Bundy and Under Secretary of State George Ball that revealed the metaphorical counter-forces still blurring the administration's image of the stakes in South Vietnam.[38]

Ball initiated the exchange by advancing a "cancer analogy" as he objected to the McNamara plan for another escalation of the war. Arguing for withdrawal of American forces, the Under Secretary pointed to the futility of "giving cobalt treatment to a terminal cancer case." Bundy defended McNamara's proposals by proffering what he regarded as a better analogy: "A non-Communist society is struggling to be born." He acknowledged that another escalation of the war would be "asking Americans to bet more to achieve less" but maintained that South Vietnamese weakness was a function of "immaturity," not a terminal disease.

Even at a point when Johnson's advisors explicitly acknowledged the policy implications of competing analogies, they missed seeing the full rhetorical potential of the birth metaphor couched by Bundy in the neutered language of non-commnism: A non-communist society, not a democratic society, was struggling to be born. An unencumbered image of giving birth to freedom in South Vietnam (and nurturing the infant through years of immaturity) would have provided the administration a potentially positive goal consistent with America's historic sense of mission and congruent with South Vietnam's status as an emerging state and revolutionary society, thus

[36]Vietnam Panel, 8 July 1965; from W.P. Bundy, 18 July 1965, NSF Aides File: McGeorge Bundy, Box 18, LBJ Library.

[37]Memorandum for the President from McGeorge Bundy, 19 July 1965, NSF Aides Files: McGeorge Bundy, Box 4, LBJ Library.

[38]Memorandum for the Record, 22 July 1965, NSF: NSC History, Box 43, LBJ Library.

precluding the need to maintain the legal fiction of Vietnamese stability and sovereignty prior to communist aggression. It could have aligned the United States squarely with support for a democratic revolution, offering the American public something for which greater risks might have seemed worth taking and larger bets worth making.

The dominance of the anti-communist containment image over a pro-freedom birth metaphor continued to stymie the administration's search for a better way to articulate America's interests in Vietnam. A strong attraction to the birth image remained apparent, however, in a speech drafted by Walt Rostow in January of 1966. Rostow explained to Presidential speech writer Jack Valenti that he had "tried to draw the problem back from the bear pit of Viet Nam to the fundamentals in our national life and policy" by introducing "new notes of tempered hope and great respect for the South Vietnamese struggle for independence and political order."[39] Valenti was impressed enough to forward the draft to the President, indicating Rostow had done a good job of setting "this whole South Vietnamese problem in full perspective."[40]

Rostow's draft was burdened with typical references to stopping communist aggression, containing "the methods of subversion, terror, and guerrilla warfare," and maintaining America's "solemn obligations in Southeast Asia." But it also featured the image of a "young nation" with its "new generation of students, profoundly anti-Communist, searching to define a democratic future for their country, [and] beginning to go out in large numbers to the villages—to build and, if necessary, to rebuild side by side with their fellow citizens." South Vietnam's government was portrayed similarly as having "recently begun to move along this constructive path. It has announced that its goal is to build a democracy. A Democracy Building Council has been created with wide representation." The "building of democracy in new, developing nations is not an easy or quick process," but America had "the same kind of basic faith in the South Vietnamese as we have had in the South

---

[39]Jack Valenti to W.W. Rostow, 29 January 1966, NSF Aides File: McGeorge Bundy, Box 17, LBJ Library.

[40]Jack Valenti to the President, 29 January 1966, NSF Aides File: McGeorge Bundy, Box 17, LBJ Library.

Koreans—faith in their vitality, their passion for independence, their determination to build in their own way a free and democratic life." Thus, "the vital interests of the United States and free men everywhere are truly involved," warranting the taking of "great risks" for the "independence of nations and the freedom of men" and the making of a "hard choice" instead of following "a safer and a softer way"—just as the "Pilgrim Fathers" had acted valiantly despite their "doubts and dangers" because they realized "all great and honorable actions are accompanied with great difficulties and must be both enterprised and overcome with answerable courage."[41]

Valenti missed the rhetorical significance of Rostow's nation-building and freedon-founding images. After advising the President that Rostow's draft had not yet "come to grips" with the problem of explaining "simply and clearly and understandably" why Vietnam was "so important to future generations in this country," Valenti put Bob Hardesty and Will Sparks to work on preparing a Vietnam booklet that would be "brief, to the point, cheap to produce, and written in language that everyone can understand."[42] The booklet, written with the assistance of Chester Cooper and William Jorden and designed for Congressmen to send to their constituents, was nearly devoid of nation-building and freedom-founding imagery, featuring instead the language of anti-communism and communist aggression. It told "the story of Vietnam" as "the age-old story of some men's refusal to let their neighbor live in peace" and concluded that America was "in Vietnam because the Communists are bent on aggression and because we must prove to them that aggression cannot succeed. If we do not prove this—and prove it now—our own security will ultimately be threatened."

Although the effect of over-emphasizing the negative doctrine of containment and understating the objective of building a new democracy was reflected in the administration's soundings of public opinion, Johnson and his advisors did not attribute the public opinion problem to the crosscurrents of metaphorical development.

---

[41]Draft, 29 January 1966, NSF Aides File: McGeorge Bundy, Box 17, LBJ Library.

[42]Jack Valenti to the President, 29 January 1966, NSF Aides File: McGeorge Bundy, Box 17, LBJ Library; Bob Hardesty/Will Sparks to Bill Moyers, 14 February 1966, Office Files of Bob Hardesty (Personal), LBJ Library. A draft of the booklet, entitled "Vietnam: The Facts Speak for Themselves," is attached to the Hardesty/Sparks memorandum to Moyers.

A memorandum from D.W. Ropa of the National Security Council noted on February 18, 1966, for instance, the "public unease over where our commitment is leading." This was "the concern of many, apparently, who still vaguely accept the necessity of blunting Communist aggression in Vietnam." Ropa's memorandum also reported "*gnawing* feelings of futility over whether anything stable, solid and popular can ever be built on the quicksand of Vietnamese life and politics."[43] The threat of communist aggression remained vague despite its prominence in administration rhetoric, and the image of nation-building had failed to take hold because of its subordination to containment imagery.

Thus, the Johnson administration never positioned itself rhetorically to address head-on the key anti-war themes, including recurrent charges that the U.S. "blocked free elections in South Vietnam," "violated the Geneva Accords," "interfered in a civil war," supported a "small upper class of landowners" who bled "the country economically at the expense of the people," and advanced an "invalid and/or obsolete domino theory" to justify "intervention" in an area where America had no "vital" interests.[44] Richard Phillips's suggestions to Fred Panzer for rebutting the "Doves" stressed the themes of "facing aggression and living up to commitments" while accepting the "unavoidable degree of immorality" associated with "our policy in Vietnam." Phillips acknowledged that the United States was "supporting social revolution and nationalism in Viet-Nam," but the primary task was "assisting the Vietnamese to defend themselves against those who would conquer them and those who would impose a retrogressive and impractical social organization upon them."[45] The image of "building" a Vietnamese nation was interpreted to mean protecting a sovereign nation from subversion and aggression while it was undergoing a social revolution rather than to mean giving birth to a new democratic state where none previously existed.

---

[43]D.W. Ropa to Mr. Bundy, 18 February 1966, NSF Aides File: McGeorge Bundy, Box 17, LBJ Library.

[44]"Recurrent Themes by Those Who Criticize the American Commitment in Vietnam," attached to memorandum from D.W. Ropa to McGeorge Bundy, 18 February 1966, NSF Aides File: McGeorge Bundy, Box 17, LBJ Library.

[45]Attachment to Memorandum from Richard I. Phillips to Fred Panzer, 24 June 1966, Office Files of Fred Panzer, Container 425, LBJ Library.

Johnson's rhetorical strategists were firmly committed to their containment-dominated heuristics when the President approved the formation of a Vietnam Information Group in August 1967. The purpose of the group, headed by Harold Kaplan, was restricted to "making the most effective use of the information coming in from Vietnam [in order] to put out our position over here at home." The assumption behind this objective was that "the American people and the American press" were "skeptical" and "cynical" because they were "uninformed." Thus, the Vietnam Information Group was envisioned as a "quick reaction team to prepare speech and background material for...use on the Hill" before the adminstration was thrown "on the defense" by "charges of escalation, increased bombing, difficulties with pacification, [and] problems with the elections."

To accomplish its main objective and to "strike a positive note" whenever possible, the group set out (1) to meet weekly with the President's closest aids in order to keep apprised of the President's "most current thinking about our policies" and what "should be getting across to the press and to the public" as well as "what speeches need to be made on the Hill," (2) to prepare speeches and "filter them to the Congress regularly," (3) to provide "well organized and effective briefing materials," (4) to "provide background material to leak to correspondents regularly," and (5) to "assist public affairs people at State and Defense so that a well-coordinated and higher quality information flow results."[46]

Within a month or two, there were clear indications that the strategy of the Vietnam Information Group was not achieving its principal goals within the confines of the established rhetoric of containment. Abe Fortas advised President Johnson that "we must get off the defensive in the propaganda battle." As he assessed the situation, support for the war was slipping as the administration tried to "sustain a shooting war on a non-emotional basis." His solution was to shift emphasis "away from helping South Vietnam to helping ourselves and the free world to combat the 'new' Communist technique of conquest by infiltration and subversion." Much like his predecessors in the business of establishing basic rhetorical strategy, Fortas spoke as though the "overthrow" of South

---

[46]George Christian to the President, 22 August 1967, 6:00 p.m., Office Files of Fred Panzer, Box 427, LBJ Library.

Vietnam would be "a monument to freedom's defeat."[47] Protecting freedom, though, was equated merely with resisting a communist victory, once again indirectly and negatively substantiating Vietnam as a weak symbol of freedom.

Thus, the administration was still at a loss, in the summer of 1967, for ways to argue that America's vital interests were involved in Vietnam. As Harry McPherson explained to the President, "Talk about defending freedom in the South ... falls on deaf ears. South Vietnam is a semi-country run by a junta of generals who were raised in the North and imposed on the South."[48] McPherson's only solution was to write more speeches emphasizing the domino effect of losing in Vietnam. He revealed no awareness of the difference between making a case based on creating a new democracy in South Vietnam and making one based on defending an established democracy from communist aggression.

The President's advisors proved incapable of revising their hierarchy of motivational images even as the failure of their rhetorical strategy became more apparent in the aftermath of the Vietcong's dramatic Tet offensive. On February 8, 1968, Rostow developed a "war leader speech," as opposed to a "peace-seeker speech," designed to "slay the credibility-gap dragon with one blow."[49] His text articulated the national interest indirectly, however, by emphasizing communist savagery rather than promoting Vietnamese democracy. In his words, "We have known savagery before. And we have known how to deal with it. We still do."

By March, the administration had prepared a remarkable, top secret analysis of its rhetorical failure, an analysis that nevertheless fell short of discovering a way to remedy the problem. It had become apparent to Johnson's advisors that "no successful plan to rally the people has been executed" even though "a large number of people have spent extensive time and effort trying to tell the story of the war." They determined that the administration's information programs had neither rallied the people nor quelled opposition to the

---

[47]Re: Vietnam, no date (c. 9/67-10/67), NSC Country File: Vietnam, Box 99, LBJ Library.

[48]Harry C. McPherson to the President, 25 August 1967, 4:15 p.m., Office Files of Harry McPherson, Box 29, LBJ Library.

[49]W.W. Rostow to the President, 8 February 1968, NSC Country File: Vietnam, Box 100, LBJ Library. A copy of his proposed speech is attached to the memorandum.

war because the government had failed to "(1) prove that it is in our national interest, (2) prove that we have a plan to win it, [and] (3) tell the people what resources are required to carry out that plan."

The memorandum recognized that "if the war is in *our* national interest, it is less important whether the ARVN are effective or not, or whether the government is corrupt or not, or whether a Vietnamese general is barbaric or not, or whether it is a civil war or an external aggression." Further, it was apparent that "if we have a plan to win, it is less important whether it takes two more years or four more, whether the Tet offensive was a victory or defeat, whether pacification is lagging, or how many crew-served weapons have been seized." Finally, "if the government lays out the required resources, the people will pay the price."

The "price to be paid for convincing America that the war is essential to our national interest would be the increased difficulty of withdrawing short of 'victory.'" Emotions would be aroused as they had been in earlier wars, giving Americans cause to "hate the enemy." The attempt to fight a limited war with limited objectives had forced the administration to avoid "emotion-arousing steps," concealing for instance "the possible torture of Americans held captive." In short, a "people moving" strategy would allow the administration to take full advantage of motivational metaphors such as savagery, risk-taking and firmness normally associated with fighting a righteous war to defend the national interests. However, such a war would require a change of policy that allowed for clear objectives and a commitment to win, rather than vague objectives and a commitment only to contain and avoid defeat. Adopting a people-moving campaign, therefore, would have to be deferred until the administration was prepared to pay the price of unleashing the military in order to unleash the emotions of the people.[50]

Johnson's advisors had encountered the limits of a rhetorical strategy featuring anti-communist containment vehicles: The national interest was defined negatively and indirectly, thus engaging the cause of freedom ambiguously; the enemy was the entire communist world, thus risking an unthinkable third world war in order to

[50]Memorandum for Meeting with the President on "Public Affairs," First Draft, 3 March 1968, NSF: NSC History, Box 49, LBJ Library.

achieve some kind of a victory; and the rest of the administration's rhetoric was constrained accordingly—projecting a confused image of firmness modified by softness, risk-taking without the promise of a clear reward, and savagery without the full satisfaction of victimage. It never occurred to Johnson's strategists to consider the rhetorical implications of placing a primary emphasis on nation-building, i.e., whether giving birth to freedom in South Vietnam and nurturing it through its troubled infancy would engage the national interests sufficiently, provide a clear and immediate objective, delimit the scope of the conflict, define the enemy less globally, and offer a real prospect of victory.

Ironically, though, birth and nation-building had been among the key images projected by Senator John F. Kennedy when he spoke of America's obligations to Vietnam as early as 1956. "It is our offspring," he said. "We cannot abandon it. We cannot ignore its needs." The United States was not in Vietnam to protect an established democracy against which communist forces had committed an act of aggression. It was there instead to defeat a communist competitor, to bring "political liberty" and establish "a strong and free Vietnamese nation" where one had not previously existed. America was creating a nation that would become "the cornerstone of the Free World in Southeast Asia, the keystone in the arch, the finger in the dike" that would hold back the "red tide of communism."[51]

Kennedy's forgotten rhetoric had integrated containment motives subtly under a dominant image of nation-building which, if it had been maintained by the Johnson administration, might have altered the public's expectations in Vietnam significantly. Johnson might have argued that the United States deliberately rejected the Geneva agreements in order to spawn a new nation in Southeast Asia that would push back the frontiers of freedom and block communism's advance in a strategic corner of the world. He might have acknowledged to his advantage that America was competing with communism for the loyalty of South Vietnamese nationalists, thus helping to explain the setbacks, the delays, and other

---

[51]John F. Kennedy, "America's Stake in Vietnam," *Vital Speeches,* 1 August 1956, 617-619.

understandable difficulties associated with establishing a new democratic nation. He might have avoided resorting to an aggression thesis that suffered rhetorically from the dual disadvantage of appealing negatively to anti-communism while presuming South Vietnam's sovereignty. Moreover, the President might have called upon Americans to protect and nourish their Vietnamese progeny by remaining firm and taking the necessary risks to defeat a savage opponent. No responsible parent would think to abandon its child under such desperate circumstances.

More importantly, though, the Johnson administration would have been better positioned, itself, to assess national interests had it not become entangled in its own rhetoric of containment. At each point where the question of whether to escalate America's involvement arose, the negative imagery of anti-communism and its various entailments obfuscated the primary issue, the stake of freedom in Vietnam, and this myopia impeded candid and thorough deliberation about the basis of our policy. The momentum of containment's anti-communism carried the nation's leaders into a vague and open-ended commitment from which they found it difficult to disengage but for which they could not express a compelling rationale.

A hierarchy of metaphors that emphasized the creation of a free nation (instead of support for any anti-communist regime, no matter how oppressive or cruel) would have been more likely to highlight the key issues necessary to assess the national interest in Vietnam. Among such issues would have been questions regarding what, if any, kind of democratic system could take hold in such soil, why the United States should plant the seed of freedom so far from home, and whether democracy's failure to germinate and grow on foreign soil would necessarily threaten freedom in America and elsewhere where conditions were more favorable. In short, the administration would have been more inclined to consider seriously whether Vietnam was a good place to foster an ideological child.

Finally, a hierarchy of metaphors dominated by nation-building heuristics would have encouraged a more considered decision on Vietnam because of its inconsistency with the traditional motives of the American war rhetor. America's concept of the just war dictates a posture of reluctant belligerence necessitated by the hostile initiatives of others, and the Johnson administration's rhetoric of anti-communism allowed the nation to respond automatically to the familiar pattern of repulsing an aggressor.[52] Thus, it was relatively easy to slip into a war of containment. Starting a war, however, for the purpose of creating a democratic state in Vietnam where none previously existed would have been far more difficult (perhaps impossible) to justify initially as a response to aggression and therefore would have required the articulation of some compelling interest in Vietnamese freedom in order to legitimize a decision for war. Thus, LBJ's rhetoric was undermined by the difficulty of developing its key metaphorical terms into a hierarchy of motives that could either maintain a war of containment against communism or justify initiating one for freedom.

Friedrich Nietzsche, as Paul Cantor explains, long ago recognized the operation of an "imperialistic principle" in metaphor. As the figurative becomes literal (or, in Burkeian terms, as the metaphor becomes perspective) its meaning is constantly extended to encompass a widening range of experience within its domain: "Man's capacity for metaphor is a special case of ... his will to power." Terms compete with one another to dominate the hierarchy of meaning by which our interpretations of political experience, and ultimately our political acts, are guided. There is no natural hierarchy of meaning, but our eventual choice of a master metaphor determines what we regard at any given point in time as literal rather than figurative.[53] This terministic warfare for motivational dominance, although arbitrary and conventional in its origins, can lead to armed conflict no matter how pointless when we mistake the conventions of linguistic creativity for the fixed laws of nature or the gods.

The tragedy of Vietnam is that the choice of a different hierarchy within the same system of motivational metaphors might have clarified the national interest before Johnson and his rhetorical strategists committed themselves even more deeply to a war that proved beyond America's ability to endure.

---

[52]Robert L. Ivie, "Presidential Motives for War," *Quarterly Journal of Speech* 60 (1974): 337-345; and Robert L. Ivie, "Images of Savagery in American Justifications for War," *Communication Monographs* 47 (1980): 279-294.

[53]Paul Cantor, "Friedrich Nietzsche: The Use and Abuse of Metaphor," in *Metaphor: Problems and Perspectives,* ed. David S. Miall (New Jersey: Humanities Press, 1982), 62.

SOME BURKEAN ROADS NOT TAKEN:
A RESPONSE TO IVIE
BARRY BRUMMETT

I come not to bury Ivie, but to play with him. The role of a respondent to a scholarly paper is not to carp peevishly but to elaborate, to foreground some of the connections, possibilities, and insights which any good essay will suggest but not develop. That is especially appropriate when the paper is as good as this one. As Ivie reminds us, it is in the best Burkean tradition to tease out the ramifications inherent in a vocabulary.[1] So I would like to follow some of Ivie's thoughts a little farther down the Burkean highway. I do this not by way of taxing him because he did not entertain these thoughts, since it is impossible to do everything in one paper. Instead, I intend simply to take us down some Burkean roads not yet taken, to get us pretty well stranded in some dramatistic woods, and to show that something there is that doesn't love scholarly closure.

If there were no form, critics would have to invent it. Without the ability to discount the obvious and literal, to look behind the surface at structure, arrangement, alignment and opposition, critics would be out of a job. Ivie does a good job of explaining the terms used by the Johnson administration and of showing how they did not sit well with each other on a surface or literal level. I propose to ask briefly about the forms of Johnson's rhetoric: What kinds of terms these are, which terms go with what, and whether certain motives and terms are being displaced into other terms.[2]

Ivie shows us the problems with a vocabulary keyed to "containment"; the immediate question his analysis raises is, why was such a master term used? The immediate answer is, because

---

[1]Kenneth Burke, *Counter-statement* (Berkeley: University of California Press, 1968), 158-160.

[2]Kenneth Burke, *The Philosophy of Literary Form,* 3rd ed. rev. (Berkeley: University of California Press, 1973).

it was popular, available, and well grounded in the rhetoric of
the Cold War. But why was it popular, available, and often
used for commie-bashing? I would suggest that containment is a
term into which is displaced a vocabulary for older and more
fundamental for the American psyche: the venerable American
drama of Good versus Evil. The form of containment underlies
a major strategy in that drama. In pentadic terms,[3] containment
is a scenic strategy in the war against Evil. We aim not to
eliminate or change Evil, but to circumscribe its location. Thus,
for instance, Prohibition fought the Demon Rum scenically by
seeking to remove it from American soil.

Our clue to the presence of a rhetorical form at work is the
clustering of negative terms within a containment vessel, in
opposition to a cluster of positive terms on this side of containment. Historically, this structure of "Good versus Evil as managed
by containment" has been aligned with the shifting interests and
prejudices of the dominant White American culture. Americans,
enlisting on the side of Good, have always sought to keep the
Old World out of the New, to keep slavery only in the South,
to keep Native Americans confined to the reservation, to keep
Japanese Americans in detention camps, to push Mexicans (after
the harvest) back south of the border, to keep Blacks in the
inner city and out of the suburbs; the notion of containing
communists within Russia and China is but the tenth verse to
an old yet catchy tune. Today, Americans are not really against
communists; we are against Evil, and communists are the Evil
Empire of the latter half of this century. But we know that
since we cannot eliminate this Evil, we must try to keep it
within a few countries.

Asking the Burkean question of what goes with what and
what is against what, then, we see that Ivie's discovery of such
terms as "savagery," "atrocities," "murder," etc., pitted against
such terms as "freedom," or "democracy," reflects the form of
the struggle between Good and Evil. While not denying the
tensions created between the terms of containment and of
birthing, formal analysis shows us that those terms could very

---

[3]Kenneth Burke, *A Grammar of Motives* (Berkeley: University of California Press,
1962).

well be on the same side in this Manichaean conflict. It could be the case that both giving birth to freedom and containing aggression were perceived to cluster on the side of Good.

But as Ivie shows us, the course of dividing Vietnam into the Good and the Bad ne'er ran smooth. Why? It would seem that the problem with Johnson's rhetoric is an inability to apply this Manichaean form to the rhetorical situation. Why couldn't Americans be the knights of Good in Vietnam? A simple answer, and the only one I will suggest here, is that improved reporting of what goes on in a war (My Lai, etc.) and of the corrupt incompetence of the South Vietnamese governments after we were already committed to one side made it impossible for many Americans to take such a noble position. Evil lay on both sides of the war, and no action was possible which did not threaten to break this venerable structure of American motives. The larger question then entailed is, to what extent was the form permanently broken? Is America's innocence forever gone, or have the contradictions of Vietnam been localized and historicized?

A second Burkean path down which I shall lead us has to do with consubstantiality.[4] Shared substance is, for Burke, the prerequisite for shared motivation and action. In English, that means that people must see others as similar before they will live, work, and cooperate with them. Now, to contain a thing is to put a circle around it and to keep it apart in there; but such a circle equally makes fellows of those who remain out here. Containment, in other words, implies a shared substance among those not contained.

Americans have always been rhetorically and symbolically strongest when constructing such barriers around people close to home (recent immigrants, gays, etc.) Such local containment allows us to consider as consubstantial only those who are closest to the locality: other "good, decent, loyal Americans." But to contain communism in Asia requires a distant circle of containment which puts out here, with us, lots of folks from far-away places with strange sounding names. And Burke's doctrine

---

[4]Kenneth Burke, *Grammar;* Kenneth Burke, *A Rhetoric of Motives* (Berkeley: University of California Press, 1969).

of consubstantiality suggests forcibly how difficult it is for most Americans to align themselves with Vietnamese who are geographically, ideologically, religiously, culturally, and perhaps most important, racially not consubstantial with us—who are indeed, as was a complaint of our soldiers during the war, practically indistinguishable from those within the containment vessel. Americans have historically relied heavily upon a scene-agent radio[5] to explain what is special, exalted, and Good about us: We are the new Adams in the new Eden. How then can we yoke ourselves with those very different agents from foreign scenes?

To consider the problem of consubstantiality helps to make clearer the difficulties Ivie found with the metaphor of giving birth to freedom. There is an ambiguity here which I am not sure Ivie noticed. The metaphor of giving birth to a new democratic nation can cast us as midwives or as parents. Most of the evidence produced by Ivie suggests the former to me: We are going to Vietnam to help the people there birth their nation-baby. But the quotation from John Kennedy is different: It explicitly casts us as parents of the Vietnamese nation. Consubstantiality helps us to understand why neither metaphor was likely to "take." The midwife version of the birth metaphor is less threatening but also less compelling; what have we to do with those people over there that we should be boiling water for them? The parent metaphor was more compelling but, for the reasons noted earlier, especially the cultural and racial reasons, more threatening because it suggested a consubstantiality which most Americans would have feared and denied: The fruits of a past indiscretion on the wrong side of the tracks showing up in a basket on our doorstep.

Let me very briefly note that Burke's concepts of the paradox of substance, or of antinomies of definition,[6] suggest another reason why the vocabularies discovered by Ivie failed. Ivie acknowledges that vocabularies must entail diversity, but he seems puzzled by their tendency to fall into contradiction. Yet Burke argues repeatedly that such is the fate of any vocabulary: it leads to its opposite, its negation, its neutralization. It is the rhetor's job to gather the flowers

---

[5]Burke, *Grammar.*
[6]Burke, *Grammar.*

of motivational possibility before the branch breaks of its own weight, falls, and withers. For instance, what could be more consubstantial than another person created out of one's own body? Your child is you, your flesh. But your child is also another's flesh and his or her own flesh. And to the extent that parents do what parents should, the child will grow away from them to cleave to somebody else's flesh. Or, we contain a thing because it harms, pollutes, and offends us. The best containment requires constant attention to maintain the containment. But such vigilance requires some sort of contact with the contained. So containment is a way of perpetuating preoccupation with that which we seek to avoid. I would suggest to Ivie that the interesting thing about Johnson's rhetoric is not that it led to contradiction, but that it did so so quickly; the half-life of vocabularies would seem to be longer. Why did this happen? Perhaps Johnson employed a vocabulary as it was in the falling arc of its cultural trajectory, on its way to disintegration.

Finally, I want to recall Burke's concept of recalcitrance,[7] in which he argues that the world offers some resistance to our making it into whatever we want to make it through words. This is an uncomfortable concept; I have always thought that it contradicted his doctrine that things are the signs of words.[8] I am also uncomfortable because it would seem to make us posit a "real" reality as opposed to a symbolic reality, a distinction which Professor Scott scared out of me some years ago in graduate school. I think one could make use of Burke's "recalcitrance" if we take it to mean a conflict between symbolic strategies currently in use and either a "real" reality or a symbolic reality privileged as unquestioned and objective for the moment.

Now, having thrown a bone to everyone's ontological bêtes noir, I want to argue that running throughout Ivie's paper is a tension between, perhaps a confusion over, certainly the lack of a direct confrontation with, "reality" and the Johnson administration's symbolic strategies. I have always found interesting the claim that Johnson failed to explain to the public why we should be in

---

[7]Kenneth Burke, *Permanence and Change: An Anatomy of Purpose,* 2nd ed. (Indianapolis: Bobbs-Merrill, 1965).

[8]Kenneth Burke, *Language as Symbolic Action* (Berkeley: University of California Press, 1966).

Vietnam, a claim Ivie repeats more than once. It is as if the reasons for our involvement were technical and objective, matters of fact or procedure, which require explanation instead of matters of value which require argument, pleading, and sermonizing. The "explanation hypothesis," usually advanced by Johnson apologists, would seem to locate reasons for our involvement in the necessities of reality, while locating failure to motivate the public in the vicissitudes of education. I also find myself wondering, as Ivie gives us a window into arguments within the Oval Office, whether these people believed what they were saying. Did they have, as we liberals told ourselves in the 'Sixties, real evil motives of gain and imperialism which they couched in the rhetoric of containment and freedom, or did they really believe that stuff that they were trying to sell the public? A third, and more subtle alternative is that motives of gain and imperialism were displaced, to return us to the concept of form, into more idealistic vocabularies.

On the one hand, Ivie says that Johnson's vocabulary kept him "from reconsidering the presumed necessity of escalating American involvement in the war." But on the other hand, Ivie seems more often to claim that the vocabulary kept Johnson from "articulating America's vital interest in Vietnam ..." What vital interests? Ivie writes as if there were some.

The tension between "reality" and rhetoric too often finds Ivie thinking about the rhetoric and not about the real results which would have followed from a Johnson success. Enough damage was done with a restrained war effort conducted by several Presidents who perceived that the public was not sufficiently persuaded to support a more vigorous action. It is not necessarily the case, as several of Ivie's references and perhaps even Ivie himself imply, that stronger resolve or more "will" was all that stood between us and victory. This kind of war may resist conventional superpower techniques of battle, as the Soviets have recently discovered in Afghanistan. Heaven forfend that rhetorical success should have emboldened Johnson to commit another half million or million soldiers, to use nuclear weapons, to invade the North. We might be there yet.

"I'VE BEEN TO THE MOUNTAINTOP":
THE CRITIC AS PARTICIPANT
MICHAEL OSBORN

What I offer here might be called a "critilogue," a critical excursion through a speech, using audio-taped segments from that speech both to illustrate and to create a sense of living presence. The procedure is nothing more than an especially vivid approach to what I have called "close criticism," which "aspires to *appreciation,* an enlightened understanding of *challenges* confronted by rhetors..., the *options* available in meeting these challenges..., an assessment of the *performance* of rhetoric..., a description of the rhetoric as *consummated* (in the evanescent moment of convergence, when rhetor-audience-message come together)..., and the moral, social, political *consequences* of the discourse."[1] If we follow traditional academic directions, and attempt to objectify, disembody, and distance the subject of criticism, we run the risk— at least in rhetorical criticism—of losing that subject. This is especially true considering that speeches normally are events that occur within dramatic contexts, are living moments that take their coloration from a symbolic environment that creates their tension and resonance. Such a moment was Martin Luther King Jr.'s final speech, often called his "Mountaintop" speech.

As I begin the task of criticizing this speech, I find myself embarrassed by my role. Clearly, I am well situated to assume the close critical stance. Living in Memphis during that time, I was immersed in the events, the tragic atmosphere, which produced this memorable moment of rhetoric. I experienced the fear and tension, the meanness and magnificence, the overall sense of looming explosiveness, that often accompanies profound social change.

But the speech stands before me like the very mountain from whch King symbolically spoke. It was surely an awesome performance. Richard Lentz in his excellent monograph, *Sixty-Five*

---

[1]I have developed this conception in more detail in my paper "A Philosophy of Criticism" presented at the Eastern Communication Association Convention, April, 1988.

Days in Memphis, calls it "one of the finest speeches of his career, matching the eloquence of his "I have a dream" peroration at the 1963 March on Washington. In it King seemed to foretell his own death."[2] Garry Wills, in a perceptive and sometimes trenchant critique in *Esquire,* argued that it was "one of his great speeches — those speeches that will outlive his labored essays."[3] Adding to my sense of intimidation is the nature of this discourse as a speech. If the great poem must seem formidable to the critic, how much more so must be the great oration. For the speech is not a disembodied text. Rather it is a point of complex convergence, in which speaker, auditors, and events can all come together in grand illumination. Time freezes in that moment, and the meaning of its panorama stands revealed: The great speech thus translates into heightened consciousness and even into revelation.

What hubris, then, is required to present oneself as a critic of such a speech? From what hill of vanity must one view Martin Luther King's mountain? My own little hill is constructed of small moments, one of which is worth remembering. When I first came to Memphis in 1966, I was asked by a friend to come to a rally announcing the candidacy of the first black candidate for Mayor in Memphis. They could get, she said, no other white person to speak in his behalf, and they did not wish him to be seen strictly as a black candidate. So I agreed, but since it was my first such involvement, I was apprehensive. "What would happen to me?" — the kind of question King shames in his speech as he tells the parable of the Good Samaritan — flashed across my mind. But I went to the rally, and it was huge, and all the audience seemed black. And I stood up finally, among the parade of black speakers, all of whom seemed so powerful and wonderful, an unknown person before an unknown audience, significant, ironically, only because of my race. And I started, "Long ago a man far wiser than any of us said, 'A house divided against itself cannot stand.'" And I paused, and from the collective throat of that great, black, wary audience there came back to me a thunderous "A-MEN."

---

[2]Richard Lentz, *Sixty-Five Days in Memphis: A Study of Culture, Symbols, and the Press,* Journalism Monographs, No. 98 (August 1986): 29.

[3]Garry Wills, "Martin Luther King: Blessed be the Name of De Lawd," *Esquire,* August, 1968, 128.

And I was startled, heckled by my own success. Finally I smiled, and they smiled, recognizing my awkwardness on first entering their rhetorical culture, and then I went on. And as I spoke there came to me in a rush what their acceptance meant, how supported I felt as they encouraged me, how large and strong and important I felt, as I talked about white obligation to open the rusted doors of opportunity to those left on the outside.

It was really a small moment, but I learned a great deal from it. Learned what the black church experience meant in forming orators who could speak to listeners who had been systematically degraded and beaten down by each week's experience in racial subjugation. Learned the cultural role of the great bold speaker in representing what they might be, relieved of that terrible subjugation. So I take this little experience and a few others like it, magnify them a hundred times, and glimpse for a moment what it might mean to be a Martin Luther King Jr.—beloved and despised, exploited as much by those who loved him as he was hated by those who feared him—as he spoke at the pinnacle and end of his life. And what I see is what follows—my view from the hill.

Much of the greatness of King's final speech on the stormy night of April 3, 1968, lay in what he had to overcome.[4] The strike of the sanitation workers, improbable from the beginning, had become a heavy burden to sustain. Over two months it had endured, involving the lives and destinies of 1,300 men and their families. They were poor people, whose salaries qualified them for public welfare. So they had no money, and there had been no pre-existing strike fund to sustain them. They were not a naturally militant group: Most of them had been conditioned both by race and by life to accept a humble role in society. They were hardly

---

[4]The facts in the description that follows of the rhetorical situation of King's speech are drawn from Lentz, *Sixty-five Days in Memphis;* from Joan Turner Beifuss, *At the River I Stand: Memphis, the 1968 Strike, and Martin Luther King* (Memphis: B & W Books, 1985); from John Bakke, "A Study of Establishment Rhetoric during the Sanitation Strike in Memphis, 1968" (Ms. housed in the Missouri Valley Collection, Memphis State University Library); and from personal experience.

the group to start a social revolution. Moreover, they had gone out at just the wrong time. To put the matter bluntly, in the winter uncollected garbage does not stink. It does not create the kind of public pressure that forces a successful conclusion to a strike. Still, from the workers' point of view, it was just the right time: That moment when their accumulation of grievances was simply intolerable, and when they must now act or surrender what claim they had on dignity and integrity. When they marched, they often carried signs asserting the simple proposition, "I am a Man." The fact that this was a metaphor for many people in Memphis, and that they had to assert such a proposition, signified the virulent racism they had to overcome. They were striking both for their jobs and for their identities. But after two months of crisis in Memphis, with no paychecks, the going was very tough indeed.

Then there was King's own embattled situation. He had won the Nobel Prize, but many thought that his brand of activism belonged to the past. Hard and brilliant new voices, like that of Malcolm X, questioned and scorned the whole doctrine of non-violent protest in America. King had just experienced a humiliating defeat in Chicago, failing to crack the entrenched institutional racism of housing patterns in that city. Adam Clayton Powell had then rechristened him, "Martin Loser King."

As though he needed additional troubles, the first march he had led in Memphis had been a tactical disaster. Poorly organized by local leaders, it had resulted in some petty violence and had disintegrated into a chaos of fleeing demonstrators and pursuing police. King himself had to be transported from the area, leaving the local newspapers to cackle over what they called this latest exhibition of "Chicken-a-la-King." The spectacle seemed to confirm to many critics that King and his movement were dangerous and ineffective anachronisms, raising further doubts about his ability to sustain the grandiose Poor People's Campaign he was planning later that year in Washington.

All these furies were swarming about King's head as he stepped onto the stage at Mason Temple on that final fateful night, and his speech may be savored now as his last triumphant response to them. To recapture the moment, Mason Temple itself is a cavernous place that can seat a multitude of souls. It is the kind of setting that requires the dramatic, Ciceronian style of oratory to challenge and fill its vastness. On the rainy, stormy night of April

3, only three thousand were in attendance, but these were the faithful, the hard-core true believers. King had been very tired and reluctant to speak that night. So he had sent Ralph Abernathy in his place, but Abernathy seeing the audience, called King at the Lorraine Motel and said, "They are your crowd." They needed the message only he could give.

And so he had come, and so he began: "I'm delighted to see each of you here tonight in spite of a storm warning. You reveal that you are determined to go on anyhow. Something is happening in Memphis, something is happening in our world. And you know, if I were standing at the beginning of time with the possibility of taking a kind of general and panoramic view of the whole of human history up to now, and the Almighty said to me, "Martin Luther King, which age would you like to live in?"

Already we see that the "Mountaintop" speech is appropriately named. At the beginning King stands on an implied mountain, outside of time but viewing its panorama up to the present. His only companion is God, with whom he talks and deals directly. He will return to that mountain again as the speech concludes, this time to proclaim his exalted moral vision of the future. He is closely identified with his listeners, but through the metaphor of the mountain he can depart from them and ascend into moral space, there to assume his lonely prophet's stance.

So he tells his audience how he would deal with God's tough question. He would consider especially vital moments in the quest for freedom, beginning in Egypt, going on through Greece and Rome, pausing with Martin Luther in the Renaissance, watching Abraham Lincoln sign the Emancipation Proclamation, and observing Franklin Roosevelt grapple with economic slavery. And he decides:

> I would turn to the Almighty and say, "If you allow me to live just a few years in the second half of the twentieth century I will be happy." [applause]
>
> Now that's a strange statement to make because the world is all messed up, the nation is sick, trouble is in the land, confusion all around. That's a strange statement. But I know somehow that only when it is dark enough can you see the stars. And I see God working in this period of the twentieth century in a way that men in some strange way are responding. Something is happening in our world. The masses of people are rising up, and

> wherever they are assembled today, whether they are in Johannes-
> burg, South Africa; Nairobi, Kenya; Accra, Ghana; New York
> City; Atlanta, Georgia; Jackson, Mississippi or Memphis, Tennes-
> see, the cry is always the same: "We want to be free!" [applause]

Notice here the beautiful diachronic and synchronic effects:
King has sketched a rising consciousness of freedom unfolding
through time, which gradually comes to focus in the present
struggle. And then he places this moment at the center of
synchronic space, in the quest for freedom extending around the
world. He lifts the tired heads and hearts of those before him:
They are important! This is not just some small garbage strike
stuck off on the margins of humanity: This moment is exalted!
(And so are they.)

Lifted with him in this exaltation, they can see the significance
of their own crisis as part of the rise of "the colored peoples of the
world." They can share King's apocalyptic vision, see that the
world's choice is between "nonviolence and nonexistence," see that
"if something isn't done and done in a hurry," then "the whole
world is doomed." Memphis has become a synecdoche for that
dark, vast foreboding, that urgency and trauma. His listeners have
become world-historical figures—precisely because they have
become figurative, representative. And they can see that in their
spiritual journey from Egypt into the now, they have assumed
transcendent new identities:

> I can remember…I can remember when Negroes were just
> going around, as Ralph has said so often, scratching where they
> didn't itch and laughing when they were not tickled. [applause]
> But that day is all over. [applause] We mean business now, and
> we are determined to gain our rightful place in God's world.
> [applause] And that's all this whole thing is about. We aren't
> engaged in any negative protests and in any negative arguments
> with anybody. We are saying that "We are determined to be
> men, we are determined to be people." We are saying, [applause]
> … we are saying that "We are God's children."

In this new religious vision of identity, the freedom quest
resonates again. Now they are depicted as on their own exodus out
of this new Egypt, escaping from a new Pharoah. The name,
Memphis, may be fortuitous, but it does reinforce the prevailing
narrative symbolism, which will climax with King himself, their
Moses, sharing his last inspired glimpse of the Promised Land.

But first the issues of the present strike, viewed in these
dramatic frames:

> The issue is injustice. The issue is the refusal of Memphis to be
> fair and honest in its dealings with its public servants who
> happen to be sanitation workers. [applause] Now we've got to
> keep attention on that. That's always the problem with a little
> violence. You know what happened the other day, and the press
> dealt only with the window-breaking. I read the articles. They
> very seldom got around to mentioning the fact that one
> thousand three hundred sanitation workers are on strike, and
> that Memphis is not being fair to them, and that Mayor Loeb is
> in dire need of a doctor. [cheers and applause] They didn't get
> around to that. Now we're gonna march again, and we've gotta
> march again in order to put the issue where it is supposed to be,
> and force everybody to see that there are thirteen hundred of
> God's children here suffering, sometimes goin' hungry, going
> through dark and dreary nights wondering how this thing is
> gonna come out. That's the issue. And we've got to say to the
> nation, "We know how it's coming out." For when people get
> caught up with that which is right, and they are willing to
> sacrifice for it, there is no stopping point short of victory!
> [applause]

One of King's favorite metaphors, that of disease and illness,
re-echoes in these words. Indeed, Mayor Loeb, already saddled
with the Pharoah symbolism, now becomes as well a living synecdoche for the sick society that was contemporary America.[5] This is
the same Mayor Loeb who boasted to Garry Wills that there was
a "good understanding" between himself and Memphis blacks.

King now puts the heart into listeners by reminding them of
glorious successes of the past, and in so doing he defends the
power and legitimacy of non-verbal protest as well. Here he

---

[5]Richard P. Fulkerson has remarked on King's attraction to archetypal metaphors,
including images of disease and health, and technological imagery in his "The Public
Letter as a Rhetorical Form: Structure, Logic, and Style in King's 'Letter from
Birmingham Jail,'" *Quarterly Journal of Speech,* 65 (1979): 131. Such archetypal and
culturetypal images, as I would identify them, connect King's vision to the timely and the
timeless, to the now as well as to the eternal. The technological (culturetypal) images
lend their subjects relevance, and are what Fulkerson would call "adaptive." The
archetypal images invest their subjects with feeling and authenticity, functioning in
Fulkerson's account as "affective" and "ethical."

remembers, and celebrates, magnificent moments in Birmingham:

> I remember in Birmingham, Alabama, when we were in that majestic struggle there, we would move out of the Sixteenth Street Baptist Church day after day. By the hundreds we would move out, and Bull Connor would tell 'em to send the dogs forth, and they did come. But we just went before the dogs singing, "Ain't gonna let nobody turn me around." [cheers] Bull Connor next would say, "Turn the firehoses on." And as I said to you the other night Bull Connor didn't know history. He knew a kind of physics that somehow didn't relate to the transphysics that we knew about, and that was the fact that there was a certain kind of fire that no water could put out. [applause] And we went before the firehoses. We had known water. If we were Baptist or some other denominations we had been immersed, if we were Methodists and some others we had been sprinkled, but we knew water. That couldn't stop us. [applause] And we just went on before the dogs and we would look at them, and we'd go on before the water hoses and we would look at it, and we'd just go on singing "Over my head I see freedom in the air." And then we would be thrown in the paddy wagons, and sometimes we were stacked in there like sardines in a can. And they would throw us in and old Bull would say, "Take 'em off," and they did. And we would just go on in the paddy wagons singin' "We Shall Overcome." And every now and then we'd get in jail and we'd see the jailers looking through the windows being moved by our prayers, and being moved by our words and our songs. And there was a power there which Bull Connor couldn't adjust to. And so we ended up transforming Bull into a steer, and we won our struggle in Birmingham. [applause]
>
> And we've got to go on in Memphis just like that.

This cameo of the past functions as a moral, rhetorical history. It helps to organize and focus time, fusing memory and desire. In rhetoric the past exists in service of the present, so here the story of Birmingham becomes an exemplar for Memphis.

Now King proceeds to tell his listeners exactly what they must do to win this strike, and how they must do it. They must proceed respectfully but with unity and determination. They must find the economic pressure points, and they must build economic strength in the black community as well. And finally, they must invest themselves personally in the desperate plight of the sanitation workers. They must stop by this dangerous road, just as King himself had stopped by Memphis: "...We've got to give ourselves to this struggle until the end. Nothing would be more tragic than to stop at this point in Memphis. We've got to see it through. [applause] And when we have our march, you need to be there. If it means leaving work, if it means leaving school, be there. [applause] Be concerned about your brother. You may not be on strike, but either we go up together or we go down together. [applause] Let us develop a kind of dangerous unselfishness." So he goes on to tell the parable of the Good Samaritan, which functions as a kind of balance for the Children of Israel narrative. While the latter provides collective identity, the former sets up models of personal, individual conduct to imitate and avoid. Moreover, the Good Samaritan, since he is "of another race," reminds listeners of their own need to maintain tolerance and acceptance:

> [Jesus]...talked about a certain man who fell among thieves. And you remember that a Levite [Voice says, "Sure"] and a priest passed by on the other side. They didn't stop to help him. And finally a man of another race came by. [Voice says, "Yes sir!] He got down from his beast, decided not to be compassionate by proxy, but he got down with him, administered first aid, and helped the man in need. Jesus ended up saying, this was the good man, this was the great man, because he had the capacity to project the "I" into the "thou," and to be concerned about his brother.
>
> Now you know we use our imagination a great deal to try to determine why the priest and the Levite didn't stop. At times we say they were busy going to a church meeting, an ecclesiastical gatherin', and they had to get on down to Jerusalem so they wouldn't be late for their meeting. At other times we would speculate that there was a religious law that one who was engaged in religious ceremonials was not to touch a human body twenty-four hours before the ceremony. And every now and then we begin to wonder whether maybe they were not going down to Jerusalem—or down to Jericho rather—to organize a Jericho Road Improvement Association. [Laughter] That's a possibility. Maybe they felt that it was better to deal with the problem from the causal root rather than to get bogged down with an individual effect....That's a dangerous road. In the days of Jesus it came to be known as the Bloody Pass. You know it's possible that the priest and the Levite looked over to

that man on the ground and wondered if the robbers were still around. [Voices agree, "Yeah."] Or it's possible that they felt that the man on the ground was merely faking, [Voice says, "Uh-huh"] and he was acting like he had been robbed and hurt in order to seize them over there, lull them there for quick and easy seizure. [Voice says, "Oh, yeah."] And so the first question that the priest asked, the first question that the Levite asked, was "If I stop to help this man, what will happen to me?" But then the good Samaritan came by, and he reversed the question: "If I do not stop to help this man, what will happen to him?" That's the question before you tonight: Not, "If I stop to help the sanitation workers, what will happen to my job?" Not, "If I stop to help the sanitation workers, what will happen to all of the hours that I usually spend in my office every day and every week as a pastor?" The question is not, "If I stop to help this man in need, what will happen to me?" The question is, "If I do *not* stop to help the sanitation workers, what will happen to them?" That's the question. [Long applause]

Let us rise up tonight with a greater readiness. Let us stand with a greater determination. And let us move on, in these powerful days, these days of challenge, to make America what it ought to be. We have an opportunity to make America a better nation....

Note here the emergence of the vertical metaphor, signifying both the strength of the rising race and the movement of the speech itself to its own elevated peroration. For now he had come to his conclusion, and who could know—could he?—that it was to be the peroration of his life, that he was actually delivering—as no one else could or would—his own eulogy? He tells first the story of how a "demented black woman" had stabbed him many years ago as he was autographing books in New York. In the hospital they found that the tip of the blade was lodged against his aorta, and the *New York Times* commented that if he had merely sneezed, he would have died. Later, while recovering in the hospital, he had received many kind letters, but one in particular remained in his memory:

But there was another letter [Voices say, "All right"] that came from a little girl, a young girl, who was a student at the White Plains High School, and I looked at that letter and I'll never forget it. It said simply, "Dear Dr. King, I am a ninth grade student at the White Plains High School." She said, "While it should not matter, I would like to mention that I'm a white girl. I read in the paper of your misfortune and of your suffering, and I read that if you had sneezed you would have died. I'm simply writing you to say that I'm so happy that you didn't sneeze."And I want to say tonight... [applause] I want to say tonight that I too am happy that I didn't sneeze, because if I had sneezed [Voice says, "All right"] I wouldn't have been around here in 1960 when students all over the South started sitting in at lunch counters. And I knew that as they were sitting in they were really standing up for the best in the American dream and taking the whole nation back to those great wells of democracy which were dug deep by the founding fathers in the Declaration of Independence and the Constitution. If I had sneezed [Crowd replies, "Yeah"] I wouldn't have been around here in 1961 when we decided to take a ride for freedom and ended segregation in interstate travel. If I had sneezed [Crowd says, "Yes"] I wouldn't have been around here in 1962 when Negroes in Albany, Georgia, decided to straighten their backs up. And whenever men and women straighten their backs up they are going somewhere because a man can't ride your back unless it is bent. If I had sneezed [Long applause!]... if I had sneezed I wouldn't have been here in 1963, when the black people of Birmingham, Alabama, aroused the conscience of this nation and brought into being the civil rights bill. If I had sneezed, [applause] I wouldn't have had a chance later in that year in August to try to tell America about a dream that I had had. If I had sneezed, [applause] I wouldn't have been down in Selma, Alabama, to see the great movement there. If I had sneezed, I wouldn't have been in Memphis to see a community rally around those brothers and sisters who are suffering. [Voices say, "Yes sir."] I'm so happy that I didn't sneeze.

And they were telling me... [applause] Now it doesn't matter now. [Voice says, "Go ahead."] It really doesn't matter what happens now. I left Atlanta this morning, and as we got started on the plane—there were six of us—the pilot said over the public address system, "We are sorry for the delay, but we have Dr. Martin Luther King on the plane, and to be sure that all of the bags were checked and to be sure that nothing would be wrong on the plane, we had to check out everything carefully, and we've had the plane protected and guarded all night."

And then I got into Memphis, and some began to say the threats, or talk about the threats that were out of what would happen to me from some of our sick white brothers. Well, I

don't know what will happen now. We've got some difficult
days ahead. But it really doesn't matter with me now because
I've been to the mountaintop. [applause] And I don't mind. Like
anybody I would like to live a long life. Longevity has its place.
But I'm not concerned about that now. I just want to do God's
will, and He's allowed me to go up to the mountain, and I've
looked over, and I've seen the Promised Land. I may not get
there with you, but I want you to know tonight that we as a
people will get to the Promised Land. [applause] So I'm happy
tonight, I'm not worried about anything, I'm not fearing any
man. Mine eyes have seen the glory of the coming of the Lord.
[Long applause, cheers.]

What finally can one say of such a mountain of a speech,
viewed from our small hill? First, perhaps, that it gives the lie to a
view one used to hear quite frequently, that the public oration is a
dying art form. King is an orator: on the page his words can seem
flat, can lose their iridescence; there the prose-patterns sometimes
appear over-blown and awkward as they strain for inflated effects.
It's when you hear them that they penetrate to your heart.[6] And it
was also in the middle of the action that King was heard best,
when the situation stripped his language of all that was unnecessary,
leaving such poetry as "Only when it is dark enough can you see
the stars."

Such, I would argue, is the language of ritual, as indeed is
much of the language of this speech. But the occasion was
certainly not epideictic, not at least in any traditional sense of that
term. Normally we think of epideictic rhetoric as belonging to an
occasion after some critical event has already occurred, in which
the event is commemorated, celebrated, and interpreted. This
occasion, it is clear, was situated in, belonged to, and constituted a
consciousness of its moment of crisis. Did King misperceive the
rhetorical situation? Clearly not. What defines the ritual of
epideictic rhetoric is not so much its place vis-a-vis events, but

---

[6]In these judgments I concur with Edwin Black, who observes that King "was often
a clumsy and overblown stylist," but concludes concerning the "I Have a Dream" speech:
"Show me a man who can *hear* that speech and not be stirred to his depths, and I'll show
you a man who has no depths to stir." ("The 'Vision' of Martin Luther King," *Literature
as Revolt and Revolt as Literature: Three Studies in the Rhetoric of Non-Oratorical Forms*
(Minneapolis: The University of Minnesota, 1970), 9.)

rather its function, which is to confer or reaffirm social identity. What both races had to confront in Memphis in the Spring of 1968 was the changing social identity of black people. In this transition, this exodus out of racism, Who were they? and Who were they to be? Those questions constituted the crisis of Memphis.

To answer them, King resorted primarily to a biblical story familiar to all in his audience—the flight of the Children of Israel from Egypt. Almost all the circumstances—the extreme poverty of the workers, the setting in Memphis, the especially adamant character of the then Mayor Loeb, the powerful *ethos* of King himself—lent special resonance to this favorite narrative-form of the black experience in America. As Malinda Snow has observed, "In the story of the children of Israel in Egypt, ... [slaves] discovered the central type of their experience, which prefigured their own deliverance from slavery. They merged biblical and contemporary time."[7] Thus as King exercised his inventional option, and selected the Children of Israel narrative as the major structural principle of his speech, his choice was far more than an exercise in cleverness. Indeed, ingenuity, a quality we may often associate with inventional excellence, had little to do with the rightness of King's selection. What is more important is that King's listeners had no doubt heard this narrative-form explored many times before as figuring and framing their racial experience. While the excellence of this particular version may have seemed unique, its primary virtue was its place within the black rhetorical tradition. For listeners, it transversed time, connecting past with present, confirming their association with generations receding into memory. Central then to the rhetorical experience of this speech was the celebration of rhetorical ritual, joining speaker and audience as they acknowledged again what it meant to be black in America, and black in Memphis. The narrative tradition made their lives coherent, invested their experience with religious meaning, and gave hope to their cause. As they had prevailed before, in so many dread situations opposed by so many other formidable Pharoahs, they would prevail again. It was the ritual

[7]Malinda Snow, "Martin Luther King's 'Letter from Birmingham Jail' as Pauline Epistle," *Quarterly Journal of Speech,* 71 (1985): 319.

repetition of this narrative then, augmented by the particular
eloquence of its statement in this performance, that gave this
speech so much of its distinctive power as epideictic utterance.

And yet, appropriate as King's narrative selection was for his
audience and for the short-term rhetorical consequences in this
situation, we may wonder at its long-term efficacy. No doubt every
selection among rhetorical options may have its shadow, its
potential negative elements. And we may wonder at the culture-
long consequences of continuing to remind people of their slave
origins, speaking of them as "children" (even transfigured as
"God's children.") The family metaphor had not been kind to
black people in America. And King's usage ran the danger of
raising the salience again of cultural metaphors that had denigrated
adult blacks as "boy," "girl," or at best "uncle." It was the family
metaphor that had created the low sense of place for blacks in the
racial hierarchy of American society, and that confined them to
that place. I believe it was these lingering images of debased
identity that Malcolm X found most objectionable in King's
approach to social reform. Again, I wish not to be misunderstood:
I believe that King's narrative selection was correct and astute, his
execution superb. But his was a human choice within an imperfect
rhetorical world, and may well have exacted its price within the
spiritual lives of his listeners.

Despite this possible weakness, the Exodus story did offer
hope to King's listeners. The reason for such reassurance, Rosteck
has observed, is that the narrative is predictive: What it predicts
for black people is an American equivalent of the Promised Land.[8]
This predictive quality is similar to the deterministic element
identified in rhetorical uses of light and dark metaphors.[9] Both the
prediction and the determinism are conditioned: the Promised
Land will come, and light will follow darkness, *if* (and only if)
auditors are true to the speaker's recommendations. Here we must
return to the parable of the Good Samaritan, and note how it
functions in this speech vis-a-vis the Exodus narrative. The latter, I

[8]Thomas Rosteck, "'I've Been to the Mountaintop': The Linkage of Narrative,
Metaphor and Argument in Martin Luther King's Final Speech," presented to the 1985
convention of the Speech Communication Association.

[9]"Archetypal Metaphor in Rhetoric: the Light-Dark Family," *Quarterly Journal of
Speech,* 53 (1967): 115-25.

observed earlier, offers cultural, collective identity for black people, while the former deals with personal moral obligation. But more than just the counterpart of the Exodus narrative, the Good Samaritan story functions as its enabling condition. The Exodus myth will become reality, will carry listeners to the Promised Land, *if* they are willing to follow with full-hearted commitment the moral example of the Good Samaritan.[10] With King they must "stop by this dangerous road" and embrace the cause of the sanitation workers in the here-and-now. Through this ingenious combination of Biblical narratives, the speech moves from the opening vision of collective identity, these Children of God who are today's Children of Israel, to the close picture of personal moral risk and choice figured in the Good Samaritan story, and back again to the grand concluding image of a people marching toward a Land that King alone has been privileged to witness. The movement of the speech is epic through moral time and space.

Besides its epideictic function expressed through the language of ritual, identity, and moral confrontation, King's speech had the immediate task of reinvigorating a faltering strike action. And so it performed the business of implementing, the work of deciding and sustaining action. It is in such moments that oratory especially comes to the center-stage of rhetoric. Nothing can take the place of the actual physical presence of orators in such moments, bringing themselves to bear witness to their own commitment, touching listeners directly with the radiance and fire of their messages, opening the eyes of auditors to the meaning of their lives and to the meaning of the events in which they are engaged. Only the great orator can hold that center-stage successfully, and King held it with a mastery and grace rarely seen in the long tradition of rhetoric. Clearly, he belongs among the great revolutionary orators. Surely, we have been witness to a phenomenon.

To speak of King's address as exemplifying the rhetoric of implementation is to depart from the close criticism of the speech and our critilogue, and to step back into what I shall call

---

[10]See the discussion of parable in general, and the Good Samaritan parable in particular, in William G. Kirkwood, "Storytelling and Self-Confrontation: Parables as Communication Strategies," *Quarterly Journal of Speech,* 69 (1983): 58-74; and "Parables as Metaphors and Examples," *Quarterly Journal of Speech,* 71 (1985): 422-40.

perspective criticism. Here we are concerned with placing King's address within the overall process of rhetoric that was working out its fateful scenario in Memphis during the early months of 1968. To understand this process, I call upon my account of rhetorical depiction, which identifies successive phases of presentation, arousal, group identification, implementation, and reaffirmation.[11] Essentially I argue that the presentation phase of rhetorical process may be most vital, because it affects how we see events, and thus how we feel, band together, act in response to them, and celebrate them. These phases enable each other in successful, coordinated rhetorical campaigns, but when they occur in competing rhetorics they can disable each other. This explains why all the passionate rhetoric of action generated by black orators during the sanitation strike, including King's several speeches, were finally subverted and limited in effect.

What undercut the reach of such rhetoric was a countervailing rhetoric of presentation which cast events and players according to presuppositions deeply rooted in the culture of racism. Presented in the mass circulation newspapers and on local television news programs, this rhetoric developed its power from an irresistible accumulation of stories, human interest features, and editorials, played out day-after-day during the strike, but consistent with plotlines that had already been established, year-after-year, decade-after-decade, in the discourse of Southern culture. There were, according to Richard Lentz, at least three themes among these powerful cultural plotlines: (1) The theme of the outsider, which "invoked the belief that outsiders were agitating blacks who otherwise would be content with their lot." (2) The fear of a black uprising, "...grounded in the concept that during a period of social unrest public order had to be maintained at any cost....The newspaper accounts resurrected in modern dress the fear of servile insurrection that haunted the antebellum South." (3) The theme of racial noblesse oblige, which "...was an amalgam of paternalism and another racial stereotype. Blacks were stereotyped as child-like creatures incapable of conducting their own affairs.... Whites

[11]Michael Osborn, "Rhetorical Depiction," *Form, Genre, and the Study of Political Discourse,* ed. Herbert W. Simons and Aram A. Aghazarian (Columbia, SC: University of South Carolina Press, 1986), 79-107.

protected and cared for 'their' blacks, usually by providing some form of largess at the back door." Blacks, in turn, owed them gratitude, and rewarded them by being content with a lower station in life. "Thus it was that the demands for equality raised by the strikers produced a mixture of puzzlement and shock that blacks would challenge the authority of those who had taken care of them."[12] These plotlines provided molds for depicting the players in the sanitation strike, for describing their motives, and for selecting and connecting their actions in presentation. They helped many Memphians make sense of the strike, and in effect rigidified the perceptions they predisposed against any counter-rhetoric rising from the black community. They limited the reach of King's rhetoric largely to the black community itself, which as this speech shows, was developing its own supporting perceptions, plotlines, group togetherness, and agenda for action. Clearly, what we are describing was a gigantic racial dialectic which reached its point of stasis in Memphis, and which would require a cataclysmic event to resolve its almost unbearable tension. The murder of Martin Luther King was that event.

I have called King a revolutionary spokesperson, and that may lift some eyebrows. What is so revolutionary about wanting to save the American dream and redeem the national conscience? If you consider just the pure ideology of King's speech, he is as conservative as red, white, and blue. He is not out to overthrow America.

Ah, but that was his secret. He was not a political speaker. He told it to us all along. He was a preacher, a converter of souls. And what he was out to redeem was cultural sin, the way people treat each other as humans, the way they betray their own ideals. As I have put it elsewhere, "His intent therefore was not so much to defeat his opponents as to save them from repudiating their own high principles. As Richard Neuhaus observed, 'A strategy for change that confronts a people with the choice of either accommodating the change or consciously surrendering the values by which they think they live is a most realistic strategy, striking at

---

[12]Lentz, *Sixty-Five Days in Memphis,* 8.

the heart of society.'"[13]

But we couldn't stand to hear all that, coming from the mouth of a black man. And moreover, a black man who could command a vast black army of humble people who were willing to assume all the risks of their own rising status and all the dangers of our own conversion. That is why this really conservative man was so hated, so feared. He threatened to rearrange our social selves, and beyond that our very souls. And so we shot him, blew away that great organ voice through an agent, a warped little man who thought, quite reasonably, given the rhetorical circumstances of that time, that he enjoyed moral license to gun down Martin Luther King. But it was fear and hatred that propelled the bullet — across a darkening street in Memphis on the quiet evening of April 4, 1968.

---

[13]Richard John Neuhaus, Letter, *Commonweal,* 88 (1968): 342; as cited in my "Rhetorical Depiction," 94.

"A DANGEROUS UNSELFISHNESS":
MARTIN LUTHER KING, JR'S SPEECH
AT MEMPHIS, APRIL 3, 1968:
A RESPONSE TO OSBORN

JOSEPH W. WENZEL

In his Foreword to the second printing of *Rhetorical Criticism,*
Edwin Black observes that criticism is inherently personal: "We
value criticism that gives us *singular* access to its subject." He
describes criticism as "a kind of discourse that acts as an extension
of a writer.... A critique represents a particular mind at work on
an object: apprehending it, examining it, coming to understand it,
placing it into history. A function of such writing is to bring its
reader to corroborate an interpretive process—not necessarily the
same one that the critic has experienced but in any case one that
will finally bring the reader to the interpretation that the critic
proposes."[1]

What does that suggest for the character of this peculiar
academic exercise I am undertaking here, a criticism of a criticism?
I suppose, on the one hand, I might set out to corroborate the
interpretation of King's speech offered by Michael Osborn; to be
candid, I will do so in the end. On the other hand, however, given
the intensely personal nature of critical interpretation, it should not
be surprising if I do not read the speech exactly as Osborn does.
So, an alternative approach might be for me to address the
question: What else can be said about the speech by another critic,
from another angle? Moreover, a respondent is expected to raise
issues, to take exceptions, challenge conclusions, and in general stir
up trouble. I will try to discharge that obligation, therefore, by

---

[1]Edwin Black, *Rhetorical Criticism: A Study in Method* (Madison: University of
Wisconsin Press, 1978), xii, xiv.

essaying an analysis of the speech rather different from Osborn's. In fact, I would disagree with Osborn's reading only in a few small details; the main point of my interpretation will be to challenge the historical frame within which Osborn views the speech, especially as it determines the starting point of his rhetorical appreciation.

In addition to critical interpretations being intensely personal in the way Black meant, each specific critique is biased by the historical perspective from which the critic views the object. Although one outcome of criticism may be to place an object in history, it is perhaps inevitable that the critic's starting point is already conditioned by his *post hoc* knowledge of the speech's significance in the flow of events both before and after. That effect is likely to be more intense to the degree that the critic is close to the rhetorical event, as when the critic is a participant on the scene, or is emotionally or ideologically bound up with the cause of the speaker.

Michael Osborn is in a uniquely privileged position to reflect on Martin Luther King Jr's involvement in the Memphis sanitation workers' strike in 1968. Memphis has been Osborn's home for many years, and he knows its politics from personal experience; he knows the civil rights movement, too, for he has been a part of it. The moving description of his first encounter with a black southern audience is testimony to his involvement and commitment. Osborn, the citizen, cares deeply about the events on which he comments. But, therein lies a problem for Osborn, the critic: his depth of feeling for Martin Luther King, Jr. and the cause he served leads him to place the speech on a monumental pedestal, to stand back and admire it, to paint his critical appreciation in broad strokes. The result is a portrayal of King's performance that seems more eulogistic than analytical, more epideictic than critical. Osborn seems to value the speech, not so much for what it is and does as rhetorical utterance, but more for what it represents as the last speech of a great man martyred for his cause on the following day. My argument will be that such a stance, leading to such a portrayal, while entirely appropriate to an historical appreciation of the speech, should be the last stage of criticism rather than the first.

That Osborn's stance is as I have described it is apparent from the opening pages of his paper. He finds himself "embarrassed by [his] role" because the speech stands before him "like [a] very mountain."[2] He wonders what *hubris,* what vanity is required of a critic who proposes to criticize this speech by King "at the pinnacle and end of his life." The image of King as martyred hero standing on a mountaintop dominates the approach to the speech. But that image owes more to our knowledge of subsequent events than to rhetorical analysis. Osborn, like others, notes the prophetic quality of the speech, in which Martin Luther King, Jr. seemed to foretell his own assassination in that line that now haunts our national conscience: "I may not get there with you but I want you to know tonight that we as a people will get to the promised land."[3] Against those interpretations that call the speech prophetic in the light of history, however, I want to urge a different reading. The last moving paragraph of King's speech, and its eloquence as a whole, can be appreciated more deeply when we understand its function in the rhetorical dynamics of the actual situation in Mason Hall on April 3, 1968. To support that statement I now turn to an interpretation of the speech.

Rather than thinking of King at a high point in his life and career as he approached this speaking situation, one can just as well think of him at a low point and faced with tremendous difficulties. Indeed, Osborn notes some of these problems. The sanitation workers' strike seemed almost hopeless in the face of an intransigent mayor and an ineffective city council. The sanitation workers were a weak group, not very militant anyway, with little material support. A short time earlier, a poorly organized demonstration in support of the strike had resulted in property damage, and the local papers had resurrected old southern fears of black violence. King himself had been accused of cowardice for leaving the scene. There were challenges to his brand of nonviolent protest, especially by young blacks. King planned a great Poor People's Campaign to begin in Washington later that summer, and a failure in Memphis would have severely damaged his credibility

---

[2]Michael Osborn, "'I've Been to the Mountaintop': A Rhetorical Appreciation," this volume.

[3]Quotations from and references to the speech are based on a text reconstructed from the following sources: Martin Luther King, Jr., "I See the Promised Land," in *A Testament of Hope: The Essential Writings of Martin Luther King, Jr.,* ed. James Melvin Washington (San Francisco: Harper & Row, 1986), 279-286; and a tape recording and transcript generously provided by Michael Osborn.

as a national leader.[4] In light of those circumstances, it seems inappropriate to begin consideration of the speech by calling it "his last triumphant response." Triumph was by no means assured; the threat of failure was very real, and the stakes were high. I agree with Osborn that the speech ends on a pinnacle, but it began at the base of some dangerous cliffs.

Martin Luther King, Jr. had much to prove when he appeared to speak at Mason Hall, and he knew it. It would be fascinating to know how he prepared, what notes he might have made, how he had briefed the speech. Perhaps, with more time and better access to his papers, someone will be able to find out. Nevertheless, judging from the topics of the speech itself, as they relate to what we know of the circumstances, it is possible to reconstruct King's specific purposes. I think he set out to prove the following points:

1. The struggle of the sanitation workers is well worth the effort, because it is a part of the world-wide struggle for freedom.
2. The struggle can be won. It would be a tragedy to stop.
3. The way to win is through nonviolent demonstration and economic boycott.
4. He was not afraid, and Memphis blacks should not be afraid.
5. Each individual must be selflessly committed to the struggle.

I used the word "prove" in introducing these points in order to emphasize the argumentative character of the speech, especially the first half. King faced an audience full of doubts about whether it was worthwhile to continue in a seemingly hopeless situation. He had to convince them of the possibility of victory, show them how it could be achieved, and insure the commitment of each individual. The first parts of the speech, therefore, built a foundation of powerful argument, supported by vivid presentation of evidence. Only on that basis could he rightfully make the demand of selfless sacrifice that emerged in the final stage.

For purposes of analysis, the speech divides naturally into two

[4]Richard Lentz, "Sixty-Five Days in Memphis: A Study of Culture, Symbols, and the Press," *Journalism Monographs* 98 (1986): 1-40. This account and Osborn's paper are my chief sources of background information.

parts. The first comprises about 60% of the whole, five of eight pages in the published version. These sections are addressed to the first three points above, and they could be read almost like a debater's affirmative case on a policy proposition. King establishes the need for action in the struggle for freedom and presents a plan in considerable practical detail. The remainder of the speech (three published pages) supports points 4 and 5 above in a manner less argumentative, but compelling in its climactic development. Let us take the parts in order.

After thanks to Ralph Abernathy for his introduction and a word of appreciation to the audience for their venturing out on a stormy night, King imagines the Almighty offering him a chance to live in any age of human history, and he reviews the possibilities by remarking on the great events and great thinkers of Egypt, Greece, Rome, the Renaissance, etc. He rejects successively each great age of human history, punctuating his choices with the words, "But I wouldn't stop there." He chooses finally "to live just a few years in the second half of the twentieth century." I agree with Osborn that there are interesting diachronic and synchronic effects here that place the Memphis sanitation strike in the forefront of the fight for freedom. But, I do not agree that the references to Greece, Rome, and so on "sketch a freedom consciousness." Rather, King wants above all to make the point that this is the most important time in all of human history: "Something is happening in our world." No doubt, Osborn is right that Memphis is made a synecdoche for the world-wide struggle to be free, but we also need to recognize the argumentative importance of this opening section as support for a specific claim essential to the case King has to make. As a first contention, he must establish that the Memphis strike is important, and he does so by comparison with high points in human history. Everyone will agree that the times he mentioned were important. Yet, by his testimony, this moment is even more important, and its focus is in Memphis. That is why he can say, "I'm just happy that God has allowed me to live in this period, to see what is unfolding. And I'm happy that he's allowed me to be in Memphis." Audience reaction (on the tape recording) indicates they have taken his meaning, and King reinforces the point by frequent subsequent references to this time in history.

The speaker moves now into the most pragmatic portion of

the speech in which he tells his listeners what they must do and how they must do it. He makes four specific points: we must stay together; we must keep a clear focus on the issue of justice for the sanitation workers; we must demonstrate through nonviolent marches; and we must use our economic power to strengthen black institutions. In developing these points, King uses very practical and concrete language much of the time. Virtually everything he says is responsive to an exigence in the present situation. Some of these are relatively small matters, as when he says, "We aren't going to let any mace stop us," or "We don't need any bricks or bottles." The Memphis police had apparently been pretty free with the use of the chemical, mace, and some young blacks had resorted to throwing missles.

Some situational exigencies are more important than others, however, and King spends more time developing his arguments about them. One of these points concerns the involvement of black ministers who had only gradually taken on leadership roles as the sanitation workers strike was transformed from a labor issue to a racial issue. So King spends some time expressing his pleasure "to see all these ministers of the Gospel. It's a marvelous picture," and he mentions several of them by name. He ends with a passage that illustrates nicely one of his favored methods of argument, comparison and contrast. Speaking of the need for relevant ministers, he says:

> It's all right to talk about "long white robes over yonder," in all of its symbolism. But ultimately people want some suits and dresses and shoes to wear down here. It's all right to talk about "streets flowing with milk and honey," but God has commanded us to be concerned about the slums down here, and his children who can't eat three square meals a day. It's all right to talk about the new Jerusalem, but one day, God's preacher must talk about the new New York, the new Atlanta, the new Philadelphia, the new Los Angeles, the new Memphis, Tennessee.

It is also characteristic of his method in this speech to continually return to Memphis, a Memphis now placed in the vanguard of a movement.

Another concrete exigence was a request by the city for a court injunction prohibiting the march planned for the following Monday. King reassures his listeners on that score by an appeal to

American values, and by contrasting American principles with totalitarian states:

> All we say to America is, "Be true to what you said on paper."
> If I lived in China, or even Russia, or any totalitarian country,
> maybe I could understand the denial of certain basic First
> Amendment privileges, because they hadn't committed them-
> selves to that over there. But somewhere I read of the freedom
> of assembly. Somewhere I read of the freedom of speech.
> Somewhere I read that the greatness of America is the right to
> protest for right. And so just as I say, we aren't going to let any
> injunction turn us around. We are going on.

The stress throughout this section of the speech is on means/end relations. King explains in practical terms what must be done, and he assures his listeners that the methods advocated will work. He argues, as I said, sometimes by comparison and contrast, especially when establishing values. But his other striking method of argument is the historical example presented in vivid imagery. King was a master of the kind of rhetorical depiction that Osborn has discussed elsewhere.[5] The best single illustration of that technique is the passage to which Osborn has already called our attention. King described in the most vivid terms how the nonviolent movement in Birmingham "ended up transforming Bull [Connor] into a steer, and we won our struggle in Birmingham." And, again, he comes right back to Memphis: "Now we've got to go on in Memphis just like that."

King ends this section with a clear transition from the practical points to what will be a lengthy development of the main theme. "Now these are some practical things we can do.... I ask you to follow through here."

The remaining 40% of the speech is the more moving part and is certainly the more interesting rhetorically. It opens rather simply with the words, "Now, let me say as I move to my conclusion...." What follows is hardly a mere conclusion. It is the best part of the speech and, I hope to show, its eloquence can be demonstrated on rhetorical grounds, without recourse to the tragedy of the following

---

[5]Michael Osborn, "Rhetorical Depiction," in *Form, Genre, and the Study of Political Discourse,* ed. Herbert W. Simons and Aram Aghazarian (Columbia: University of South Carolina Press, 1986), 79-107.

day. King's rhetorical creativity emerges in two ways: first, in the deliberately designed elaboration of his major theme and, second, in his instinctive response to a special moment at the very end.

I believe Martin Luther King, Jr. had a theme in mind as he prepared for this speech. As noted before, he faced some demands for proof that the Memphis cause offered the chance of victory, and these he had discharged. But I think he felt the need to stiffen the resolve of his followers, to insure their dedication, and to demonstrate his own willingness to sacrifice. He begins to develop this theme in these words: "Now, let me say as I move to my conclusion that we've got to give ourselves to this struggle until the end. Nothing would be more tragic than to stop at this point, in Memphis. We've got to see it through. And when we have our march, you need to be there. If it means leaving work, if it means leaving school, be there. Be concerned about your brother. You may not be on strike. But either we go up together, or we go down together. Let us develop a kind of *dangerous unselfishness.*" (Emphasis added)

Numerous phrases might be plucked from the speech to capture the theme, for like any speaker rich in invention, Martin Luther King, Jr. had in mind a cluster of ideas and a plentitude of ways of expressing them. One of the most striking carries echoes of John Kennedy's famous line, "Ask not what your country can do for you; ask what you can do for your country." King concludes his version of the good Samaritan story with this central moral:

> And so the first question that the Levite asked was, "If I stop to help this man, what will happen to me?" But then the good Samaritan came by. And he reversed the question: "If I do not stop to help this man, what will happen to him?"
>
> That's the question before you tonight. Not, "If I stop to help the sanitation workers, what will happen to my job?" Not, "If I stop to help the sanitation workers, what will happen to all of the hours that I usually spend in my office every day and every week as a pastor?" The question is not, "If I stop to help this man in need, what will happen to me?" "If I do not stop to help the sanitation workers, what will happen to them?" That's the question.

The way King tells the story of the good Samaritan seems labored, even clumsy in spots. But, he was concerned to drive home the parallel with Memphis and to ridicule all the excuses that might be given for hanging back. No matter how awkward the story might seem when read, or even heard on tape at this remove from the event, in the context it must have built beautifully to the conclusion just quoted. The audience response was frequent and enthusiastic.

This whole section of the speech circles around, illustrates, reiterates, and reinforces the theme. I think the central theme is captured best in the phrase "a dangerous unselfishness," and so I chose that as a title. Listening to the tape recording, one hears Martin Luther King, Jr. draw out the words. Not only does he emphasize the phrase, but he also seems to be musing on it, as if those particular words had just come to him, as if he himself is just being struck by their implications. What is wanted is not merely unselfishness, but a "dangerous unselfishness."

That theme is powerful, appropriate, and moving. Moreover, it was necessary to the completion of his case. He has been telling his listeners: if you believe that this is an important moment in history when progress can be made toward freedom, if you believe that Memphis is the scene of the immediate struggle and is part of the world movement, if you believe that we can win through nonviolent protest (as we have elsewhere), then you must be with us when we march. You must be prepared to risk all in "dangerous unselfishness."

It seems reasonable to suppose that the development of ideas just reviewed was consciously planned by King. He knew he had to strike this note, and he knew the story of the good Samaritan would be an appropriate vehicle. What I have been suggesting is that some of the language came to him in the inspiration of the moment, as no doubt it often does to great speakers. But, there is another significant moment of inspiration yet to come. Near the very end of the speech, we can discern a convergence of rhetorical forces that produce a moment of oratorical brilliance. Here is how I think it happens.

King begins to tell the story of the attack on his life and his brush with death, and the passage appears to serve two purposes. First, he wants to reinforce the claim made at the very beginning of the speech about the importance of the time and place in which he and his listeners find themselves. The transition from the good Samaritan passage into this next story refers to "these powerful days, these days of challenge to make America what it ought to be." Secondly, he wants to prove his own commitment, his own courage, in order to inspire his listeners not to be daunted by fear. So, he begins the account of his being stabbed, the blade lodging so close to his aorta that "if I had merely sneezed I would have died." There follows the touching story of the young girl who wrote King a letter to express her happiness that he "didn't sneeze." On that foundation, he builds the beautiful passage marked by the refrain "If I had sneezed...." The passage reinforces his claim about the importance of the time and expresses his joy in the struggle for freedom. Like so many important passages in the speech, this one reaches its climax in Memphis: "If I had sneezed, I wouldn't have been in Memphis to see a community rally around those brothers and sisters who are suffering. I'm so happy that I didn't sneeze."

Immediately, King starts some new thought: "And they were telling me...," apparently referring to the "brothers and sisters" just mentioned. But then his speech is arrested by something from the audience. At first there is applause almost drowning the phrase just quoted—the audience is still savoring the passage that ended "I'm so happy that I didn't sneeze"—but there are also voices, faintly heard (on the tape recording) and impossible to understand. Perhaps someone is calling out, "Don't ever sneeze," or something of like import. No matter, it is clear that King changes his line of thought in response to his audience and here, I believe, something wonderful happens.

The enthusiastic applause is an outpouring of respect, admiration, and love for Martin Luther King, Jr. Perhaps a lesser person, a less astute rhetor, or a person less committed to the full implications of his message might have accepted that response as a sign of rhetorical success. But not King. He was not seeking personal tribute. He was seeking commitment to a cause, and he had been telling them not to be concerned about themselves. How, then, could he accept their cries to be concerned about himself? To do so would be to deny his central message of "dangerous unselfishness." Perhaps, in just that moment, Martin Luther King, Jr. realized the full implications of the phrase for himself. For others, dangerous unselfishness meant a risk of school or job; for him, it meant the risk of life itself.

Despite their affectionate intentions, it seems, the audience had unwittingly corrected King, pulled him up short. He had gone too far in personalizing the triumphs of the nonviolent civil rights movement. And so, he stopped, to offer them correction in turn. And he did so in a way that revealed extraordinary rhetorical insight, and extraordinary moral courage. He made himself face death once again, not this time as a danger passed, one to be made light of—"If I had sneezed"—but as a real, and constant, possibility. This is "the evanescent moment of convergence" Osborn speaks of, "when rhetor—audience—message come together." It is an amazing convergence, considering all that happens in the space of a few seconds: King wins the audience completely; their response tells him they are in danger of missing the point; he shifts abruptly to a topic designed to correct them. Again, consider the shift from narrative of personal triumphs to the denial of personal importance.

The story of his stabbing and the litany of his personal triumphs (e.g. "If I had sneezed, I wouldn't have had a chance… to tell America about a dream that I had had.") are dominated by the first person pronoun. The whole tone of that section is egocentric, and perhaps properly so. Martin Luther King, Jr. had great ethical appeal with his audiences, after all, and he knew how to use it. Yet, at the moment of the warmest audience response, he realized, apparently, that his ethos was about to overwhelm his message. I feel confident in supposing that the audience was telling him, in some way, "not to sneeze." Whatever words were spoken from the audience, they had to be something encouraging King to have a care for his own life. Only something of that kind can explain his reaction at that instant: "…now it doesn't matter now. It really doesn't matter what happens now."

King knew, because the audience forced him to see it, that even as he contemplated the possibility of his own death, he had to deny its importance. He had called them to sacrifice. He had told them that the individual was not important in the great struggle for freedom. And now he proved it by symbolically sacrificing himself:

> Well, I don't know what will happen now. We've got some difficult days ahead. But it doesn't matter with me now. Because I've been to the mountaintop. And I don't mind. Like anybody, I would like to live a long life. Longevity has its place. But I'm not concerned about that now. I just want to do God's will. And He's allowed me to go up to the mountain. And I've looked

> over. And I've seen the promised land. I may not get there with
> you. But, I want you to know tonight, that we, as a people, will
> get to the promised land. And I'm happy tonight. I'm not
> worried about anything. I'm not fearing any man. Mine eyes
> have seen the glory of the coming of the Lord!

This passage, too, is dominated by the first person. But the
pronouns no longer refer just to Martin Luther King, Jr. the man.
Rather, they refer to Martin Luther King, Jr. as a symbol for all
that he wanted his people to become. In his final words, Martin
Luther King, Jr. became for all of them the embodiment of
"dangerous unselfishness."

In telling the story of the good Samaritan, King had reported
that Jesus said "this was the good man, this was the great man,
because he had the capacity to project the 'I' into the 'thou.'" In a
sense, that is what King did in closing his speech. He projected
himself into his audience as a symbol of the sacrifice each "I"
must make to forge a greater "we as a people." To see the
necessity of that discursive move—denying his own significance—
in the very instant that the audience was disposed to adulation,
and to find just the right words to make the move—this was
instinctive rhetorical genius. I say "instinctive" in the sense of
capacities sharpened by long experience to sum up a situation and
instantly respond with the fitting words. Yet, the eloquence of this
speech was not the product of the moment, alone. Martin Luther
King, Jr. was prepared for this response in two important ways: he
was prepared rhetorically by a career of leadership through the
power of speech; he was prepared morally by the deepest
commitment to dangerous unselfishness.

Therein lies the greatness of this speech—in what it shows us
of the power of great moral courage combined with rhetorical
brilliance. I come to that conclusion by means of rhetorical
analysis, so far as possible unburdened by knowledge of the fact
that King died the following day. Those who reflect on the
apparent prophetic quality of this speech might consider these
questions: Why did Martin Luther King, Jr. choose to talk about
his own death? Why in this speech? Why at that precise moment
in the speech? The frequent threats against his life must have
forced him to live with a terrible sense of vulnerability, and the
possibility of assassination must have been a constant, looming
presence in the background of his consciousness. But, that does not

explain why he brought it to the foreground in his Memphis speech. The answer, I believe, is that Martin Luther King, Jr. bravely faced that spectre because it was rhetorically necessary.

As rhetorical critics, we need not, indeed should not, stand in awe of a speech just because it occupies a prominent place on the canvas of history. Rather, we should endeavor to understand it and evaluate it on its own terms, as a real response to a particular situation. On those terms, Martin Luther King, Jr's final speech is a monument to his genius and his courage. In the end, my interpretation corroborates Mike Osborn's evaluation, although I have come at the task from a different angle. Certainly, Martin Luther King, Jr. deserves a place in the pantheon of great orators who succeed in: "...bringing themselves to bear witness to their own commitment, touching listeners directly with the radiance and fire of their messages, opening the eyes of auditors to the meaning of their lives and to the meaning of the events in which they are engaged." Those are fitting words, indeed, to describe the accomplishments of Martin Luther King, Jr. So, I have tried to show that, as we place King's final speech in the literature of American public address, we should regard it, first, from the perspective of rhetoric. Appreciating the speech as an eloquent response to particular rhetorical challenges enhances our appreciation of it as an enduring document in the chronicle of human striving for freedom. We see more clearly why Martin Luther King, Jr. was not just a man for the moment on April 3, 1968 in Memphis, Tennessee. He was, too, a man for the ages.

THE FULFILLMENT OF TIME: KING'S "I HAVE A DREAM" SPEECH (AUGUST 28, 1963)

J. ROBERT COX

All such relationships will work themselves out gradually,
naturally, quietly, in the long course of the years: and
the less they are talked about the better.
　　　　　　　-Ray Standard Baker
　　　　　　　Following the Color Line *(1908)*

Now is the time to make real the promises of democracy.
　　　　　　　-Martin Luther King, Jr. (1963)

Martin Luther King Jr.'s speech "I Have a Dream" has become a moral compass in American political culture. Delivered before approximately 250,000 persons at the Lincoln Memorial on August 28, 1963, the speech won immediate and sustained praise. King's biographer David Garrow has called it "the rhetorical achievement of a lifetime, the clarion call that conveyed the moral power of the movement's cause to the millions who had watched the live national network coverage."[1] Thomas Gentile believes that King's speech forever "legitimized" civil rights in the minds of most Americans.[2]

Yet, surprisingly, rhetorical critics have paid little attention to

---

[1]David J. Garrow, *Bearing the Cross: Martin Luther King, Jr., and the Southern Christian Leadership Conference* (New York: Vintage, 1988), 284.

[2]Thomas Gentile, *March on Washington: August 28, 1963* (Washington, D.C.: New Day Publications, 1983), 249.

the "I Have a Dream" speech.[3] Nor have accounts by contemporary observers and biographers of King lessened the enigma of its success. Senator Hubert Humphrey, who witnessed the speeches of that day, admitted: "All this probably hasn't changed any votes on the civil rights bill, but it's a good thing for Washington and the nation and the world."[4] And David Lewis, speaking of King's "dream," says only, "This was rhetoric almost without content, but this was, after all, a day of heroic fantasy."[5] Such views express a common interpretation of the "I Have a Dream" speech. Lewis, especially, implies that it succeeds as a kind of emotional or "display" oratory. Yet, this clearly was not King's purpose. Its metaphors and stylized rhythms cannot alone account for Schulke and McPhee's judgment that the "I Have a Dream" speech continues to "live today as one of the most moving orations of our time."[6]

I believe, however, we can discover another basis for the "moral power" of this address. Specifically, I believe that King's dream addresses an important source of legitimation in political culture: public time or the sense of "timing" of social change. As Michael Leff suggests, "Time as experienced in the text becomes a vehicle for transforming time as experienced in the world to which

---

[3]To the author's knowledge, no full-length study of this speech has appeared in an SCA journal. Among recent papers at professional meetings are Michael C. Leff, "Metaphoric Action in King's 'I Have a Dream' Speech," and David Zarefsky, "Coming to Terms with the Rhetoric of Martin Luther King," both papers presented at the Speech Communication Association convention, Boston, November 1987. Cf. also John Pattons' brief comments in "Martin Luther King, Jr.," in *American Orators of the Twentieth Century: Critical Studies and Sources,* ed. Bernard K. Duffy and Halford R. Ryan (New York: Greenwood Press, 1987), 268-269.

An encouraging development was the SCA-King Center for Nonviolent Social Change conference "The Power of the Spoken Word: The Oratory of Dr. Martin Luther King, Jr.," held in Atlanta, Georgia, January 9-10, 1988. The conference included a symposium on King's "I Have a Dream" speech, though papers have not yet been published.

[4]Quoted in David L. Lewis, *King: A Critical Biography* (New York: Praeger, 1970), 229-230.

[5]Lewis, 228-229.

[6]Flip Schulke and Penelope McPhee, *King Remembered* (New York: Pocket Books, 1986), 157.

the text refers."[7] For Martin Luther King, Jr., America in August 1963 was a world in which "the tranquilizing drug of gradualism" had become a major obstacle to justice.

In the months before his August 28th address, King had expressed an increasing concern with the view of time that white moderates relied upon as a defense of the racial status quo. He wrote in his "Letter" from the Birmingham city jail in April 1963, "The Negro's great stumbling block in the stride toward freedom is not the White Citizens' 'Councilor'... but the white moderate who... lives by the myth of time and who constantly advises the Negro to wait until a 'more convenient season.' "[8] King believed such "gradualism" was a tragic misconception of time: "It is the strangely irrational notion that there is something in the very flow of time that will inevitably cure all ills."[9] It sanctioned the long-suffering of millions of Americans. "For years now I have heard the word 'Wait!'," King said. "It rings in the ear of every Negro with piercing familiarity. This 'Wait' has always meant 'Never.' "[10]

I want to begin, then, by describing the origins of gradualism in the efforts of Southern moderates to maintain an agenda of control in the 1950s and early '60s. My intention is to locate King's speech in relation to this larger *agon* of social change. The significance of "I Have a Dream" can ultimately be seen in the powerful critique it offers of this political culture: King's address reconstitutes public time as urgent and the struggles of civil rights activists as redemptive.

GRADUALISM AND CIVIL RIGHTS

The nature of opposition to civil rights visibly changed during the turbulent years following the U.S. Supreme Court's ruling in *Brown v. Board of Education* (1954). By the late 1950s, the strategy

---

[7]Michael C. Leff, "Time and Timing in the Argument of Cicero's *Pro Murena*," paper presented at the meeting of the Central States Speech Association, Chicago, April 1984, 1-2.

[8]Martin Luther King, Jr., "Letter from Birmingham City Jail," in Haig A. Bosmajian and Hamida Bosmajian, ed., *The Rhetoric of the Civil Rights Movement* (New York: Random House, 1969), 45-46.

[9]King, 47.

[10]Quoted in Arthur M. Schlesinger, Jr., *A Thousand Days* (New York: Fawcett Crest, 1967 [1965]), 873.

of massive resistance had lost the initiative in Southern politics.[11]
On the eve of the March on Washington, King could acknowledge,
"We are able to see that even in the Deep South hardcore states, the
overwhelming majority of white people say, 'later,' instead of
'never.' "[12] Despite its defeat, however, the legacy of massive
resistance prevented an authentic moderate rhetoric from forming in
Southern politics. Bartley notes massive resistance pulled the
political spectrum far to the right and oriented public discourse
toward the more conservative aspects of the southern tradition.
"Even the more progressively oriented 'moderates' usually felt
compelled to avow their devotion to segregation before timidly
suggesting token alternatives," he observes. "And token efforts to
comply nominally with the letter of the law . . . , while often evading
its spirit, came to be hailed as 'progress.' "[13] For such leaders, the
question of civil rights was no longer phrased, at least publicly, as
"race," but as *kairos* or the proper timing of change.

In appearance, at least, this argument had a respected lineage.
Gradualism had been an assumption of moderate forces in Southern
politics since the early twentieth century. Such a view held generally
that change cannot be achieved by sudden or disruptive practices
but by slow, steady steps. Even organizations such as the
Commission on Interracial Cooperation felt compelled in the 1930s
and '40s to adopt a gradualist approach. R.B. Eleazer, Educational
Director of the Commission, explained, "The philosophy of the
movement is not that of 'seeking to solve the race problem,' but
simply that of taking the next practical step in the direction of
interracial justice and good will."[14]

---

[11]Numan V. Bartley, *The Rise of Massive Resistance: Race and Politics in the South During the 1950's* (Baton Rouge: LSU Press, 1969), 341.

[12]"What the Marchers Really Want," *The New York Times Magazine,* August 25, 1963: 60.

[13]Bartley, 343.

Also, cf. William H. Chafe, *Civilities and Civil Rights* (Oxford and New York: Oxford University Press, 1980, 1981). Chafe defines white "moderates" (as opposed to "liberals") as those "who welcomed an atmosphere of tolerance but did not initiate or endorse change in the racial status quo" (p. 43n).

[14]R.B. Eleazer, quoted in Gunnar Myrdal, *An American Dilemma: The Negro Problem and Modern Democracy* (New York: Harper and Brothers, 1944), 844-5. Cf. also Myrdal, 786-88, 1022.

In post-*Brown* Southern politics, however, the timeliness of social and political change was seized upon as an argument by white self-styled moderates. Racists' belief in the inferiority of blacks (voiced less often publicly) was sublimated in a discourse of gradual evolution. Since this construction was derived from racist assumptions, substantial change would be forever postponed. Gradualism, therefore, became the rationalization of the status quo.

Ironically, moderates discovered an important premise in *Brown* for mystifying time. The Court had followed its initial ruling with an order, in May 1955, to proceed "with all deliberate speed...." The Court, however, left the timetable and means of integration open to interpretation. The decree had ordered that the desegregation of public schools proceed gradually but with "a prompt and reasonable start." "Once such a start has been made, " it conceded, "the [district] courts may find that *additional time* is necessary to carry out the ruling in an effective manner."[15] One Southern lieutenant governor was quick to argue, "A 'reasonable' time can be construed as one year or two hundred.... Thank God we've got good federal judges."[16]

As the Southern strategy unfolded, gradualism — as an argument — assumed an ideological form. Self-styled moderates represented their claims for continued racial segregation as being derived from the natural timing of change. Change had its season, its order in the workings of practical politics. Thus, The Greensboro, North Carolina, *Daily News* could editorialize: "During fifty years, the Negro race has moved rapidly to take its rightful place in the mainstream of the nation. But these extremists on both sides — the Talmadges and the NAACP — should remember the moderate views held by most Southerners. They cannot be pushed too fast...."[17] The message to those who had hoped the Court's ruling in *Brown* would speed a new day was unmistakably clear: blacks must go slowly or wait. They must respect the normal order of social evolution if change was to occur at all. If, on the other hand, civil

---

[15]"Final Decision of Relief," *Brown et al. v. Board of Education of Topeka et al.,* 349 U.S. 294, May 31, 1955, 535, 534. (Emphasis added)

[16]John Frederick Martin, *Civil Rights and the Crisis of Liberalism: The Democratic Party 1945-1976* (Boulder, CO: Westview Press, 1979), 135.

[17]Chafe, 41.

rights activists continued to agitate this issue in the South, "southern moderates would be driven to the wall and hard-core *segs* (segregationists) would prevail."[18]

At the same time, moderates were able to rationalize the expression of blacks' demands by reference to this transcendent construction of the polity. Gradualism simultaneously held forth the promise of progress while restricting change to a form of tokenism. During the 1963 marches in Birmingham, for example, municipal and clergy leaders issued "An Appeal for Law and Order and Common Sense." "We recognize the natural impatience of people who feel that their hopes are slow in being realized," explained Bishop C.C.J. Carpenter and other clergy who signed this appeal. "But we are convinced that these demonstrations are *unwise and untimely.*"[19]

By renouncing the harsh language of massive resistance, Southern moderates had been successful in distancing a rhetoric of promised change from the world of political praxis. In 1960, six years after the Court had called for desegregation with "all deliberate speed," not a single school was integrated in South Carolina, Georgia, Alabama, Mississippi, or Louisiana.[20] The civil rights movement, King lamented, "instead of breaking out into the open plains of progress, remains constricted and confined. A sweeping revolutionary force is pressed into a narrow tunnel."[21]

---

[18]E. Culpepper Clark and Raymie E. McKerrow, "The Historiographical Dilemma in Myrdal's American Creed: Rhetoric's Role in Rescuing a Historical Moment," *Quarterly Journal of Speech* 73 (1987), 306.

To the dismay of blacks and also white liberals, such arguments were finding their way into national political discourse. During the 1956 presidential campaign, Adlai Stevenson had used similar language before a black audience in Los Angeles. A *New York Times* reporter noted that the crowd "murmured" when Stevenson said as president he would not cut off funds from segregated schools nor use force: "It can't be done by troops, or bayonets. We must proceed gradually, not upsetting habits or traditions that are older than the Republic." W.H. Lawrence, "Stevenson Backs 'Gradual' Moves for Integration," *The New York Times,* Feb. 8, 1956, 1. "Later, when Stevenson abandoned 'gradualism,' his staff discarded those texts referring to it, fearing they might be used inadvertently. And today few references to gradualism remain in his papers" (Martin, 282).

[19]"Public Statement by Eight Alabama Clergymen, April 12, 1963," in Bosmajian and Bosmajian, 35.

[20]Samuel Eliot Morison, Henry Steele Commager, William E. Leuchtenburg, *A Concise History of the American Republic,* 2nd ed., v. 2 (New York and Oxford: Oxford University Press, 1983), 696.

[21]Martin Luther King, Jr., quoted in Morison, et al., 726.

Although sit-ins and marches for civil rights would occur in the years immediately preceding the March on Washington in 1963, King anguished over the "slow pace of progress."[22] Time seemd to grow more urgent for him. In his "Letter," four months before the March, he wrote that without the struggle for change, "time itself becomes an ally of the forces of social stagnation."[23] It was this concern that continued to dominate King's thinking and to create tension between King and the Kennedy Administration as the date for the March grew nearer. John Seigenthaler, assistant to Attorney General Robert Kennedy, noted the President and Attorney General "hoped for time. King thought that time was an enemy."[24] King returned to this theme in an interview with Kenneth B. Clark prior to the March. He reiterated his belief that the administration did not fully appreciate the relationship of civil rights to the deeper impatience among black Americans and remarked, "there is a necessity now to see the urgency of the moment. There isn't a lot of time; time is running out, and the Negro is making it palpably clear that he wants all of his rights...now."[25]

As August 28th approached, most of the press commentary linked the purpose of the planned speeches and activities to the passage of Kennedy's civil rights bill. King supported this goal obviously, but other speakers would address the specific features of this legislation. He had been scheduled as the last speaker that afternoon and would use this opportunity to highlight another event. The year 1963 was the centennial of President Lincoln's

---

[22]Martin Luther King, Jr., *Why We Can't Wait* (New York: Harper & Row, 1963, 1964), 6.

[23]King, "Letter," 47.

[24]John Seigenthaler, interview with Martin Strobel, May 18, 1987.

Ironically, Kennedy himself was criticized for moving too "fast" on civil rights. The *Wall Street Journal,* commented on his June 19, 1963, civil rights message to Congress: "We find this tone of haste...deeply disturbing.... The President's only real justification is that the progress is not fast enough. That seems to us a dubious justification for a law of this nature." *Wall Street Journal,* June 20, 1963; quoted in *Civil Rights—the President's Program,* Hearings Before the Committee on the Judiciary, U.S. Senate, 88th Congress, 1st Sess. (Washington, D.C.: Government Printing Office, 1964), 235.

[25]"Kenneth B. Clark Interview," in *A Testament of Hope: The Essential Writings of Martin Luther King, Jr.,* ed. James Melvin Washington (San Francisco: Harper and Row, 1986), 338.

TABLE ONE

Temporal Movement in Martin Luther King, Jr.'s "I Have a Dream"

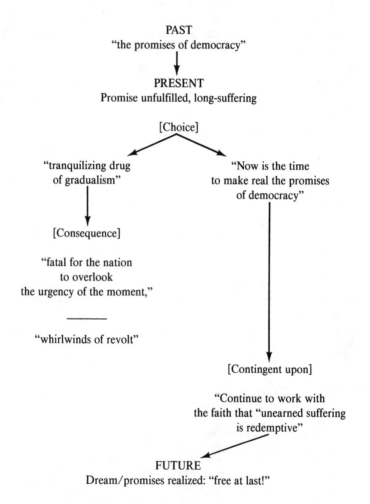

PAST
"the promises of democracy"

PRESENT
Promise unfulfilled, long-suffering

[Choice]

"tranquilizing drug
of gradualism"

"Now is the time
to make real the promises
of democracy"

[Consequence]

"fatal for the nation
to overlook
the urgency of the moment,"

"whirlwinds of revolt"

[Contingent upon]

"Continue to work with
the faith that "unearned suffering
is redemptive"

FUTURE
Dream/promises realized: "free at last!"

signing of the Emancipation Proclamation. King believed this was a critical moment for those blacks who would attend the Washington March: "This was [their] recognition that one hundred years had passed since emancipation, with no profound effect on [their] plight."[26] The milestone of this promise offered King an occasion to address the larger *agon* of change in the culture. If this centennial were to be meaningful, he wrote, it must be observed not as a celebration, "but rather as a commemoration of the one moment in the country's history when a bold, brave *start* had been made, and a rededication to the obvious fact that urgent business was at hand—the resumption of that noble journey toward the goals reflected in the Preamble to the Constitution...."[27] With this in mind, Martin Luther King, Jr. began to work on an address that would attempt to reconstitute public time as urgent and the continued struggle in history as "redemptive."

MARTIN LUTHER KING, JR'S ADDRESS OF AUGUST 28, 1963

The speech that King delivered at 3:40 p.m. on Wednesday afternoon, August 28, 1963, had been more carefully prepared than any he had made before, "more worried over by paragraph, line, and comma...."[28] Yet, its most famous refrain ("I have a dream today") was quite spontaneously added by King as he arrived at his peroration. The speech, internally, had become a rhetorical whole. With this important final section, King's "I Have a Dream" articulated a temporal movement of long-suffering and the redemption of human struggle.

In the first half of the address, King identifies an essential *agon* between the "promises" of democracy and a state of justice delayed. (TABLE ONE.) The urgency of this confrontation, he believed,

---

[26]King, *Why We Can't Wait*, 10.

[27]King, *Why We Can't Wait*, 13.

[28]Lewis, 227. "During the preceding two days and even late into the last night, he had written and rewritten the text.... Ed Clayton, the SCLC public relations agent in the Atlanta office and frequently a polisher of Martin's speeches, spent hours with his employer on Monday [Aug. 26th]. That night, Martin telephoned to read Ed his latest revisions. Revisions continued on the plane to Washington" (Lewis 227). Mrs. King reports he continued his revisions at the Willard Hotel during the night of the 27-28th. Coretta Scott King, *My Life with Martin Luther King, Jr.* (New York: Holt, Rinehart and Winston, 1969). 236.

presents two visions of social change in America, each of which interprets the experience of time differently. In the final third of the speech, King's "dream," resolves this *agon* by articulating one vision—the fulfillment of the dream of freedom and justice.

"The Promises of Democracy"

In his opening words, King introduces the moral and temporal frame of interpretation that guides the remainder of his address: "Five score years ago, a great American, in whose symbolic shadow we stand today, signed the Emancipation Proclamation."[29] King's choice of words also recalls Lincoln's voice at Gettysburg, in 1863. "Four score and seven years ago our fathers brought forth on this continent a new nation," Lincoln had proclaimed. "Now we are engaged in a great civil war, testing whether that nation...can long endure." Lincoln had given meaning to the moment by placing it in a story with a past and a future: "a myth of origin [and] a glimpse of a future placed in jeopardy by a present crisis...."[30]

In a similar effort, King remembers the Emancipation Proclamation as a site of meaning and as origin of his dream of a future time. He continues, "This momentous decree came as a great beacon light of hope to millions of Negro slaves, who had been seared in the flames of withering injustice. It came as a joyous daybreak to end the long night of their captivity." King had often spoken of a "beacon light" and of blacks' long night of "captivity." Such phrases were used interchangeably with their struggles for freedom and were, of course, familiar to his predominantly Christian and Jewish audience as the stories of bondage in Egypt

---

[29] All references to the "I Have a Dream" speech are from an original audio recording of August 28, 1963. Transcriptions have been further verified by reference to Haig Bosmajian, "The Inaccuracies in the Reprintings of Martin Luther King, Jr.,'s 'I Have a Dream' Speech," *Communication Education* 31 (April 1982): 107-114.

[30] David Carr, *Time, Narrative, and History* (Bloomington/Indianapolis: Indiana University Press, 1986), 156.

and Babylon.[31] King had also used these phrases in a May 17, 1957 prayer pilgrimage at the Lincoln Memorial to describe the resistance that had arisen to the court's ruling in *Brown*. That ruling, he said, was a "beacon light" that had come as a "joyous daybreak to end the long night of enforced segregation."[32]

King's use of such metaphors reflected an ability to blend biblical references with the civic tradition of American culture. We know that stories of exile and freedom, in particular, were meaningful for King and also for his audience. In an April 1957 sermon, for example, King had compared the civil rights movement to the Exodus struggle. The effort, he said, of the Israelites to leave Egypt and to reach the promised land "is something of *the story of every people struggling for freedom....* And it demonstrates the *stages* that seem inevitably to follow the quest for freedom."[33] The narrative of bondage (Egypt), struggle (Sinai wilderness), and deliverance (Canaan), and their reference to time past, present, and future offer important cues, therefore, for our own understanding of the temporal movement of the "I Have a Dream" speech.

The story of the "beacon light" of Exodus/Emancipation/*Brown* is, for King and for us, the story of moral promise and also of direction in difficult times. The first sentences of this address, therefore, help to form our anticipation of the section that follows. This is the experience of the present: a time of long-suffering and

---

[31]King's use of the phrase "Long night of captivity" appears first in his speech at the Holt Street Baptist Church, Dec. 5, 1955: "We, the disinherited of this land, we who have been oppressed so long are tired of going through the long night of captivity" (personal transcript).

Compare also King's use of "beacon light" with the account in *Exodus* 13:21, "And the Lord went before [the Israelites]...by night in a pillar of fire, to give them light; to go by day and night."

[32]Martin Luther King, Jr., "Give Us the Ballot—We Will Transform the South," speech at the Lincoln Memorial, Washington, May 17, 1957, in Washington, *Testament of Hope,* 197. The same theme, of course, appears prominently in the "I've been to the mountaintop" speech. See Osborn's essay in this volume.

[33]Martin Luther King, Jr., "The Birth of a New Nation," (Atlanta, April 1957), King Center transcript, p. 1; quoted in Frederick L. Downing, "Martin Luther King, Jr. as Public Theologian," *Theology Today* XLIV (1987): 19. (Emphasis added.)

I am indebted to Frederick L. Downing's insightful commentary on the "geo-existential" stages in the Exodus story and also to Michael Walzer's analysis of the uses of this story in progressive movements in history, in his *Exodus and Revolution* (New York: Basic, 1985).

"whirlwinds of revolt." King turns to this experience: "But one hundred years later, the Negro still is not free." Blacks had hoped to march toward freedom with the aid of the "beacon light" of emancipation. But what they now confronted was quite different: "One hundred years later, the life of the Negro is still sadly crippled by the manacles of segregation and the chains of discrimination.... One hundred years later, the Negro is still languished in the corners of American society and finds himself an exile in his own land." The last line returns to the theme of exile and invites our memory of a time of bondage. In the narrative categories of the Exodus story, "Egypt" is a condition of suffering. (King had referred to America, in his May 1957 speech, as "a bewildering Egypt.")

Temporally, this refrain is encompassed by the preceding section and by the hope of a "time-when." But "one hundred years later" was a time of waiting. Such feelings of long-suffering had lain below the surface of the crowd at the Lincoln Memorial on August 28th. Just before King began to speak, a moment occurred when these feelings erupted into the open. Mahalia Jackson was singing *I've Been 'Buked and I've Been Scorned:* "I'm gonna tell my Lord when I get home, ... Just how long you've been treating me wrong." "And then, suddenly, it happened." one man later reported. "A spasm ran through the crowd. The button-down men in front and the old women way back came to their feet, screaming and shouting. They had not known that this thing was in them and that they wanted it touched."[34]

King's articulation of this experience of time also prepares us for the significance of the March itself and for the demand King now announces: "So we've come here today to dramatize a shameful condition. In a sense we've come to our Nation's Capital to cash a check." The metaphor of a check assumes, of course, that a promise has been made. As though for emphasis, King returns to time-past and restates the nature of America's obligation: "When the architects of our Republic wrote the magnificent words of the Constitution and the Declaration of Independence, they were signing a promissory note to which every American was to fall heir. This note was a promise that all men — yes, black men as well as

---

[34]Lerone Bennett, Jr., "Biggest Protest March — Masses Were March Heroes," *Ebony* (November 1963): 120.

white men—would be guaranteed the unalienable rights of life, liberty, and the pursuit of happiness."

It is important, I believe, to grasp both the temporal and moral nature of this "promise" for King. As an illocutionary act, "promising" implies that one predicates a future act and, further, that one's making of the promise will place that person under an obligation to do this act.[35] It is this temporal quality that gives us the sense of King's metaphor. A check is time-binding; it has a moral claim in subsequent time upon the one who utters the promise.

The past promise thus provides a basis for King's appraisal of the performance of American political culture in mid-twentieth-century: "It is obvious today that America has defaulted on this promissory note insofar as her citizens of color are concerned. Instead of honoring this sacred obligation, America has given the Negro people a bad check, a check which has come back marked 'insufficient funds'." This temporal and moral failure allows us to understand the dissatisfaction of blacks; and it prompts us to consider seriously the "whirlwinds of revolt" that are fueled by this default.

But, King introduces a break in the temporal form that has guided his narration up to this point: "We refuse to believe that the bank of justice is bankrupt. We refuse to believe that there are insufficient funds in the great vaults of opportunity of this nation." King's refusal is an effort to dissociate the promise from the record of temporal failure. This record does not exhaust the "heritage" of moral promise—the temporal horizon of past possibilities not yet manifested in history.[36] King recalls this heritage in his description of Lincoln's act, "the one moment in the country's history when a bold, brave start had been made...." In eloquent terms, King's dream will attempt to recapture this possibility: the resumption of that "noble journey" whose goal had been defined in the Constitution and in Lincoln's Proclamation one hundred years ago. "So we've come to cash this check, a check that will give us upon

[35]John R. Searle, *Speech Acts: An Essay in the Philsophy of Language* (Cambridge: University Press, 1969): 57-61.

[36]J. Robert Cox, *Cultural Memory and Public Moral Argument,* The Van Zelst Lecture in Communication (Evanston, IL: Northwestern School of Speech, 1987), 11. The distinction between tradition and heritage is drawn from Martin Heidegger, *Being and Time,* trans. John Macquarrie and Edward Robinson (New York: Harper & Row, 1962), 388, 437n.

demand the riches of freedom and the security of justice." The
metaphor of a check introduces the moral choice that King believes
is posed by contemporary political culture: whether we shall
continue in the belief of moderates that "all such relationships will
work themselves out gradually, naturally,"[37] or whether we shall
recognize the urgency of this moment.

"The Fierce Urgency of Now"

By framing the present in relation to the promises of democracy,
King is able to bring focus to the timeliness of the choice before
America. "We have also come to this hallowed spot to remind
America of the fierce urgency of now." This sense of urgency is
disclosed by the scandal of promises delayed and by the understandable resentment of those who are told to wait. The lines that follow,
therefore, outline what King believes are the alternatives now facing
America and the consequences of each: "This is no time to engage
in the luxury of cooling off or to take the tranquilizing drug of
gradualism." The moderate doctrine of "gradualism" had been the
dominant assumption of the polity. Now, the time of waiting had
come to an end. The urgency of this moment finds expression in
King's insistence: "Now is the time to make real the promises of
Democracy. Now is the time to rise from the dark and desolate
valley of segregation to the sunlit path of racial justice.[38].... Now is
the time to make justice a reality for all of God's children." (Coretta
Scott King recalled "When he got to the rhythmic part of
demanding freedom now...the crowd caught the timing and shouted
now in a cadence."[39])

King had not been alone that afternoon in his militant plea of
"now." Minutes before King spoke, John Lewis, chair of the Student
Non-Violent Coordinating Committee, had made a similar plea for
the completion of the "unfinished revolution of 1776." In spare,

---

[37]Ray Stannard Baker, *Following the Color Line* (1908), quoted in Myrdal, 1022.

[38]Compare Hubert Humphrey's speech in support of the (liberal) minority plank on
civil rights at the 1948 Democratic Party convention: "My friends, to those who say that
we are rushing this issue of civil rights, I say to them, we are 172 years late.... The time
has arrived for the Democratic Party to get out of the shadow of states' rights and walk
forthrightly into the bright sunshine of human rights" (Martin, 85).

[39]Coretta Scott King, 239.

angry words, the charismatic Lewis warned: "To those who have said be patient and wait, we must say that we cannot be patient, *we do not want to be free gradually.* We want our freedom and we want it *now.*"[40]

King is, therefore, drawn at this moment to spell out the consequences of further rejection of fundamental change. In the following passage, he signifies the need for the nation to act and warns of the danger of quiescence. It was the warning Moses gave to Pharaoh: "It would be fatal for the nation to overlook the urgency of the moment." The time of waiting had ended; now was the time to begin again. "This sweltering summer of the Negro's legitimate discontent will not pass until there is an invigorating autumn of freedom and equality." (In the months ahead, King would describe the depth of this impatience: "How many people understood, during the first two years of the Kennedy administration, that the Negroes' 'Now' was becoming as militant as the segregationists' 'Never'?")[41]

King warns that America's choice cannot be indefinitely postponed. The pretense of gradual change can now be sustained only in the face of growing turmoil: "There will be neither rest nor tranquillity in America until the Negro is granted his citizenship rights. The whirlwinds of revolt will continue to shake the foundations of our nation until the bright day of justice emerges."

This is a critical point within the text; for, if left unanswered, the "whirlwinds of revolt" may produce consequences that are harmful for the movement itself. King must also speak to those who live in the face of the betrayal of the present and whose awakening has fueled the urgency of this moment. "There is something that I must say to my people who stand on the warm threshold which leads into the palace of justice." (This alternating emphasis upon militant arousal and commitment to non-violence had been a conscious rhetorical choice since King first spoke to

[40]Quoted in Nicolaus Mills, "Heard and Unheard Speeches: What Really Happened at the March on Washington? *Dissent,* Summer 1988: 289. (Emphasis added.)

[41]King, *Why,* 8.

supporters of the bus boycott in Montgomery in 1955.[42]) Thus, the warning of the "whirlwinds of revolt" is now set against King's caution: "In the process of gaining our rightful place, we must not be guilty of wrongful deeds.... We must not allow our creative protest to degenerate into physical violence. Again and again we must rise to the majestic heights of meeting physical force with "soul force" [Ghandi's *satyagraha*]." King's words implicitly recognized a tension in the civil rights movement that had threatened to spill into the March itself. He does not address this directly, but moves instead to the teleological ideal of a civic community and the duties incumbent on its members. He urges: "The marvelous new militancy which had engulfed the Negro community must not lead us to a distrust of all white people, for many of our white brothers, as evidenced by their presence here today, have come to realize that their destiny is tied up with our destiny.... We cannot walk alone." Potential differences within the movement become submerged (perhaps unjustly[43]) in King's plea for common action. The focus now begins to shift to another tension; it is a focus on the journey ahead: "And as we walk, we must make the pledge that we shall always march ahead." The nature of this march must be understood as a plane of movement, of going forward in time. "We cannot turn back," King says.

Yet, King turns aside from this forward movement in the lines immediately following. Why? Perhaps he was concerned that there be no uncertainty as to the goals of this "noble journey," after so many efforts had ended in tokenism. Thus, it was appropriate for

---

[42]King discusses this rhetorical choice in his account of the Montgomery bus boycott: "How could I make a speech that would be militant enough to keep my people aroused to positive action and yet moderate enough to keep this fervor within controllable and Christian bounds?... I decided that I had to face the challenge head on, and attempt to combine two apparent irreconcilables. I would seek to arouse the group to action by insisting that their self-respect was at stake and that if they accepted such injustices without protesting, they would betray their own sense of dignity.... But I would balance this with a strong affirmation of the Christian doctrine of love." Martin Luther King, Jr., *Stride Toward Freedom: The Montgomery Story* (New York: Harper & Row, 1958), 434.

[43]At the last minute, March leaders had persuaded John Lewis of SNCC to alter a harsh denunciation of the Kennedy Administration. Lewis' original speech had announced: "In good conscience, we cannot support the Administration's civil rights bill, for it is too little, and too late" (Lewis, 223).

King to acknowledge that "There are those who are asking the devotees of civil rights, 'When will you be satisfied?'" King has returned here to his public audience—"those who are asking"— and to their view of time. The traditional assumptions of gradualism are now set against the expectation of change; time becomes the horizon of hope, the ancient dream of deliverance. In the parallel stanzas that follow, King sets what *is* in tension with this horizon:

> We can never be satisfied as long as the Negro is the victim of the unspeakable horrors of police brutality....
>
> We cannot be satisfied as long as the Negro's basic mobility is from a smaller ghetto to a larger one....
>
> We can never be satisfied as long as a Negro in Mississippi cannot vote and a Negro in New York believes he has nothing for which to vote.

The rejection of the false present implies an Other, the promise of what was "not yet." For theologians as Jurgen Moltmann, the challenge to the *present order of things* is derived from this promise. "The event of the promise, therefore, is the beginning of the criticism of everything that is."[44] It is the persona of prophet that finally condemns the old *agon* of time and change: "No, no we are not satisfied, and we will not be satisfied until justice rolls down like waters and righteousness like a mighty stream." This is, of course, the prophet Amos' report of God's judgment of Israel for its sins.[45] "Therefore will I cause you to go into captivity..." (*Amos* 5:27). Significantly, the prophet Jeremiah also blames the Babylonian exile on the failure of the people to "proclaim liberty" as they had convenanted to do (*Jeremiah* 34:8 ff.).

---

[44]Jurgen Moltmann, *Theology of Hope,* 59-60; quoted in Gustavo Gutierrez, *A Theory of Liberation,* Sr. Caridad Inda and John Eagleson, tr. and eds. (Maryknoll, NY: Orbis Books, 1973), 215-217.

The author wishes to express appreciation to Stephen D. O'Leary for references to the theology of Jurgen Moltmann.

[45]*Amos* 5:24, "But let judgment run down as waters, and righteousness as a mighty stream."

198 TEXTS IN CONTEXT

"Unearned Suffering is Redemptive"

With this final warning, King returns to the march/struggle at the heart of his foregrounding of future time. He now addresses the difficulties of this journey: "I am not unmindful that some of you have come here out of great trials and tribulations. Some of you have come fresh from narrow jail cells." The civil rights campaigns had taken a toll. Intimidation, beatings, arrests, and lynchings had confronted the followers of *satyagraha* in rural counties and towns throughout the South. How, then, could those who had endured too long in the shadow of Lincoln's promise continue to march ahead? How could the image of a march (over time) be reconciled with King's more militant insistence that *"Now* is the time..."?

King had to convey some sense of the possibilities for transformation in continuing a non-violent struggle. He returns, therefore, to the voice of the wilderness prophets: "You have been the veterans of creative suffering. Continue to work with the faith that unearned suffering is redemptive." The fact of the Promise has always implied the hope of redemption; i.e., continued struggle can bring about a people's liberation. The re-telling of the Exodus in black preaching has also drawn upon this hope. Generations in the pews of Southern churches had listened to the words of *Exodus* 6:6. The Lord commanded Moses: "Wherefore say unto the children of Israel,...I will bring you out from under the burdens of the Egyptians, and...*I will redeem you....*"[46] King had incorporated this powerful theological term in his civil rights rhetoric early. Redemption had been the theme of the first convention of King's Southern Christian Leadership Conference, and later became the motto of SCLC: "To Redeem the Soul of America."[47]

---

[46]Michael Walzer recounts the following experience in the early months of 1960: "In Montgomery, Alabama, in a small Baptist church, I listened to the most extraordinary sermon that I have ever heard—on the Book of Exodus and the political struggle of southern blacks. There on his pulpit, the preacher...acted out the 'going out' from Egypt and expounded its contemporary analogues: he cringed under the lash, challenged the pharaoh, hesitated fearfully at the sea, accepted the covenant and the law at the foot of the mountain." Walzer, *Exodus and Revolution,* 3. Cf. also Joseph R. Washington, *Black Religion* (Boston: Beacon Press, 1964), 99-102.

[47]Andrew Fairclough. *To Redeem the Soul of America: The Southern Christian Leadership Conference and Martin Luther King, Jr.* (Athens and London: University of Georgia Press, 1987), 32.

With this declaration, King turns somewhat abruptly to his
planned peroration: "Go back to Mississippi; go back to Alabama;
go back to South Carolina; go back to Georgia; go back to
Louisiana; go back to the slums and ghettos of our northern cities,
knowing that somehow this situation can and will be changed."
The call to "go back" to scenes of struggle was crucial. Yet, the
hoped-for transformation of this struggle had not been fully articulated. King's call ("somehow") is unconvincing. David Zarefsky
has noted, "This was small assurance especially to those who were
concerned with material gains."[48]

"A Dream Deeply Rooted in the American Dream"

It is at this point, however, that King adds, quite spontaneously,
another vision of the future. (It will occupy fully one-third of the
speech.) It is his own proclamation of hope: "I say to you today
my friends, so even though we face the difficulties of today and
tomorrow, I still have a dream." It is King's articulation of this
"dream" for which his address that day is remembered and from
which it derives its name. "I started out reading the speech," King
recalled in a private interview three months later. "Then, just all of
a sudden—the audience response was wonderful that day—and
all of a sudden this thing came to me that I have used—I'd used it
many times before, that thing about 'I have a dream'—and I just
felt that I wanted to use it here. I don't know why, I hadn't
thought about it before the speech."[49] Garrow notes that King had
used the same passage previously—at a mass meeting in Birmingham in early April, and in a speech two months before at Detroit's
huge civil rights rally.[50]

King's "dream" completed the temporal movement begun with
the promises of democracy: "It is a dream deeply rooted in the
American dream. I have a dream that one day this nation will rise
up and live out the true meaning of its creed: 'We hold these
truths to be self-evident; that all men are created equal.'"

The allusion to the Declaration of Independence links the first
part of the speech (as past, heritage) with its promised fulfillment

---

[48]Zarefsky, 10.
[49]Garrow, 283.
[50]Garrow, 283.

in history. Past and future are identified in the image of "sons of former slaves and the sons of former slave-owners" who "will be able to sit down together at the table of brotherhood." The dream is fulfilled in the lives of those who have inherited the legacy of slavery but who chose to struggle as brothers and sisters. King's dream can therefore include even former sites of slavery: "I have a dream that one day even the state of Mississippi, a state sweltering with the heat of injustice, sweltering with the heat of oppression, will be transformed into an oasis of freedom and justice." It is a dream that returns to the hope that had been and recalls it as what can still be: "I have a dream that my four little children will one day live in a nation where they will not be judged by the color of their skin but by the content of their character. I have a dream today."

The dream finds its denouement in the words of comfort Isaiah spoke to those whose exile in Babylon in the sixth century B.C.E. would soon end: "I have a dream that one day every valley shall be exalted; every hill and mountain shall be made low; the rough places will be made plain, and the crooked places will be made straight, and the glory of the Lord shall be revealed...."[51] God's message to Isaiah (familiar also from the libretto of Handel's *Messiah*) comes as the Israelites are permitted to return to Jerusalem. As theologian George A.F. Knight explains, the reference to making "straight" the "crooked places" heralds "both a factual and an eschatological situation...."[52] In the time of Babylonian exile, "servants" would go ahead of the king's party in order to "level the hillocks and build up the ditches and fill in the holes so that the royal chariot might" pass.[53] More importantly, the command "Prepare ye the way" (*Isaiah* 40:3), recalls a similar deliverance in the Exodus. Isaiah's promise of an end to captivity raises an eschatological vision of a time when a people will be redeemed and the promise realized.

---

[51]*Isaiah* 40:4-5, "Every valley shall be exalted, and every mountain and hill shall be made low: and the crooked shall be made straight, and the rough places plain: And the glory of the Lord shall be revealed, and all flesh shall see it together...."

[52]George Knight, A.F. *Deutero-Isaiah: A Theological Commentary on Isaiah 40-55* (New York: Abingdon Press, 1965), 25.

[53]Knight, 24.

Far from Lewis' heroic fantasy, the words of Isaiah were a source of assurance to those gathered at the Lincoln Memorial. It is King/Isaiah's assurance to those in bondage that "the redemption announced by the Voice is bound to become event, and when it does, that event will take place *in history*."[54]

"This is our hope," King proclaims. "This is the faith that I go back to the South with." This is the strength to "always march ahead": "With this faith, we will be able to work together,...to struggle together, to go to jail together, to stand up for freedom together, knowing that we will be free one day." The door of hope is still open; things can and will be changed.

As eschatological vision, time is both what has been promised but is "not yet." Now, in his peroration, King articulates such a time in secular and patriotic images of song ("My country 'tis of thee, sweet land of liberty, of thee I sing") and American history ("land of the pilgrims' pride"). In the quasi-mythical time of this vision, past and future are reconciled; no longer is there any tension between promise and reality, or between struggle and deliverance. King enacts this fulfillment in his injunction, "So let freedom ring from the prodigious hilltops of New Hampshire," and from the mountains of New York and Pennsylvania, the "snow-capped Rockies of Colorado," and the "curvaceous slopes of California!" In its sweeping arc across the continent, King's cry of "let freedom ring!" recalls the natality and western movement of a new nation in history.

The moral-temporal movement begun earlier in King's address is able to reconcile the sites and history of America's racial conflicts—the Civil War (Lookout Mountain, Tennessee) and the birthplace of the Ku-Klux Klan ("let freedom ring from Stone Mountain of Georgia!"). Again, the movement in this panorama is as much moral as geographical. This is the eschatological experience of exile and the promise of deliverance. As Michael Walzer argues, "The Exodus is a journey forward—not only in time and space. It is a march toward a goal, a moral progress, a transformation."[55]

It is as a fulfillment of this goal that King sings a song of arrival in Canaan/America. It is a celebratory time when all will

---

[54]Knight, 27.
[55]Walzer, 12.

be able to sing the words of the old Negro spiritual, "Free at last! Free at last! Thank God almighty, we are free at last!"

THE FULFILLMENT OF TIME

"Free at last!" The words, as King says, are from an old spiritual in which oppressed people will rise in the air to meet the Lord. Much criticism of the "I Have a Dream" speech has focused on the use of such religious imagery and has either been hostile for this reason[56] or has praised such motifs as rhetoric "without content."[57]

Alternately, we can argue that King's dream is a story of liberation from the heart of the Judeo-Christian tradition that has power to imbue contemporary struggle with meaning. This interpretation urges us to take the religious imagery of King's speech seriously. It invites us to consider the "dream" in terms of the redemptive motif of eschatological time and the implications this has for political action.

The dream of "Free at last!" is a fulfillment—within the temporal space of the text—of a heritage that King had articulated in the Lincolnian words of his opening sentence. King incorporates Exodus history and the national and patriotic symbols of American experience into the movement of the text, thus rehearsing his listeners in what Horton terms "the practice of social change."[58] The timing of change in the polity and eschatological time are merged. King's dream becomes an empowering vision of the fulfillment of time.

Gustavo Gutierrez offers an important insight, in his discussion of Moltmann's theology of hope, that sheds light on this interpretation. "The statements of the Promise," he says, "'do not seek to illuminate the reality which exists, but the reality which is coming,' and therefore establish the conditions for the possibility of 'new

---

[56]Cf. the discussion of King's language, generally, in Andrew A. King, "The Rhetorical Legacy of the Black Church," *Central States Speech Journal* 22 (1971): 184.

[57]Lewis, 228.

[58]John Horton, "Class Struggle and the American Dream: A Marxist Analysis of Communication," *Studies in Communications* 2 (1982): 122.

experiences.'"[59] I believe this has two consequences, rhetorically, for the dream: (1) The dream redeems past suffering and the continued struggle of those working toward Canaan by referring to a time when there will be justice in the land. And (2) the dream of future time, therefore, reconfigures the significance of the present as the horizon of action.

First, midway through the speech, King assures those who had been "battered by the storms of persecution" that they had been "the veterans of creative suffering." His effort to redefine the nature of their experience as redemptive, however, cannot fully succeed until he moves from this focus on the present to his foregrounding of future-time. This is fully embodied in the dream. The dream provides textual continuity with King's opening allusion to the "symbolic shadow" of Lincoln: the dream follows from and is a fulfillment of the promises of democracy. As such, it provides a site of meaning and a source of transformation (the dream redeems suffering). It is King's articulation of this dream, therefore, that calls back the experience of suffering and makes it whole. As Lerone Bennett observed, it

> called back all the old men and women who had had this dream and had died dishonored; called back rickety Negro churches on dirt roads and the men and women who sat in them, called them back and found them not wanting, nor their hoping in vain. The rhythms and the intonation called back all the struggle and all the pain and all the agony, and held forth the possibility of triumph;...called them back and said they would soon be over.[60]

By disclosing "the difficulties of today and tomorrow" in a moral arc of history, King could ask those assembled to continue to work with the faith that their actions would ultimately be redemptive.

Second, eschatological time (as the memory of what is "not yet") places what "is" in tension with its alternatives. Such memory problematizes the present. "Thus there is maintained" says Gutierrez, "'a specific *inadequatio rei et intellectus*' regarding 'the existing and given reality,' inaugurating a promising and productive

---

[59]Gutierrez, 217.
[60]Bennett, 122, 124.

'open stage for history.'"[61] The dream enters the present as hope. King reminds us, however, this hope is contingent upon struggle, the need always to "march ahead." Thus, an eschatological perspective, "is not an escape from history...it has clear and strong implications for the political sphere, for social praxis."[62]

The dream of a future time orients our action now, as instrumental to this end. By articulating this experience within a heritage and an eschatological vision, King redefines public time as morally-charged, urgent; continued struggle within history is purposeful. "*Now* is the time to make real the promises of democracy."

King's speech continues to instruct us on the meaning and possibilities of epideictic discourse in civic life. His "dream" still evokes the memory of Exodus — of oppression but also deliverance. "There... in the shadow of Lincoln and the presence of God, they recalled (in Archibald MacLeish's phrase) 'the holy dream we were to be'...."[63] King taught us that collective struggle despite its difficulties is a redemptive praxis. This was a theme King returned to again and again and which he proclaimed, in Memphis, on April 3, 1968: "We, as a people, will get to the promised land."

[61]Gutierrez, 217. Cf. also Elizabeth Schussler Fiorenza, *The Book of Revelation: Justice and Judgment* (Philadelphia: Fortress Press, 1985).

[62]Gutierrez, 215.

[63]Bennett, 92-3.

TIME AND THE RECONSTITUTION OF GRADUALISM IN KING'S ADDRESS: A RESPONSE TO COX

ROBERT HARIMAN

> *The stork in the sky*
> *knows the time to migrate*
> *the dove and the swift and the wryneck*
> *know the season of return;*
> *but my people do not know the ordinances of the Lord.*
> *-Jeremiah* 8:7

> For years I labored with the idea of reforming the existing institutions of the society, a little change here, a little change there. Now I feel quite differently.
> -Martin Luther King, Jr. (1966)

Rhetoric has long been defined as essentially temporal. Rhetorical purposes and appeals must be timely, rhetorical power depends upon some phenomenon of the moment such as the crowd or the crisis, and rhetoric has been distinguished from the other arts because it is ephemeral while they are enduring. When time figures within oratory it often represents the most profound concerns of rhetorical practice: the moral order of the political community and the means for preserving and changing that community. When a critic examines the uses of time in a public address, we have an opportunity to grapple with significant questions about the nature of rhetoric and the practice of rhetorical criticism.

Robert Cox's fine study of King's address of August 28, 1963 begins with the insight that the legitimation of the American system of racial discrimination came to depend largely upon the belief that there is a natural time for social change. This belief was based upon a sense of time as a gradual movement independent of human intervention. King's use of the temporal progression of Biblical narrative then seems a masterful strategy for challenging this temporal figure: if the immoral social order has its natural time, then sacred time must express another higher moral order; if this better order is not possible within natural time, then the advent of sacred time creates the conditions of possibility; if natural time defeats human actions, then actions are the sign of this sacred time; if natural time is a matter of belief, then sacred time becomes an article of faith.

Or so we would like to believe. As much as I, too, feel the profound power of King's vision of America free at last, I want to challenge Cox's critical affirmation of that vision. Cox argues that King succeeded in the task of establishing the conditions for legitimizing urgent action on behalf of civil rights. I shall argue that Cox's conclusion depends upon his overlooking the conflict within the civil rights movement between those who were advocates of radical change and those who were advocates of modern reform. King's rhetoric does aim to legitimize change, but that change only appears to require urgent action if it is set against the ideology of white resistance. When we recognize that King also was struggling against more radical speakers for continued control of his movement, we see how his speech reasserts a moderate voice and some of the assumptions of gradualism. My comments will challenge Cox's definition of the situation of the speech, his analysis of its structure, and his evaluation of its vision.

THE RHETORICAL SITUATION

Why did Martin Luther King, Jr. believe that time was running out? Cox suggests that King's arguments with the Kennedy administration played some part in this conclusion, but they were not likely to have been compelling by the time of the March. The ground rules for the March had been settled on June 25: "No disruptive modes of protest would be acceptable.... No civil disobedience could occur, and the Kennedy administration had to be consulted at every stage."[1] The basic agreement was that,

---

[1]Manning Marable, *Black American Politics: From the Washington Marches to Jesse Jackson* (London: Verso, 1985), 91.

contrary to the intentions of SNCC and others, the March would not be a massive demonstration to apply pressure directly to the national legislature, and in return the administration would encourage support of the March by white liberals. The March became a promotion for the Kennedy civil rights bill, and the administration maintained tight control over the proceedings, right down to the two aides standing ready to "pull the plug" on the public address system.[2]

Nor does King's urgency make sense in respect to the momentum of the civil rights movement itself. In recent years it had achieved a striking series of victories, developed a powerful arsenal of political techniques, and incorporated thousands into the movement. Just prior to the March, they had broken the resistance at Birmingham, the citadel of segregation. That campaign had included huge, integrated rallies in Northern cities and the support of Robert Kennedy's Justice Department. As the March was organized, President Kennedy was lobbying for the toughest civil rights legislation in history. Any sense of desperation, then, seems to arise from a retrospective on the rioting of subsequent years rather than from the events of the early 1960's.

I submit that King's sense of urgency came primarily from the struggle for leadership that was occurring within the civil rights movement. King's "Letter from Birmingham City Jail" shows us that he not only recognized this conflict within the movement but also was already defining himself in terms of it: "I stand in the middle of two opposing forces in the Negro community. One is a force of complacency.... The other force is one of bitterness and

---

[2]David J. Garrow, *Bearing the Cross: Martin Luther King, Jr., and the Southern Christian Leadership Conference* (New York: Vintage, 1988), 283.

hatred, and comes perilously close to advocating violence."[3] King's
SCLC had begun as a challenge to the NAACP from the left, and
SNCC in turn had developed as a similar challenge to King's organization.[4] The successes of the sit-ins "broke decisively the NAACP's
hegemony in the civil rights arena and inaugurated a period of
unprecedented rivalry among the racial advancement groups."[5]
Thus, for more than a decade, the movement experienced simul-
taneous increases in external influence and internal tensions. The gap
between SCLS and SNCC was already pronounced by Birmingham,[6]
and the Muslims, especially Malcolm X, were beginning to influence
left-leaning organizers.[7] The pressure from the right also intensified
during the preparations for the March, culminating in Wilkins'
victory at the June 25th meeting, when "the entire civil rights
movement took a decisive shift to the right."[8] As the day of the
March approached, "the movement was threatening to split apart in

---

[3]James Melvin Washington, ed. *A Testament of Hope: The Essential Writings of
Martin Luther King, Jr.* (San Francisco: Harper & Row, 1986), 296. We should note the
similarity in stance between this letter and the address of August 28th. The letter directly
confronts the "myth of time" used by the white ministers of Birmingham when they
counseled that the march would be "unwise and untimely," yet it also inveighs against
Black militancy and defines King as the voice of moderation. Note also how a subsequent
text illustrates King's tendency to align himself with figures of time when aligning himself
against the militant leaders within the movement. King's book *Why We Can't Wait*
presents his plea for non-violent resistence—in opposition to the challenge of Black
militancy—through the "titular" figure of urgency; the temporal definition is used to
displace a similar sense of public time, the time of revolution, in order to inculcate a
more restrained sense of political responsibility.

[4]Marable, *Politics*, 88.

[5]August Meier and Elliott Rudwick, *CORE: A Study in the Civil Rights Movement,
1962-1968* (New York: Oxford University Press, 1973), 101.

[6]Garrow, p. 254; Manning Marable, *Race, Reform and Rebellion: The Second
Reconstruction in Black America, 1945-1982* (Jackson: University of Mississippi Press,
1984), 75.

[7]"Malcolm's base of supporters cut deeply into the Civil Rights Movement"
(Marable, *Race*, 100). Garrow describes King as being uncharacteristically angry with the
Muslims (275); they are the only radical organization mentioned by name in the Letter
from Birmingham (*Testament*, 296).

[8]Marable, *Politics*, 91.

public just as it reached its highest level of potential influence."[9]

If the movement had split apart, the center would have had the most to lose. Nor was King's increasing concern about the left unfounded, for the radicals presented the greater challenge to his vision of the movement: they challenged his most dearly felt commitments to integration through non-violent resistance, and they lent credence to the major allegation against his method—that it would degenerate into violence; the radicals were less familiar and less tractable than the leaders of the NAACP, in part because their political attitudes reflected differences in age, background, and experience; they were vital to the recent successes of the movement; and history seemed to be on their side, for coercion was proving more effective than persuasive appeals addressed to southern whites. King became "preoccupied with the rapidly accelerating pace of black activism."[10]

This preoccupation was matched by increasing signs of militant discontent about the direction the movement was taking that summer. In June, Muslims threw eggs at King during a speech in Harlem;[11] in July, SNCC leaders complained when they received only $15,000 of $565,000 distributed for the March;[12] in August, controversy developed over the speech John Lewis had distributed in advance of the March. Lewis's original text denounced the Kennedy bill and declared that the "revolution is at hand."[13] Robert Kennedy thought that Lewis could deliver a better speech, and friction continued until the final hour, when King and other leaders of the March persuaded Lewis to present a different speech. The Lewis compromise seemed final confirmation of the objections militant organizers had been voicing all summer: "Many movement radicals who attended the gathering agreed with Malcolm X that the event was nothing but a 'farce on Washington.'"[14]

---

[9]Garrow, 270.
[10]Garrow, 273.
[11]Marable, *Race,* 83.
[12]Garrow, 278.
[13]Garrow, 281-82.
[14]Marable, *Race,* 81.

THE SPEECH

When King was drafting his address of August 28, he faced not one but two conflicts; when he rose to speak it was both to persuade whites that they should not countenance gradualism and to persuade blacks that they should not pursue radical change. As we consider how King crafted a strategy to meet these divergent purposes, we can understand why critics might come to contrary interpretations of the speech. As I shall suggest later, the key difference in interpretation between Cox and myself stems not from our critical assumptions or methods, but from King's participation, and our participation, in the larger contradictions of American liberal democracy.

My basic point is that, although King is indeed "time-binding" his audiences, each of the figures he uses to do so also can be used to resist the temporal consciousness of ordinary political action and so displace a sense of urgency with a more "formal" satisfaction. Consider the metaphor of cashing a check. King uses this figure to explain the basic purpose of the March — "In a sense we've come to our Nation's Capital to cash a check" — and he used it to communicate both the condition of promises being deferred past their time and the moral necesssity — the "sacred obligation" — to honor those promises. Cox tells us that "in his use of the check metaphor, King introduces a fundamental moral choice" between gradualism and the "the 'urgency' of this moment." But is a check always a figure of urgency? You write it out methodically; it takes three or four days to be processed, then it's mailed back to you in a month or two so that you can file it away in a drawer for seven years. Moreover, checks are issued by banks, a premier symbol of the institutional order. When King affirms that "we refuse to believe that the bank of justice is bankrupt," he is affirming more than our commitment to justice. A check can be a sacred obligation only if capitalism is a religion. Thus, the metaphor of the check communicates one of the basic assumptions of the moderate voice, which is that the institutional order is essentially sound, legitimate, in need only of reform.[15] The metaphor also suggests a sense of time that is closer to the gradualism King is opposing than to any sense of

---

[15]For a reading of this metaphor midway between Cox and myself, see David Zarefsky, "Coming to Terms with the Rhetoric of Martin Luther King," Speech Communication Association annual convention, Boston, Massachusetts, November 1987, 4-5.

urgency. Banks themselves are outfitted in the trappings of temporal regularity—they display clocks, keep "banker's hours," etc.—this sense of time is thoroughly secular, even quotidian, and always regular, routine, gradual.

This assertion of the moderate voice in the first sustained analogy of the speech is matched by the two sustained figures in its conclusion. "I have a dream" is indeed a powerful evocation of an ideal state and wholly consistent with the narrative structure Cox identifies. Perhaps it can pull us forward in time, or help us pull the future into the present, but it also, in its most simple sense, takes us out of time. A dream is by definition not part of real time. Dreams have no secure, measurable sense of duration; dreams regularly scramble time and still make sense. Moreover, King's dream evokes the American Dream, that mythic celebration of prosperity for all achieved by individual initiative and effort. Again, we are pulled out of time and into those myths used to legitimate the status quo.[16] The concluding coda of "let freedom ring" follows a similar movement. The church and town hall bells evoked in the image do toll the time, but here they are marking a special occasion, a ceremonial sounding, which in turn echoes with colonial celebrations and liberty bells. The speech concludes its Biblical narrative of the last days by evoking our myth of origin. The mode is indeed temporal, but the temporality remains ambivalent, capable of motivating action toward the ideal state but perhaps also capable of occluding the present behind a miasma of myth.

Even King's most explicit calls to action in time carry this ambivalence. My argument here relies upon the following observation: many of King's figures of time also are followed by a figure of space that may serve as a reduction of the first figure. The opening reference to history is matched by the reference to the demonstration massed in the public space before King; the "five score years ago" is matched by the allusion to Lincoln's shadow and thus to the place where the speech is being delivered (that is, at the base of the Lincoln Memorial.) The same pattern of balancing the temporal against the spatial continues through the speech: "one hundred years later" the negro lives on "a lonely island of poverty" and in the "corners of American society"; "now is the time" to leave a "valley

---

[16]See also Zarefsky, 6-7.

of segregation"; "I have a dream that one day on the red hills of
Georgia" we can sit at "the table of brotherhood"; and, most
powerfully, the final call to "let freedom ring" is followed by a
calling out of the names of American promontories. This last figure
illustrates the possibilities in them all, for it combines the narrative
of God's time arriving with the archetypal figure of physical
ascension while creating a mythic panorama of the American
landscape. As he calls out the names of the mountains, the
American *mythos* is evoked in all its power: a special place for a
special people, set outside of history, reaching toward heaven by
virtue of its timeless harmony with nature.[17]

Since this transformation of time into space is ambivalent, it
cannot stand *prima facie* for or against any evaluation of the speech.
The question is, do these combined figures of time and space present
complementary figures of public time and public space, or a
reduction of public time to mythic space? They can work either
way. "Let freedom ring from the mighty mountains of New York"
can mean that New York is the place and now is the time to achieve
racial justice, and that if justice is to be in the public space then
urgency must be present in public time. But it can also mean that a
disturbing sense of public time is being reduced to a reassuring sense
of public space. Time not only functions in the text as a "scenic"
container of action, "expressing in fixed properties the same quality

---

[17]For fine studies of the role of this theme in American historiography and in
American literature, see David Noble, *Historians Against History: The Frontier Thesis
and the National Covenant in American Historical Writing since 1830* (Minneapolis:
University of Minnesota Press, 1965); *The Eternal Adam in the New World Garden: The
Central Myth in the American Novel Since 1830* (New York: Grosset & Dunlap, 1966);
*The End of American History: Democracy, Capitalism, and the Metaphor of Two Worlds
in Anglo-American Historical Writing 1880-1980* (Minneapolis: University of Minnesota
Press, 1985). Noble documents "the assumption that the United States, unlike the
European nations, has a covenant that makes Americans a chosen people who have
escaped from the terror of historical change to live in timeless harmony with nature"
(*New American Adam,* ix). In King's speech, the American theocratic myth of an ideal
polity outside of history sounds through the Negro spiritual's eschatological vision of
being "Free at Last." See also Sacvan Bercovitch, *The American Jeremiad* (Madison:
University of Wisconsin Press, 1978). King is indeed a preacher, but perhaps more in the
sense of those Puritans who imposed "original Heaven's time" upon the imperfect,
worldly time of their people in order to legitimate theocratic government.

that the action expresses in terms of development,"[18] but it also can be converted into a scene that could construe motivation differently. As Mircea Eliade has taught us, the essential operation for creating and maintaining the mythic consciousness is to convert time to space, and this is done to escape the anxiety of living in history.[19] If, as Cox and I agree, political consciousness is constituted in temporality, then the reduction of temporal to spatial consciousness should have political consequences. It seems to me that although King's peroration can activate a mutually reinforcing sense of public space and time, its panoramic structure and coordination with the mythic escape from history into nature make it more capable of displacing the consciouness necessary for *praxis* with a consciousness that is formally satisfying but morally limiting. Cox's argument hinges upon the idea that the audience will transfer the consciouness created (through temporal definition) within the text of the speech into the world outside the text. As Kenneth Burke has also suggested, we need to beware of the alternative inducement to substitute the satisfactions of the text for the labor of working in the world it supposedly describes.[20]

The ambivalence in King's speech can be registered further by looking to that moment in the speech when King explicitly addresses the black audience. The first 29 paragraphs of the speech are addressed to the national (and so largely white) audience.[21] Then King allows that "there is something that I must say to my people"; that something is expressed as caution regarding the "marvelous new militancy that has engulfed the Negro community." Cox sees this section as the temporal pivot of the speech, the point

[18]Kenneth Burke, *A Grammar of Motives* (Berkeley: University of California Press, 1969), 3.

[19]Mircea Eliade, *The Myth of the Eternal Return,* trans. Willard R. Trask (1954; Princeton: Princeton University Press, 1971).

[20]Kenneth Burke, "Literature as Equipment for Living," in *The Philosophy of Literary Form,* 3rd ed. (Berkeley: University of California Press, 1973). Burke illustrates this warning by discussing self-help books: *"The reading of a book on the attaining of success is in itself the symbolic attaining of that success.* It is *while they read* that these readers are 'succeeding'" (299, his italics).

[21]My division of the speech by its implied audiences is as follows: paragraphs 1-29, the national audience; 30-40, black audience, especially those on or influenced by the left; 41-47, national audience; 48-55, black audience, especially those activists who have practiced King's program of civil disobedience; 55-84, all audiences.

when the Biblical narrative shifts from past-present to present-future. He gives only minor recognition to the fact that King is addressing a special audience, and there responding to serious pressure from within the movement, and Cox reads the narrative figure of walking (paragraphs 38-40) and the use of "destiny" as indicative of how King is overcoming gradualism with "the ancient dream of deliverance" out of the wilderness, which in turn carries Isaiah's assurance to those in bondage that redemption will come in historical time. I think it is more plausible, however, to see King modulating time at this point in the speech to suppress and control the political conflict within the movement. The response to the challenge from the left is specific and comprehensive: the "cup of bitterness" had been used in the Birmingham letter to describe Elijiah Mohammed; the twin issues of non-violence and integration are defended explicitly; and the decorum of the institutional order is upheld as "dignity and discipline." The implicit narrative is used to displace this militancy, just as the term "destiny" supplants the historical materialism articulated more and more frequently by many of the radicals. Moreover, the Biblical structure has an emphasis Cox ignores: King's designation of his black audience as "my people" evokes the form of patriarchal authority well known to those SNCC organizers who referred to him as "de Lawd."[22] Just as the segregationist claimed to recognize the natural time of social change, so does the prophet claim to have special knowledge of God's appointed time. Moreover, notice how the strong temporal figures of the preceding section — which announced that "now is the time" for the "fierce urgency of now" — have receded while more explicitly spatial figures have appeared. We are to avoid the cup of bitterness, take to the high plane and the majestic heights, and walk (down a road). (Notice also how Cox actually had to reverse the transformation, deriving the temporal figure of narrative from King's spatial figure of walking.) As King turns from a more conservative to a more radical audience his speech shifts from temporal to spatial figures while his tone becomes more conservative. A transformation has occurred, and with it a reduction of possibilities for action. Gradualism has been reconstituted.

---

[22]Marable, *Race,* 75.

Evaluation

When King finished his speech of August 28, 1963, he stood at the heights of American oratory. There is little question that this speech is a masterpiece. This judgment should not terminate the process of evaluation, however, for as critics we are committed to taking questions of value so seriously as to see them as the means for establishing and reviewing our basic relationships in the political world. Criticism is at times politics pursued by other means, and the evaluative stage in any criticism can be a time for reviewing the political relationships shaped by the speech. The differences between Cox and myself become most clear at this point, and the choice turns out to be more difficult than one might expect of an academic argument.

The evaluation of King's ambivalence about historical change has to include an account of the effects of his speech and a political commitment in respect to those effects. This is where the difficult choice emerges. For just as the speech has two audiences and two attitudes toward history, so did it have dual effects. I think Cox and I disagree because he sees more of the "good" effects, and I see more of the "bad," but the choice is not so easily simplified. On the one hand, Cox sees a story of the genius of our political system. King's inspired union of the Bible and the Constitution, the two foundational texts of our political culture, overcame a corrupt rhetoric of law and order. A good man speaking well inspired genuine reform toward a more just civil order without recourse to violence. (What rhetorical critic could fault that?) And the reforms did come, including the strongest desegregation legislation in American history, the collapse of massive resistance in the South, the tough 1965 voting rights act which transformed Southern politics, and significant gains in black economic and social conditions.[23] The moderate leadership could claim legitimately that their deal with the Kennedy administration had been a good one. In exchange for giving up the self-indulgence of youth and suppressing an unrealistic yen for revolutionary rhetoric, they had gained quickly those goods the political system could deliver.

But there is another side to it. "Militants were bitterly

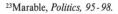

[23]Marable, *Politics, 95-98.*

disappointed that King had chosen not to include extensive critical remarks on the recent racist violence in the South, and the failure of most white liberals to respond concretely or adequately to the Negro's economic plight."[24] King's ascension to international celebrity was accompanied by increasing conformity with the administration line. His "betrayal" of the organizers at Selma, his speeches on behalf of law and order and against criticism of the Vietnam war, were in each case evocations of gradualism and all suggested the hidden costs of the moderate stance. As "the strain between the moderates and the militants that existed during the March mobilization rapidly became an ideological chasm,"[25] the civil rights movement itself went into a convulsion that ended only in its complete collapse several years later. As the moderate rhetoric came to dominate the movement, the left became ever more extreme, just as the moderates found they were indeed compromised. This story is the story of the tragedy of our political system. The norms of consensus and compromise, and the fact that the system really does honor its compromises, promote the self-destruction of those movements that are essential for the polity's achievement of justice and community. As virtuous leaders are driven to extremism rather than critique and to rebellion rather than reform, we lose honest, intelligent accounts of the banality of evil, as well as authentic affirmations of the good life. In order to live without conflict we diminish our capacity for action. In repulsing one form of evil we deny ourselves the opportunity for another form of the good.

The question then is, to what extent should King, because of his speech at the Lincoln Memorial, bear some of the responsibility for the self-destruction of the civil rights movement? My analysis suggests that although he may have established that the time had come for legislative action against Southern resistance, his speech also suggested that civil disobedience and the radical demand for social transformation had become untimely, out of synch with the American Dream. King legitimated one kind of action by driving competing speakers into marginality, and they were speakers we needed to hear.

Furthermore, King may have done us an additional disservice.

---

[24]Marable, *Race,* 82.
[25]Marable, *Politics,* 97.

To complete our judgment of his speech, we need to ask how Americans should constitute their sense of public time. The status quo continues to be maintained by a sense of secular time, the time of gradualism, and so can be challenged by either an affirmation of sacred time or a redefinition of secular time. Examples here include the use of Biblical narrative by the radical right and the development of radical history on the left. The story I have recounted suggests that one opportunity for testing and tempering the American character lies in those moments when it can confront its myth of the New American Adam transcending history. The opportunity is lost when the myth is re-invoked. If King's speech re-invoked this myth, those gains from doing so have to be set against the price, perhaps yet to be paid in full, for once again failing to accept that American racial conflict has not just a present, but a past, and that solutions to our problems lie not in divining the future, or even in calling it to us, but in challenging the continuities of injustice in our time.

NIXON'S "FUND": TIME AS IDEOLOGICAL RESOURCE IN THE "CHECKERS" SPEECH

CELESTE MICHELLE CONDIT

The concept of "free speech" is absolutely central to representative and democratic government, and has been so recognized both in Anglo-American history and rhetorical theory.[1] The ability of freedom of expression to generate rational, consensual decisions through argumentation in a "marketplace of ideas" is, however, seriously challenged by the merging of capitalist economic forms with mass communication. When the major forms of effective communication cost thousands of dollars per second, public argument is no longer "free" speech—in at least one very important sense. The ability of large sums of money to buy disproportionate representation in the "marketplace of ideas" threatens to twist the public space ever more fully into an arena of mere persuasion devoid of legitimate argumentation.[2] Such configurations of economics and politics may gravely affect the character of public decision-making and ultimately may threaten the legitimacy of democratic government.

Republican Vice-Presidential candidate Richard Nixon's televised address of September 23, 1952, with its multiple, ideologically loaded labels—"Checkers," "My Side of the Story," or "The Fund"—provides a concrete, historically situated understanding of the modern problem of free speech in contemporary America. This mass-mediated apologia, costing $75,000, was given

---

[1]"Free speech" is, of course, protected by the United States' Constitution; in Britain it was argued for perhaps most thoroughly in the political context by Milton in the *Areopagetica,* and in America in the alien and sedition debates.

[2]Throughout this essay, I borrow the concepts of Jürgen Habermas with regard to the system problems of late capitalism. I am indebted to Claudia Salazar for this focus. It was her class paper, arguing that the "Checkers" speech was an example of the legitimization problems cited by Habermas, that originally influenced me to pursue this topic in this way. She has also assisted in reading this essay and in developing the theoretical statements. However, in general I prefer the Anglo-American inflections and assumptions describing the character and role of free speech. See: Jürgen Habermas, *Legitimation Crisis,* (Boston: Beacon Press, 1975).

to defend a fund of $18,000 dedicated to mass political communication. It occurred at a critical historical juncture and therefore created a complex web of rhetorical relationships, including ideology, time, and governance. To explore these relationships I will first describe the historical period and the ideological problems posed by campaign financing. I will then offer an interpretation of how Nixon's apology strategetically deploys to resolve both immediate and more far ranging problems connected with campaign funding in the age of mass media.

A TIME FOR TELEVISION

1952 was a pivotal election year in the history of "free speech" in the United States of America. It was the year in which television emerged as the central form of communication in electoral campaigns.[3] Until 1952, the cost per vote in presidential elections had remained about the same throughout the nation's history.[4] After 1952 and the introduction of television, costs escalated rapidly, largely because television advertising is expensive. In 1952, the Presidential candidates spent $11 million; in 1960 they spent $25 million (up 46% from 1956), and in 1968, they spent $60 million on television time alone.[5] Not only television, but the airplane as well, made campaigning into a significantly different activity. Together, these two technologies of mass communication

---

[3]George Thayer, *Who Shakes The Money Tree? American Campaign Financing Practices From 1789 to the Present* (New York: Simon and Schuster, 1973), 76, 22. Jasper B. Shannon, *Money and Politics* (New York: Random House, 1959), 61. Alexander Heard, *The Costs of Democracy* (Chapel Hill: The University of North Carolina Press, 1960), 403.

[4]Alexander Heard 376, 380, estimates that the cost was about 18- 20 cents per vote. (This assumes adjustment for changes in the value of the dollar or cost of living; there were some exceptionally high expenditure years by some candidates that break this trend to some degree — e.g. Willkie apparently spent as much as fifteen million dollars in 1940, Thayer, p. 73). For campaign financing history, see Thayer.

[5]Thayer, 107; for 1952 figures, Heard reports national committee expenditures, 376-377, 380. By 1968 the cost per vote was 60 cents; Alexander Heard, *Financing the 1968 Election* (Princeton, NJ: Citizen's Research Foundation, 1971). Estimating the relative costs of campaigns is not a straight-forward matter because it is influenced by inflation rates, by the difficulty of getting accurate figures on fund dispersal, by rising numbers of voters, and by declining percentages of voting by eligible voters. Noticeably, the television age has featured a decline in voting percentages.

made possible the intense, national, ideological crusade.

Richard Nixon was not the only party caught in the cross-currents of this political vortex, but it was Nixon who was forced to give a speech specifically embedded within this new political environment. And it was therefore Nixon's articulation of ideological choices that had serious consequences, not only for himself, but for our shared political history.

Nixon had emerged as a spokesperson for the Republican version of the "American way" (i.e. Free Enterprise) through his vigorous prosecution of the Alger Hiss case, his vehement anti-communist campaigns against California Democrats, and his boisterous support of Republican candidates throughout the country. He engaged not only in the traditional ebb and flow of California elections, but also in the larger, national dialogue linking party, policy, and ideology. This sort of activity, made possible by the dissemination of one's speech to large audiences, is expensive. Few would doubt that Nixon had a right to this activity—his Free Speech—but Nixon could not personally afford freedom to speak on this scale. He became, therefore, a hireling—a paid voice for others, who wished to convey a "free enterprise" message but who found it more convenient or effective to open their wallets instead of their mouths.

A group of California businessmen established a fund to support Nixon's ideological/political activities. With businesslike efficiency, they carefully kept track of the income and outflow of the fund, which was disbursed solely for political communication, not for salary for the Nixon family or others. If one accepted the moral correctness of the existence of such a fund (as eventually almost everyone seemed to do), it clearly met Eisenhower's criterion—it was clean as "a hound's tooth."[6]

Nixon, however, was involved in a dirty and hotly contested presidential campaign. He, as much as anyone, had contributed to the muddy environment,[7] and one of his central claims had been that the Democrats were corrupt and Eisenhower was clean. When

---

[6]Eisenhower's "off the record" criterion for finding Nixon innocent. See: Garry Wills, *Nixon Agonistes: The Crisis of the Self-Made Man* (Boston, Houghton Mifflin, 1970), 99.

[7]Stephen E. Ambrose, *Nixon: The Education of a Politician 1913-1962,* (New York: Simon and Shuster, 1987), 271-274.

the fund was discovered, therefore, it created a journalistic sensation, and the issue was prolonged by the inaction of the Eisenhower entourage, who had long found Nixon's tactics and allegiances somewhat distasteful.[8] Having gradually been moved to a resign-or-act position, Nixon decided to give a nationally televised address to vindicate himself—a decision that responded to the urgings of Dewey and Eisenhower and that accorded with his own combative style.[9]

The ensuing speech is troublesome for scholars of rhetoric and public address. Nixon's talk appears to be an example of the schools of rhetoric Aristotle had in mind in condemning those who paid too little attention to logos and the enthymeme in favor of other aspects of persuasion.[10] The address presents us with a persuasive discourse which, although devoid of stylistic elegance or grace and seriously defective in argumentation, nonetheless succeeded through the use of ethos and pathos. It served its immediate purpose—to generate enough favorable telegrams to keep Nixon on the ticket.[11] Consequently, although we would not

---

[8]See, e.g., Wills, 97 or Henry D. Spalding, *The Nixon Nobody Knows* (Middle Village, N.Y.: Jonathan David Publishers, 1972), 316.

[9]There seems to be a general consensus about Nixon's combativeness; see Wills and Ambrose, also Celeste Michelle Condit, "Richard Milhous Nixon," in *American Orators of the Twentieth Century: Critical Studies and Sources,* ed. Bernard K. Duffy and Halford R. Ryan (New York: Greewood Press, 1987), 323-330; Carol Jablonski, "Richard Nixon's Irish Wake: A Case of Generic Transference," *Central States Speech Journal* 30 (Summer 1979): 164; Russel Windes, "The Republican Convention," *Quarterly Journal of Speech* 46 (October 1960): 249-252; L.W. Rosenfield, "A Case Study in Speech Criticism: The Nixon-Truman Analog," *Communication Monographs* 35 (November 1968): 435-450. For a more nuanced, situational interpretation, see Roderick P. Hart, "Absolutism and Situation: Prolegomena to a Rhetorical Biography of Richard M. Nixon," *Communication Monographs* 43 (August 1976): 226; and Theodore White, *Breach of Faith* (New York: Dell Publishing Co., Inc., 1975), 89.

[10]See Aristotle's *Rhetoric,* I:1.

[11]I will deal more fully with the "speech effects" below; the emphasis on ethos and the lack of logos have been noted by many commentators, including Henry E. McGuckin, Jr. "A Value Analysis of Richard Nixon's 1952 Campaign-Fund Speech," in Halford Ross Ryan, ed., *American Rhetoric From Roosevelt to Reagan* (Prospect Heights, IL: Waveland Press, Inc., 1983), 124-133; Kathleen Hall Jamieson, *Packaging the Presidency* (New York: Oxford University Press, 1984), 73-77; Barnet Baskerville, "The Illusion of Proof," *Western Journal of Speech Communication* 25 (Fall 1961); 231-236; Barnet Baskerville, "The New Nixon," *Quarterly Journal of Speech,* 43 (February 1957); 41; it was also noted at the time by opponents in the popular press, but for an opposing view see Rosenfield, 450.

take the "Fund Speech" as a touchstone of eloquence, we ought to investigate it as a sign of the political choices facing the nation at the time.

Nixon's "crisis" can be described as a singular case of a more general problem facing American governance. As a consequence of the expense of the mass media, political speech could no longer be effectively free. The time had passed for most individuals to exercise freedom of expression that could have a truly meaningful impact on the public discourse. The inheritance from Milton, Locke, and Mill no longer was viable—individual rights were no longer a sufficient guarantee of a fair and rational political decision-making process.

This problem had, to some extent, always been present in American representative government because of its reliance on cyclical elections. That problem had been addressed, however, after an embarrassing history of electoral corruption;[12] a series of campaign finance laws required public disclosure of financial influences and established maximum contributions to limit disproportionate access.[13] While these mechanisms often were circumvented, they nonetheless exerted a salutary general effect.

These campaign finance provisions, however, were powerless against the national ideological crusade. Once politicians became convinced that controlling the ideological environment—the "marketplace of ideas" in general—could help them to influence election outcomes, and once the new mass communication technologies made possible a disproportionate influence on that marketplace, the national ideological campaign was born. Because campaign financing laws were tied to the ebb and flow of election seasons, this broader type of hired political speech, directed at the more general target of "public opinion," was in no manner controlled.

Therefore, when television surfaced as a new, expensive, and

---

[12]See Thayer.

[13]Discussions of campaign finance laws, history, and practices can be found in Thayer; Shannon; Thomas J. Schwarz and Benjamin M. Vandergraft, co-chairmen of Corporate Law and Practice, *The Corporation in Politics 1978* (New York: Practicing Law Institute, 1978); Herbert Alexander and Laura L. Denny, *Regulation of Political Finance* (Berkeley: Institute of Governmental Studies, 1966); David W. Adamany and George A. Agree, *Political Money* (Baltimore and London: Johns Hopkins University Press, 1975).

dominant medium of political communication in 1952, it almost inevitably raised the issue of control of the distortive impact of special-interest financing of national ideological campaigns.[14] Nixon, through a series of historical "accidents,"[15] was the person around whom this problem first visibly coalesced. His choices in dealing with his personal version of this essentially systemic problem influenced the manner in which the nation at large dealt with the issue.

TENSE AND DISPOSITIO IN TIME

In order to explore Nixon's treatment or personal resolution of the ideological problem, I wish to borrow and stretch the notion of time in rhetorical action which has recently been employed by Michael Leff.[16] Time enters into the rhetorical process in multiple ways. Speeches are given in real historical moments—and so there is the question of the *timeliness* of a speech (which in Nixon's case was nothing less than masterful).[17] There is also the intrinsic timing employed by the rhetor; this is the characteristic Leff has focused on most fully, and it can be divided into the *tenses* used by the rhetor and the temporal progression of the speech, that is, its order or *dispositio*. Finally, the aggregate of these three temporal elements combine to describe the character of rhetoric as "work."

---

[14]This argument might plausibly have been subsumed in the larger social question about the functioning of Anglo-American political theory, but given the particular historical confluence, it was the impact of the demands of mass communication that was of immediate significance. Whether we see 1952 as a new challenge to the American decision-making system or as simply one more step on the stairs toward a crystallized legitimacy crisis, however, the problem for officials and would-be officials of the system was the same—how to integrate the mass-mediated power of disproportionate speech into the government form in such a way as to make it appear legitimate and function well, i.e. eliminate or minimize its distortive impacts.

[15]While there was no necessity that Nixon be the one to be caught in this issue, there were a group of factors that made it likely for him to be the "victim" or "representative" of the underlying social problem. I would therefore describe this as a "systemically probable accident."

[16]See Michael Leff, "Dimensions of Temporality in Lincoln's Second Inaugural," *Communication Reports* 1 (Winter 1988): 26-31; Leff, "Rhetorical Timing in Lincoln's House Divided Speech," Van Zelst Lecture in Communication. Evanston: Northwestern University; Leff, "Textual Criticism: the Legacy of G.P. Mohrmann," *Quarterly Journal of Speech* 72 (November 1986): 377-389.

[17]Leff; see also Bruce Gronbeck, "Rhetorical Timing in Public Communication," *Central States Speech Journal* 25 (Summer 1974): 84-94.

Any rhetorical act occurs in a specific historical juncture and does work at that site (place + time) to bring about or forestall change. As Leff points out, every oration therefore contains and constitutes "rhetorical action." Additionally, however, to perform that action, to accomplish the speech's rhetorical work, the rhetor must move the audience (in time) through the ideological constellation or dominant public vocabulary that constructs the particular rhetorical problem she or he (and/or the society) faces. Each of the moves the rhetor makes is a *disposition* of a reigning ideological constellation, and it shifts the audience into new "places" where, because of new perspectives, key terms take on new significance. The rhetor may make many alternative moves, but the character of the ideological terrain at the given historical site constrains the repertoire of choices available and shapes the ideological consequences of each move. Moreover, because the rhetor's discourse constitutes "moves through time" *through* the ideological terrain, timing alone (in the form of tense or disposition) often is capable of doing the necessary work to make ideological moves persuasive. Richard Nixon relied heavily on these temporal resources in constructing a persuasive response to the allegations about his fund.

NIXON'S MOVES IN THE "CHECKERS" GAME

The stance from which Nixon chose to open his address to the record television audience of sixty million Americans was influenced, as Halford Ross Ryan has suggested, by the way the topic had been framed by his attackers.[18] In raising the fund as an issue, Nixon's opponents had repeatedly phrased the matter as one concerning the young Vice-Presidential candidate's personal integrity, demanding that Nixon get off the Republican ticket. This is quite evident in Leo Katcher's headline in the *New York Post:* "Secret Rich Men's Trust Fund Keeps Nixon in Style Far Beyond His Salary," and in the National Democratic Party Chairman Stephen A. Mitchell's attack: "Senator Nixon has been accepting

---

[18]Halford Ross Ryan, "Senator Richard M. Nixon's Apology for 'The Fund'," in *Oratorical Encounters: Selected Studies and Sources of Twentieth-Century Political Accusations and Apologies,* ed. Halford Ross Ryan (Westport, CT: Greenwood Press, 1988), 99-120.

donations from wealthy California businessmen to supplement his salary as a Senator. Senator Nixon knows that is morally wrong."[19] This general frame was shared by almost all the attackers as well as the defenders, in spite of the fact that, as historian Stephen Ambrose has argued, the personal attack was in large measure a sham, insubstantial, and sure to fail.[20] Crucially, however, this attack was comprised of two parts: first that Nixon had acted without integrity for the purpose of personal gain, and second, that he had sold out the public to a special "rich men's trust." Nixon's address focused primarily on the issue of his own personal gain, thus deflecting public attention from the more general "special interest" issue that was implicit in the personal attack (and this was in direct contrast to his strategy of generalization in his Watergate speeches).[21] He made this choice, moreover, fully aware that the funding problem was shared not only by Adlai Stevenson, but also, according to campaign finance expert George Thayer, by many others. Thayer noted that "there was nothing unique in the fund; many earlier politicians were beneficiaries of similar arrangements."[22] In fact, I will suggest, through careful shepherding of temporal resources, Nixon's address employed the personal issue not simply *instead of* the more general finance issue but rather as a uniquely suitable substitute for and cover-up of that important general concern. Nixon's text began this

---

[19]*New York Post,* 22 September 1952, 25, and "Mitchell's Statement," *New York Tribune,* 19 September 1952, 11.

[20]Ambrose calls the Democrats "criminally stupid" for playing up the issue, 284-285. The single exception seems to have been Taft, who discussed the general propriety of the fund and noted the need for permanent campaigning that had arisen; "Taft says Nixon Did No Wrong In Taking Gifts," *New York Tribune,* 20 September 1952, 6. There was a good deal of discussion in the newspapers about the "special interest" or "special favors" question and also about Nixon's role as a "spokesman for free enterprise," but no consideration about the relationship between these two facets of the issue.

[21]President Nixon, for example, employed the principles of "confidentiality" and "executive privilege" to counter attacks on his personal integrity in the Watergate scandal. On Watergate see Jackson Harrell, B.L. Ware, and Wil A. Linkugel, "Failure of Apology in American Politics: Nixon on Watergate," *Speech Monographs* 42 (November 1975), or William L. Benoit, "Richard M. Nixon's Rhetorical Strategies in his Public Statements on Watergate," *Southern Speech Communication Journal* 47 (Winter 1982): 192-211.

[22]See also Spalding, who argued, "most Representatives and Senators had, or hoped to have, a similar fund," 307; Ambrose, 284-285.

temporizing with the following salutation: "My Fellow Americans: I come before you tonight as a candidate for the Vice Presidency and as a man whose honesty and integrity have been questioned."[23]

This introduction of the issue employed a tense structure that recurred throughout the speech. I will call that structure "present-subordinated past." This easily-caricatured feature of Nixon's speaking style consisted of a lead-in phrase or sentence in the present tense followed by phrases or sentences in the past tense. This structure repeatedly signaled that the past contained the primary clue to the present. As the speech opened, the most important consequence of the usage of this tense was that it designated the rhetorical situation as a judicial rather than a deliberative one; as Aristotle noted, the rhetoric of the past is judiciary, rhetoric of the future, deliberative.[24] Deftly and unobtrusively, the tense solidified the audience's position as judges of Richard Nixon's fate rather than deliberators on an important social issue.

This use of tense was quickly reinforced by a description of the particular character of the judgment the polity was to render. Nixon specified that the issue was not to be one of political effect, or even legality, but simply a judgment on the moral character of Richard Nixon. Intensifying the focus on the past, he asked awkwardly: "Now, was that wrong? And let me say that it was wrong—I'm saying, incidentally, that it was wrong and not just illegal. Because it isn't a question of whether it was legal or illegal, that isn't enough. The question is, was it morally wrong?" (para. 6, 114). Almost at once, then, the tense structure of the speech encouraged the audience to focus on Nixon's personal morality.

Once the issue was firmly and safely framed as a forensic matter, the text could set out the criteria for this moral judgment (para. 7, 114). Of course Nixon naturalized these criteria, making them seem like the only relevant measuring sticks, but his choices were largely unobjectionable, covering, at least briefly, the important issues. As we will come to see, however, the order in which these topics were arranged was of surprising importance for the

---

[23] All citations from the speech will hereafter be listed by paragraph (para.) and page number from Ryan, (para. 1, 114).

[24] Aristotle, I:3.

speech; the least consequential and most easily answerable question came first and the most serious and problematic issue last. Nixon asked first if he had used the fund for personal advantage, second, if it had been secret, and finally, whether the fund had produced special favors (a serious distortion in the political process — one which might have challenged its legitimacy).

This section of the discourse continued in the present-subordinate past, repressing questions of any future advantages to be given to fund contributors as it pushed the attention of the polity again, back to the past. And, it was in the past tense that Nixon introduced his first response to the charges in light of these criteria. He asserted that he had not used the fund for personal use, that it had not been secret, and that he had given no rewards to contributors (para. 8-12, 115).

These assertions carried persuasive force because they were devoutly attested to. However, this demonstration of the "cleanli-ness" of the fund instantly called up the more potent question, "Why did you have to have it?" (para. 13, 115). Given that the fund had been portrayed by papers and politicians as atypical, once Nixon had claimed that his use of it was fully moral, the audience needed to know why he had atypical needs. The question naturally could have been read as raising the systemic issue — what purpose does such money serve if not to gain political advantage for contributors? However, because the issue was raised only as a subordinate one (the true "moral" criteria having already been met), and because it was dealt with only after the issue was safely embedded in the past, the text reshaped the query, dodging its problematic potential.

Two devices assisted the maneuvering around this ideological hotspot. First, Nixon denied that the need for a fund was atypical. He did not do so by describing the generality of the practice of soliciting such funds — that might merely have implicated all politicians and hence challenged the legitimacy of the system as a whole. Instead, he portrayed a long-standing and widely shared need for such funds. A shift to a new tense helped to make this move persuasive. The description of the need for special political funding was executed in what I would call a "transcendent" tense (borrowing but modifying Leff's concept of transcendent time). This tense appears to use a present verb form, but it implies a permanent standard by framing the issue either in continuing terms (this is how Senate offices [always] work) or as a moral principle applicable to all behavior at all times (this is how you would [always] want us to behave). This transcendent, permanent standard replaced a deliberative orientation, that is, an orientation toward the future, while still providing some kind of generalized measure for judgment.

The second move by which Nixon avoided the deliberative issue his text had raised was to shift the question from a systemic one (why do politicians need such "extra" funds) to a personal one (back to Nixon's personal choices). He did so by gradually deepening the personal focus he had established from the first sentence. In describing the official business of the Senate, he emphasized, for example, that the staff money was not paid personally to him and that it was individuals who were helped by this money "for example, when a constituent writes in and wants you to go down to the Veterans Administration and get some information about his GI policy" (para. 16, 115). But Nixon needed to argue that he had to finance more than "official business," and this was the difficult claim to make (as we will see in more detail when it arises again later). At this point, therefore, the text relied upon a series of rhetorical questions to address the funding of political broadcasts and travel, for example: "Do you think that when I or any other Senator makes a political speech, has it printed, [sic] should charge the printing of that speech and the mailing of that speech to the taxpayers?" (para. 17, 116).

These rhetorical questions performed an important shift. They took up the topic the rhetorical action of the text had made visible (the costs of non-official business), but they avoided making that topic itself into an issue. Instead, in Nixon's questions it was the source of the funding that was at issue. Nixon thereby introduced and naturalized the necessity of such political expenses on a national scale, without having to address their necessity as a contentious political issue. Notice here how tense and *dispositio* cooperated. The transcendent tense and the placement following "official business" of a personal nature, in juxtaposition with the "purely political" raised only in question form, served to urge the audience to ask not about the desirability of theoretically unlimited amounts of political funds for political speech, but instead about the appropriate source for obtaining such funds.

Thus, at one of the crucial points where the action of the text had itself raised the underlying deliberative issue about the political system as a whole, Nixon was able to avoid the issue through careful disposition, bolstered by choices of tense and the clever shift to rhetorical questions. He shifted the question to the legitimacy of alternative sources of funds rather than the legitimacy of the need for such funds. There was, however, a cost. Something had to be substituted for attention to the ideological problem — the audience had to be moved to some new ideological terrain. It was by sacrificing the privacy of his personal life that Nixon found the means to disguise the political issue (and this, I will eventually argue, was itself a virtually necessary product of the ideological terrain).

The next section of the speech therefore introduced the strongest, most sustained theme of the address — the building of Nixon's own ethos (para. 22-28, 116). This shift to the personal was accomplished by a dispositional move that bridged the system issue and his personal character. Nixon measured his conduct against a systemic standard, portraying himself as having made the best choice among the available alternatives. This move required the re-appearance of the transcendent tense, through which he set up a kind of checklist of permanently available financing options. He juxtaposed his own conduct against these options, indicating that he had in each case made the morally superior choice. By the time the section was completed, the focus had shifted from the general problems raised by the "need" for such money to a flattering portrait of Nixon as enactor of the American mythos — a common man of common means, one who did not allow his wife to work for wages, and one who devoted all his energy to public service.[25]

The section concluded by proclaiming the necessity of such political expenses as an accomplished ideological fact. Nixon summarized, "the best way to handle these *necessary* political expenses of getting my message to the American people...was to accept the aid which people in my home state of California...were glad to make" (My emphasis, ellipses for focus; para. 29, 117). Conceivably, that might have made an end to the speech. However, unsatisfied with the rhetorical action of his text, debator Nixon tried to reinforce the necessity of such admittedly political speeches

---

[25]McGuckin.

by emphasizing the worthiness of his message—"exposing this Administration, the communism in it, the corruption in it."

Here the progression of Nixon's text had led him fully into the darkest part of the ideological labyrinth. Following the line of personalization, Nixon had tried to justify the need for political funds in general, by referring to the value and significance of his own political discourse. This entailed the dubious move of claiming universal validity for a particular ideology and a clearly partisan position. In short, the personal focus Nixon preferred was inherently insufficient; in the ideological configuration within which he found himself, each attempt to absolve himself on exclusively personal grounds seemed merely to bring up, in a new guise, the issue of partisanship, special interest, and gain—the larger issues his address continually moved to avoid.

While his intended audience might have accepted the equivalence of anti-communism and universal truth, Nixon apparently recognized the gap at some level. His address moved immediately to "dispose" of that newly resuscitated issue, the third issue—the linkages among special interest, partisanship, and political or personal gain. He flatly asserted that "I am proud of the fact that not one of them [the contributors] has ever asked me for a special favor" (para. 30, 117), and then, implicitly indicating his recognition of the weakness of his position, moved again to the rhetorical question "Let me say, incidentally, that some of you may say, 'Well, that's all right, Senator; that's your explanation, but have you got any proof?' (para. 31, 117)."

Before we look at the proof offered by Nixon at this critical juncture, it is important, given my underlying claim that the speech has serious argumentative flaws, and is representative of a dangerous political trend, to establish that Nixon's central, crucial position here—that he did not accept special interest money targeted toward distortion of "freely" arrived at political decisions—was problematic, unverifiable, or even false.

Nixon not only claimed that none of his contributors had asked him for special favors, but also that they had not attempted to influence his vote (para 30, 117). We have good reason to believe that this is not true (depending, of course, on our definitions of special favors and voting). Ironically, our informant was one of Nixon's sycophantic biographers. Bela Kornitzer made a feeble attempt to prove that Nixon had never voted for any bill these contributors asked him to support.[26] In doing so, Kornitzer quoted Thomas R. Knudsen, one of the important contributors to the fund, as having said "The Danish cheese quota was the only issue I ever talked about to Nixon. During one of his visits to California, shortly after becoming Senator, I brought up the matter of the quota and said I was hoping that it could be lifted. I argued that, if Denmark could sell its products in the United States, it would need no aid from the United States."[27]

Knudsen's admission, therefore, was that he quite definitely did attempt to influence Nixon's vote. Moreover, the story does not end there. Kornitzer claimed that "He (Nixon) did not vote to lift the quota. In other words, he did not follow Knudsen's stated request as Pearson had alleged" (p. 191). But this denial was a bit too carefully phrased. In fact, Nixon would never have had a chance to vote this bill up or down. During his period in the Senate, the only chance he had to vote on the bill was a vote to commit it to committee (from whence it was not resuscitated during his service in the Congress). In the face of massive pressure from other constituents who publicly opposed lifting the quota, Nixon did not cast a vote on the move to commit, even though he

---

[26]Bela Kornitzer, *The Real Nixon: An Intimate Biography* (Chicago: Rand McNally and Co., 1960), 190-191. In addition, Ambrose reports that "Nixon's office requested information about or urged speed in the resolution of problems specific to contributors to the fund. In one case, the office interceded on behalf of Dana Smith himself in a Justice Department case in which a firm owned by Smith's family was asking for a $500,000 rebate." Ambrose (258) notes that these were common practices, but that Nixon had claimed a higher standard of conduct.

[27]Knudsen makes this statement as proof that Pearson was wrong in his allegations that Nixon was being supported to influence him to OPPOSING the quota's elimination. Knudsen therefore portrays himself as arguing against his immediate, "special" self-interest, and in favor of the broader principle of free enterprise. All of this becomes a complex matter in two ways. First, the distinction between special interest and partisan political/ideological interest is crucial here. Knudsen is still issuing a vote in his "self-interest" in that he perceives that he will benefit from a free enterprise move (e.g reduced aid, therefore reduced taxes). This becomes especially clear when Dana Smith argues that, as a salesman for free enterprise, "Dick did just what we wanted him to do" (Ambrose, 275). Additionally, the portrayal of Knudsen's self interest as in favor of a quota assumes that his position vis a vis other DOMESTIC producers would not be advanced by their greater vulnerability to the influx of imported blue cheese. In any case, the point remains that Knudsen claims here that his only contact with Nixon was with regard to promoting a particular position on a particular bill.

had answered a quorum call earlier that day.[28]

What we have here is a plausible argument that the only talk Nixon had with a special contributor was a request that Nixon vote opposite to the way that a large group of Nixon's constituents publicly argued he should vote. Pushed from two directions, Nixon decided not to vote to offend either group, but to abstain.

Now all of this is, of course, circumstantial evidence. We can hardly prove that Nixon's actions were "against his conscience" (another criterion he listed in the speech, para. 30, 117). The point here is larger than Nixon's honesty, for our problem is larger than an import quota on Danish blue cheese. The problem here is that the American electorate can never know when special interests are being "disproportionately," "irrationally," and therefore "unfairly" served. It is impossible to know whether Nixon's failure to vote was caused by a necessary absence, by his having no authentic preference on the bill, or by some other motive. Moreover, we have no clean test to separate "ideological" interests (which take a partisan line, but claim a general good arising through policies favorable to a limited sector of the population) from "special favors" (which provide direct benefit to single groups or individuals with reckless disregard for the general good). We most certainly cannot scan the consciences of those who make the decisions. All of these limitations center around the fact that our system depends, for its sole guarantee of legitimacy, on the *process* of open argumentation itself, and a faith that the best decisions are arrived at when all factions have their opportunity to participate in forming compromise and consensus in a fair way. Thus, the very presence of special funds represents a problem, regardless of any ability to discern specific influences resulting from those funds. Nixon's circumnavigation of this issue can once again be traced in the temporality of the speech.

Nixon had raised the possibility that special funds brought special influence; his immediate response was a denial of the charge and an offering of an audit as objective proof. The games

---

[28]*Congressional Record,* 30 January 1952, 638; he missed the quorum call immediately preceding the vote.

of *dispositio* and tense thickened here precisely because Nixon could not have any objective proof of his innocence (for the same reasons that it could not be conclusively proven that he did succumb to special pressure). In the absence of positive evidence at this crucial juncture in the speech, timing and order performed all the persuasive work.

Note first that the introduction to this section returned the audience to the present-subordinate past tense (para 31-55, 117-119). Remember also that throughout the speech the issues had been disposed of in the order (1) personal gain, (2) secrecy/legality, and finally (3) special favors. Nixon's text relied here on the expectations generated by that repeated order to make the citation of an independent audit appear appropriate as a response to the serious charges of special influence.

Nixon opened the section by answering his own rhetorical demand for proof in this way, "I'd like to tell you this evening [present] that just about an hour ago we received an independent audit of this entire fund [subordinate past]." (para. 32, 117). Significantly, however, the audit established at most only the first and second issues—that Nixon did not gain from the fund personally (privately) and that it was not illegal. The proof did not touch the third issue (the special favor question), which as you will recall, was the question that had sparked the demand for a move toward external proof and that had determined the organization of this section of the speech.

The audience was disposed to accept the audit section in spite of its substantive irrelevance, as an appropriate response, for two reasons. First, the tense structure set the audience's expectations in such a way that the past personal account fitted; it sounded appropriate because the tense structure had set up a looking toward the past, and that was what the audit provided. More crucially, the move worked because the dispositional structure functioned cunningly here. The question raised was with regard to proof for question #3, but the audience had been prepared by the dispositional structure used throughout the speech—the repetitive pattern of 1, 2, 3—to work through the questions in that order. Consequently, when the audit did not immediately address question #3, instead returning to issue #1, the shift did not appear as a non sequitur, but merely as an orderly approach to the issue. The audience was disposed to wait a while until issue #3 was reached.

By the time a proof for #3 would be in order—nineteen paragraphs later—the audience had been encouraged to forget the urgent need for proof of that issue. Moreover, the energy and commitments to those concerns had been displaced by two other moves I will note momentarily.

Meanwhile, however, in using time and tense as replacement structures, the rhetorical action of Nixon's text had only delayed but had not overcome the fundamental problem. Nixon could not simply stop the speech after proving items #1 and #2. Precisely because of the dispositional expectations (used to displace the earlier expectations generated by earlier moves), such a move might have made it obvious that something was missing. Instead, he inserted a filler—an extended proof of his innocence of charge #1 through a full accounting of his financial holdings. But this move entailed its own problems.

As a number of writers have argued, the relationship of the public and private realms is extremely problematic for Western governmental systems.[29] Habermas and others have claimed that it is only through "civil privatism" and "familial vocational privatism" that the necessary passive support is maintained for a government riddled with inequity.[30] That is, capitalist private appropriation of socially-produced wealth can only be legitimized through the structural depoliticization of the public realm. Only if participation in the democratic system consists solely of formal mechanisms like voting, rather than substantive involvement in issues and policies, and only if that form of participation is passively supported because of contentment with familial-vocational approaches to life,

[29]Hannah Arendt, *The Human Condition* (New York: 1959); Zillah R. Eisenstein, *The Radical Future of Liberal Feminism* (Boston: Northeastern University Press, 1981); Mary O'Brien, *The Politics of Reproduction* (1981; rpt. Boston: Routledge and Kegan Paul, 1983); Habermas, e.g. 36, 70, 75.

[30]Habermas defines civil privatism as "political abstinence combined with an orientation to career, leisure, and consumption" and which "promotes the expectation of suitable rewards within the system (money, leisure, time, and security)" (37). He defines familial-vocational privatism as "family orientation with developed interests in consumption and leisure on the one hand, and in career orientation suitable to status competition on the other" (75).

will wide-spread support for systematic misappropriation of social goods continue. However, there is an ironic flip side to this capitalist coin, revealed uniquely in Nixon's situation. If disproportionate access to the process of political argumentation and decision-making is to be permitted (and Nixon's address simply attempted to re-routinize the new, expanded disproportions offered by television), the only way the populace can continue to have faith in the political system is to have faith in the integrity of those who are elected. The people must trust that the personal character of elected officials will prevent them from becoming purchased pawns of special interests, that politicians will continue to make decisions based on fairly weighed assessments of the public good. In order to establish such "character," politicians must bare their entire selves in public view (or at least skillfully appear to do so), presenting themselves as representatives of traditional lifestyles and values. In abandoning their own privacy and private identity to become fully political animals, the politicians thereby further promote civil privatism both by quieting the concerns of the people and by giving heightened presence to the traditional familial-professional values. Ironically, therefore, the maintenance of civil privatism for the populace occurred with the *de*-privatization of the politician and a consequent professionalization of politics that hastened the demise of the citizen-orator.

Nixon's choices in the "Fund Address" were therefore simply a crucial step in a long line of ideological moves which, by using personal and private substance to cover ideological issues, destroyed the private realm for all politicians by inviting the media and the public into their lives. The rhetorical action of Nixon's "Side of the Story" sacrificed his private life not by accident, but because revelations about personal character provided the most appropriate replacement for a direct resolution of the special interest problem.

At least at one level, Nixon was aware that he was making such a move. He emphasized in the speech that this rhetorical action was "unprecedented in the history of American politics" (para. 40, 118) and that it amounted to a baring of his soul (para. 71, 121). While it is peculiarly and extremely capitalist to equate one's soul with one's financial history, Nixon was certainly sincere about the trauma involved in such personal revelations. Other politicians, most notably Eisenhower, were extremely disturbed by Nixon's assertion that all politicians should thereafter share such personal exposure if the voters were to be able to trust them.[31] We also know that the issue was a matter of some dispute within Nixon's own family. Pat had claimed that "it seems to me that we're entitled to at least some privacy," but the candidate had replied "these are not normal circumstances. Right now we're living in a fishbowl. If I don't itemize everything we've earned and everything we've spent, the broadcast won't convince the public. I just don't have a choice."[32] The "Fund Speech" was reportedly a major turning point in Pat's disdain for politics and campaigning.[33] Nixon's mother reported similar difficulty with the exposure: "At the point when he gave that itemized account of his personal expenditures, I didn't think I could take it. But I drew courage from my faith. That carried me through."[34] Although it may not seem like a major disclosure today, Nixon arguably was sacrificing something of serious value to cover the underlying ideological issue in the only way that could make the "broadcast convince the public."

The dispositional structure of this personalizing of politics and deprivatizing of politicians was itself interesting. The first half of the "personal disclosure" was nothing more than campaign biography—Nixon's birth, education, marriage and "war record." However, at paragraph 44, he completed this portion of the personal defense and its rather standard ethos-building by inserting the first particular, private, financial reference. He claimed "the total [savings] for that entire period was just a little less than $10,000" (para. 44, 118).

Nixon began the political/financial disclosure section with an extremely awkward tense structure: "Well, that's where we start when I got into politics" (para. 45, 118). This sentence is in a very strange version of the present-subordinate past tense. The present

---

[31]Wills, 108. Eisenhower in fact had insisted that Nixon provide such a disclosure, but he was incensed at Nixon's generalization of the issue to others; Ambrose, 282. Ambrose (108) notes further that after this point all the candidates did make financial disclosures.

[32]Spalding, 335; see also Nixon's own accounts in *Six Crises* (Garden City, New York: Doubleday and Company, 1962); *RN: The Memoirs of Richard Nixon* (New York: Grosset and Dunlap, 1978). Jamieson (78) also argues that the speech represented a turning point towards personal financial disclosure.

[33]Ambrose, 295, 296.

[34]Kornitzer, 205.

section ("that is where") serves to obscure the temporal and, therefore, ideological relationships in the narrative. Is it fully in the past ("that is where we started"), subsuming Nixon's entire biography under the political realm, or is it in the present ("that is where we start now"), indicating that only one's biography after entry into political life is a test for present character? I suggest here that the tension in the structural transference of private to political was simply too great and Nixon therefore did not control it. In any case, Nixon then gradually shifted to a "real" present tense and began the "real proof"—that he did not have a lot of money currently in his bank account and credits. The fact that this section did not match the past (judicial) form very well and that it only dealt with charge #1 rather than #3 was also reflected in the disposition. By dividing the personal account into two parts, Nixon attempted to maintain some separation between private life (the sanitized pre-political campaign biography safely in the past tense) and the real blending of public and private life through financial disclosure (which appears in a more present tense).

The story of the gift of Checkers, which closed the section, tied the tensions between the two forces together in a neat package. It attempted to reassert some boundaries around the disclosure of privacy—children are off limits—while providing a transition back to the political issue, the issue of personal attack and smear. In addition to setting ideological boundaries, the distractive quality of the Checkers incident was important for this transition. Recall that at this point, dispositionally, it was again time for Nixon to address issue number three with concrete proof similar to that he had offered for charges number one and two. Because he could not do so, he had to re-focus the audience's attention in a different direction. The emotional quality of the Checkers example allowed him to hide the topic shift. Following the Checkers story, he took relevant topics and tenses from the previous section to move in a new direction. He employed the present/transcendent tense to make a transition to the impersonal, political, future-oriented attack.

I will not describe these moves in detail, but gradually, by see-sawing back and forth between present, past and transcendentally tensed expectations, Nixon worked his way out of the personal, back into the political. It was, however, a different political issue from the one that had opened the speech. The speech had begun with the question—what does the Nixon fund mean (about the system/about Nixon)? In the meantime Nixon's character had been established and the issues about the system displaced. Consequently, he could now frame the matter as a question about why others might have attempted to smear his character. Nixon informed the public that it was for political (ideological) reasons—because of his anti-communist message.

This political focus allowed him to shift from defense to a full attack. He gradually aligned the battle between communism and free enterprise (the ideological battle) with the electoral battle between corrupt Democrats and clean Republicans. Here, finally, Nixon provided the deliberative section of the speech and the bulk of the very rare future-oriented tenses in the speech. It was, however, deliberation not about the historically situated ideological problem that had given rise to the speech—the status of paid free speech and its links to politicians (especially Nixon)—but rather about the normal, electoral cycle itself (about Nixon as Veep). Nixon had accomplished this rhetorical work through the rhetorical action of a major public address which persuaded a crucial segment of the public through clever disposition, disposition-setting tenses, and the sacrifice of his privacy.

CONCLUSION

This account of Nixon's journey through time can best be summarized, I believe, through a reflective judgment of the text's accomplishments. In telling "his side of the story," Nixon negotiated a complex and problematic ideological positioning with complex outcomes. He gained immediate success—300,000 letters and telegrams to the Republican National Committee, 2 million letters overall, 350 to 1 in favor of his staying on the ticket.[35] He also advanced his party's position. By conspicuously avoiding the finance issue, the Republican party would gradually amass a two-to-one

---

[35]Ambrose, 290; Jamieson, 77; Spalding, 355.

financial advantage over the Democrats.[36] To achieve their goals, the well-to-do could continue to contribute money to gain disproportionate access to the marketplace of ideas in an effort to drown out opposition voices.

There were, however, other effects stemming from this success. There were clear personal costs to Nixon as a person and to his family. As Garry Wills argued: "He vindicated himself in the 'Checkers' speech." But to do so he had to violate his own privacy, and the experience left him with a permanent air of violation, not of vindication."[37] There were also, as Stephen Ambrose has indicated, costs to Nixon as politician:

> The impression that the speech was a personal triumph for Nixon is also incorrect. He held on to that part of the Republican Party faithful who were always his supporters no matter what, but he failed to use his unique opportunity to win new supporters. He made new enemies. Despite the flood of telegrams, a majority in the audience found the speech objectionable, if not nauseating. In the years that followed, one never heard Republicans bring it up, while Democrats quoted it to one another gleefully.... Even at 350 to 1 on the wires, Nixon did not win a majority of the viewers.[38]

The political effects may also have extended far and dramatically into Nixon's future. Candidate Nixon's conservative fixation with a present subordinated to the past and his related failure to face directly the campaign finance issue with critical awareness of its significance arguably may have been what led to President Nixon's unprecedented demise.

The final effect of the speech was on the polity at large. Through this address, the American public was urged to ignore rather than address a vital public issue—the standard of free speech in an era of purchased communication. It is perhaps unfair, however, for liberal academics with the benefit of hindsight to

---

[36]For example, in Nixon's 1972 campaign; see Lester A. Sobel, ed. *Money and Politics: Contributions, Campaign Abuses, and the Law* (New York: Facts on File, 1974), 11. A similar analysis, but from a view critical of the Democratic party is offered by David Nichols, *Financing Elections: The Politics of an American Ruling Class* (New York: New Viewpoints, 1974), 56, 87, 93.

[37]Wills, 6.

[38]Ambrose, 294.

condemn Richard Nixon for obscuring the major ideological issue of his time for the sake of personal and partisan advantage. After all, Nixon may not have been fully aware of the problem. At the least, the rhetorical action of Nixon's text was not solely of his own making—it was a product both of the resilient shape of the ideological terrain (or Nixon's rhetorical situation) and of Nixon's own attempts to move across that terrain.

Consequently, to judge harshly a text's historical role and to treat it as an indication of serious political problems should not necessarily be to judge its maker with equal severity. Although Nixon's text may have been pivotal in the historical trend toward fusing political issues almost inseparably to a political persona, Nixon may stand guilty of nothing more than being the common man he sought so earnestly to present himself as being. If so, it would seem harsh to judge him negatively for failing to rise to the insight of a Roosevelt or a Lincoln, leaders who recognized how their personal rhetorical situations reflected larger rhetorical positions and who shaped the two together.

Nixon, however, did more than simply fail to recognize a serious problem in the political system. He provided the mechanism by which that problem could be concealed. He devised a way to re-legitimate civil privatism and protect the faith of the people in the formal electoral republic. He was able to inflate the ordinariness and mediocrity of the common man into the ideal persona of the politician, and he was able to make that persona outshine the financial interests that had paid for the communication of that persona. That is clearly an achievement of great rhetorical skill, if not exactly a matter of rhetorical artistry. The ultimate judgment of the stature of that accomplishment rests, of course, on our satisfaction with the political system he preserved and our attitude toward mediocrity.

THE CARNIVAL AS CONFESSIONAL: RE-READING THE FIGURATIVE DIMENSION IN NIXON'S 'CHECKERS' SPEECH

THOMAS B. FARRELL

I don't know if every late-Capitalist culture must have its own Gothic, anti-heroic figure: someone to represent a corporeal version of the soul's dark night. This is partly because I am not sure that every late-Capitalist culture even has a soul. But were all these unlikely conditions true, there could be little doubt as to the identity of our own dark trope.

Of all the scholars in all the disciplines in all the world, I am surely among the least suitable to be an audience for this serious analysis of the "Checkers" speech. This is despite the fact that I have heard the speech many times. An anecdote may help to explain. My most frequent exposure to this address came about twenty years ago—at the old *Majestic* theater off the Square in Madison. This was before the midnight cult success of "The Rocky Horror Picture Show." But the idea was quite similar. There, I and scores of other future scholars and felons—aided by what I can best describe here as reception enhancement devices—would watch weekend midnight madness showings of "The Checkers Speech." The second feature varied. Sometimes it was "Reefer Madness." Other times it was "Tricia's Wedding." But there was never any doubt as to the main attraction. It brought down the house.

Perhaps you appreciate the nature of my dilemma. One of the most remarkable achievements of Professor Condit's lively and very provocative essay is that it forces someone like me to take this speech seriously. It is as if Dostoevsky's great character, Stavrogin, had never even expected laughter from the priest-confessor in response to his notorious confession. In other words, at least some of the surreality is gone.

In this response to Professor Condit's paper, I want to offer my best understanding of what she has managed to do, along with some issues that might frame a useful discussion of what might still be done. I would like to work through this in my customary style — backwards: from implication, to theme, to method, and then perhaps add my own two cents.

Professor Condit's analysis of "Checkers" is the best evidence I have yet seen that the engaged criticism of a text helps to recreate that text — to refashion it for new forms of appreciation. I have already alluded to the marginal status of the Checkers speech in the library of so-called "great works." And if anyone had raised the question, I would have thought that when objects of camp humor get old and in the way, they should just slink out of our attention span, better to die quietly than to be a continual burden on already strapped scholars and colleagues.

Well, for whatever it is worth, I would have been wrong. Richard Nixon's speech was made farcical by two decades of questions and suspicions revolving largely around his character. It was, remember, no less a humorist than Hubert Humphrey who referred to him as Richard Milltown Nixon. So, it is not surprising that the whole late sixties crowd derived enormous hilarity from the fact that the old (young) Nixon and the new (old) Nixon were all of a piece after all. What Professor Condit has done is to interrupt all the chuckles by taking the joke seriously. In doing this successfully, she forces us to do the same. To the extent that she forces political content from all the shenanigans, we teacher-scholars can no longer go around winking and elbowing each other in the ribs every time we show this speech to our undergraduates.

Well, as you can probably tell by now, I am not totally comfortable with this development. In the celebrated Burkean spirit of political debunkery, I have always kind of enjoyed jabbing away at the new, the old, the borrowed, the blue Nixon. With new cold war treatises on foreign policy appearing every campaign season, I also think Nixon is being taken seriously enough as it is. But Professor Condit forces me to consider something else. If you stop and consider the number of basic speech classes that have whizzed through the Checkers speech every quarter or semester for the better part of two decades, is there any wonder that people have trouble taking political discourse seriously?

At this point, I am tempted to stop and add, solemnly, that renewed serious consideration of the Checkers speech is but another sign that our discipline now has new-found legitimacy.

I'll stop short of that, and I am comforted by the fact that Professor Condit does not want to step aside and welcome this artifact into the pantheon of eloquence. Early in her study, she refers to the discourse as, "devoid of stylistic elegance or grace and seriously defective in argumentation." Obviously, taking the discourse seriously is not equivalent to commending its qualities. But it does mean that, in a larger sense, we should take every political discourse seriously. The era of politics as burlesque has hurt no one so much as ourselves. So, if my reading of this one implication is correct, I can only applaud its forceful expression here.

However, as students of rhetoric, we all like to look over each other's shoulders while we work. So I thought it might be useful to offer one person's opinion on how Professor Condit was able to work the critical magic of taking Nixon's Checkers speech seriously. This brings me to her theme.

Bluntly put, Professor Condit changes the thematic context for reading and interpreting the work. I think it is safe to say that almost everyone, Nixon included, has seen this speech as addressing an overblown scandal about Nixon's character. It was one of the original *Six Crises*. Regardless of the reader's political leanings, it is usually conceded that Nixon acquitted himself with a highly sentimental, but effective *apologia* which helped define the use of television in a media age. Professor Condit brings in the much larger historical context of paying for political speech in the era of television: the money-equals-time logic that resulted in Nixon's own campaign spending abuses in 1972, and finally—in the wake of Watergate—forced the highly convoluted campaign financing reforms which currently afflict us.

This choice of interpretative context is ingenious, for several reasons. First, it is undeniably true that the persons who took sides on Nixon's "secret fund" were concerned about influence-peddling rather than the much more remote horizon of preserving symmetrical political speech in the era of late Capitalism. This means that Professor Condit is able to supply a fascinating sense of the way our social knowledge norms have shifted during the ensuing decades. The very premises of Nixon's argument would never hold up today. Second, there can be little doubt that Professor Condit's larger historical context is valid. In the very acceptance of independent funds for communication, political elites of the Fifties probably paved the way for the unprecedented scandals and political upheavals of decades to come. Third, and here you will sense that I don't let go of farce very easily, I think Professor Condit's analysis could be invoked to explain why some people in the early Seventies found Nixon's defense of an illegal campaign fund from the early Fifties so hilarious. Of course, I would never do such a thing. It would be wrong.

In any case, I think the whole conception and direction of this undertaking should be applauded. This is the first social symptom criticism I have read in some time that manages to take its subject seriously. At its best, this study is direct evidence of Mikhail Bakhtin's remarkable insight that utterances continue to respond, In a multiplicity of voices, through time and history. In the remaining part of my commentary, I want to mention some small quibbles over method and execution, and raise a couple of related issues.

Professor Condit occasionally writes as if Nixon is actively evading or even dissembling about this larger historical context of accountability whenever he addresses (or fails to address) the question of improper influence. For instance, she professes surprise that Nixon the orator does not take on the most serious charge against him (i.e. improper influence, special favors) right away, instead of deferring it to the third claim in his defense. Later on, when addressing the third claim, she finds him in an ideological labyrinth, because no evidence can be decisive for this most important larger question. Later still, she accuses him of covering up this central thematic question.

Well, I would not want this to get around (i.e., that I have anything but numbed nerve endings where Nixon is concerned), but it seems to me that the same seriousness which a new horizon of reading forces upon the text also revives the principle of interpretive charity. What I am saying is that I don't think Nixon could have been expected to even know about Professor Condit's larger political issue: "What are we to do to control the distortive impact of special-interest financing of national ideological campaigns?" I mean, we are not exactly dealing with the Max Horkheimer of the Republican party here. And after all, Adlai Stevenson, the liberal conscience of America, had a similar fund, and he didn't feel guilty about it.

Granted, the subject of our discussion has always at least

appeared to have something to feel guilty about. Granted, also, that no one can conclusively disprove charges of special interest favoritism. Still, I think it was surely possible in the early Fifties to debate more localized questions of special interest influence without turning to the larger thematic horizon that Professor Condit's Eighties sensibility affords. So my first quibble might be rephrased as an ungrammatical issue: To what extent is it fair to blame the symptom—however rotten and disgusting the symptom might be—for what he or she is a symptom of?

Now if we grant, for the sake of argument, that it was possible to address the more localized question of special interest influence in this fund without the full-scale ideological critique implied here, then perhaps a simpler interpretation might be suggested. The explanation turns upon the fact that this is an instance of *apologia,* a sub-species of forensic discourse. It is a commonplace to establish the coloration of an act—its circumstances, its legal status—before turning to the basic forensic question of justification itself. Nixon, being an old debater, knew that much, just as he probably knew that if the fund was perfectly legal, if it was not secret, if others had similar funds, if he derived no private gain from the fund—if all these colorations of circumstance and appearance could be established, it would be much easier to make plausible the claim that he had not been guilty of any special interest favoritism through the fund's influence. After all, why should he? Where is the motive? And wouldn't he have hidden the fund, had he been so influenced?

A second issue might be derived from this counter-interpretation. This is just a suggestion, but I wonder if Professor Condit's dichotomy of temporal *dispositio* and logical inference might not be a bit too neat. At least, where the stasis points of forensic controversy are concerned, might these two not come together in natural structure of issues in the argument itself? This is just a suggestion, for I found myself wondering if Professor Condit's wonderfully suspenseful depiction of tense-subordination might be made even more powerful and depictive within the frame of such a synthesis.

While I am on the subject of terminology, there is a very subtle change of meaning that affects the dominant terminology of this study. Early on, we are given rhetoric which moves through time in certain ways. But then, following that section—and on the same page — we are given rhetoric as work comprised of "moves" through an ideological constellation. The move (forgive me) is from the dynamic through the strategic. I don't mean to suggest that anything sinister is going on here. In fact, if I haven't said so explicitly, I find the intricacy of "moves" in tense and *dispositio* detected here to be nothing short of masterful. My only point is that the predilection toward the strategic in "Checkers" (which this writer interprets as "moves" in a game) may overdetermine the analysis toward the "evasion" hypothesis, while under-emphasizing other relevant factors.

Here I am again coming painfully close to a certain empathy for Nixon. So I'll just come to the point. I think that greater emphasis upon a figurative dimension to the speech — what Bakhtin would call its voice(s), tone, key focus, the way unlikely tropes, synecdoches and anecdotes are forced and hurled together — might strengthen the very perceptive points this essay already makes. Of course Professor Condit does not find much of stylistic interest here, calling the speech "devoid of stylistic grace and elegance." I cannot but agree. And it is her intent to look in an exterior direction toward an historical issue rather than to gaze too deeply inward upon the dark night of this Gothic personality. Here I can hardly blame her. But I would argue, just for fun really, that the intersection of *kairos* and the figurative domain might actually help to answer one of Professor Condit's major questions: Why have we become obsessed with private qualities while simultaneously denying and distorting equitable public speech?

Given the de-emphasis of a figurative dimension in Nixon's "Checkers game," I find it interesting that the two figurative allusions for which the speech became most famous get little attention in Professor Condit's study. The first is the "respectable Republican cloth coat" allusion, which follows Nixon's painfully detailed recitation of his personal financial history, and which is designed to dramatize his party identification with the common man. There is not really much to the figure, so I can understand why Professor Condit does not pursue it. But recall that this figure is followed by that "old smoothie" Nixon turning to his wife (whose smile is frozen in place) and saying "and I always tell her that [pause] she'd look good in anything...." Invariably, some wag in the Majestic audience would yell out, "How about a prison uniform?" We were a cruel bunch. Anyway, this is a nice example of third person, depersonalized reference, or "the wife as inartistic proof." Sometimes, as I watch Pat Nixon return that same frozen smile to her husband, I imagine that—were she possessed of, say, Carrie's telekinetic gifts—there would be nothing left behind the desk on camera but a vapor trail.

This transcendent figurative moment is followed by one even more famous: the Checkers anecdote. I am making the assumption here that when a conspicuous public figure offers a conspicuous anecdote to encapsulate his discourse, then that anecdote becomes figurative—for the character of the speech, perhaps even for the character of the person giving the speech. I realize that this view runs counter to Professor Condit's view of the anecdote. She regards the anecdote as primarily diversionary, a distraction designed to deflect attention from the aforementioned third claim of special interest favoritism. This actually allows each of our views to be sustained without contradiction. If, in fact, this anecdote succeeds in encapsulating the discourse and the character of the speaker, as I have suggested, then it could be argued that Professor Condit is right: it also succeeded in distracting everyone from the flimsiness of Nixon's third claim.

I don't want to question whether this story might have a diversionary function, but rather whether this function exhausts the significance of the tale. After all, Professor Condit cites Stephen Ambrose's testimony that "a majority of the audience found the speech objectionable, if not nauseating. In the years that followed, one never heard Republicans bring it up, while Democrats quoted it to one another gleefully." I doubt that this existential repulsion and political reversal is due solely to Nixon's elusiveness with the facts.

So let us look briefly to the figurative anecdote itself. Recall that Nixon moves directly to this tale from the "cloth coat" anecdote. His transition is, "There is one other thing I should probably tell you about, because if I don't, they'll probably be saying that about me too." Nixon continues with the now familiar story. The radio interview with Pat, where an anonymous benefactor from Texas learned that the children wanted a pet dog. A package arrived at the Baltimore train station. Nixon lingers lovingly over the cocker spaniel's features, floppy ears and black and white spots. (Contrast this, if you will, with "My wife is a wonderful stenographer.") Then, the long-awaited punch line: "And, you know, the children, like all children, love the dog, and I just want to say this right now, no matter what they say, we're going to keep him."

Very clearly, this is intended to be a kind of figurative *reductio.* Where will my anonymous and evil tormentors draw the line? My family? My dog? Do they have no shame, no sense of decency? Of course, that is not exactly how history has treated the anecdote or its perpetrator. To see why, I thought it might be useful to turn to the clearest rhetorical antecedent to Nixon's tale, the much more effective and ingenious "Falla" story told by Franklin Roosevelt.

While not everyone has heard the story, probably everyone is familiar with its theme. At the height of his wartime popularity, and in the midst of the 1944 election campaign, rumors circulated that the four-term President had sent a destroyer to one of the Aleutian islands to pick up his dog, Falla. This was apparently supposed to symbolize the President's aristocratic heritage, his growing monarchical air. Before a frenzied audience of labor partisans, the President replied. He said: "These Republican leaders have not been content with attacks on me, or on my wife, or on my sons. No, not content with that. They now include my little dog, 'Falla.' Now of course, I do not resent these attacks, and my family don't resent these attacks. But Falla does resent these attacks." Roosevelt went on to point out that, since Falla was a scottie, his little scottish soul was furious at the cost involved. FDR's masterful bit of impish humor was delivered only eight years before Nixon's own speech in the midst of yet another war. The similarity of subject and purported intent could hardly have been accidental.

But there the resemblance ends. And a simple glance at the figurative qualities will show us why. Roosevelt's persona soars so far above the battle that he is inclined to introduce the voice of his own dog to respond. And note, the dog will not even stoop to respond. He merely "resents" these charges. I would suggest that here righteous indignation has been repaid with the ultimate humorous indignity. In this light, consider Nixon. Until this moment, all of his aggressiveness has taken the form of baring his soul, opening his own business to the intrusive gaze of others. Now, he comes charging forward, putting character on the line for the family dog. Here, in other words, his own public voice finally invests itself and is lowered in consequence. There is one other difference. Roosevelt delivered his feisty polemic in the midst of an army of working class supporters. They rolled in the aisles at his every winking aside. Nixon delivers his strangely somber "vindication" before a vast silent television studio. When he pauses during the "Checkers" story, the silence is almost deafening.

The *reductio,* in other words, at least appears to turn inward. "Checkers" inaugurates for us the Nixon whose characteristic pattern has been to deconstruct and mutilate himself so completely as to career toward nihilism, only then to stop abruptly and blame the whole grotesque result upon his nameless opponents. They'd had enough? Or stop, stop — I'm killing me. We find it in the rueful comment, "You won't have Nixon to kick around anymore," in the Watergate tapes, in giving them the "sword," in his own memorable words. In that book about Watergate, Nixon variously wrote about his nameless opponents as vultures, searching for whatever meat was left on the bones, or as trying to exact the last pound of flesh. He avowed that he would not give it to them. But he always has. Thus the vindication becomes a kind of continual monologic confession.

This is all a way of saying that I politely and genially disagree with Professor Condit's rendering of the figuration in this discourse, particularly with respect to Checkers. But the difference of opinion helps to prove her larger point. I don't see Checkers as "reassert (ing) some limits around the disclosure of privacy — children are off limits." After all, this man has just invited us through his financial history, his checking accounts and mortgage records, his wife's wardrobe. He wants to stay on the ticket that badly. He is going to stop with a dog? He's already used children and dogs as emotional proof. The boundaries have already been crossed, the sacrifice rendered. By the time Nixon reaches this stage of the accounting, it has become apparent to everyone that Richard Nixon would have eaten Checkers smothered in barbecue sauce if it would have helped him become Vice President.

I am greatly in sympathy with the larger theme of Professor Condit's analysis, but only want to suggest that the terminology of *logos* and figuration might enhance its appreciation. Timing, figuration, and movement of inference all come together in the individuated quality of the discourse as a whole, in its unique character as *utterance.* That is why the central problem, encircled and finally violated by Nixon's entire discourse is that of *propriety.*

The choices of voice and tone, as well as the disposition of time and inference, are responsible for the primary differences between "Checkers" and my own little analogue. FDR could wave off opponents and rumors and soar forever above the battle; Richard Nixon came to inhabit and finally even caricature "the maudlin self."

Professor Condit is correct, I think, in noting a disturbing new equivalency between the loss of representative public voices in media channels and the erosion of elite distinctions between private and public self. This is a curious mutation of the mass society, which I do not think can be explained entirely by the failure to address questions of free speech early on. Bakhtin introduced the notion of "carnival" to describe an earlier, but, I think reminiscent, form of encounter-setting. He wrote that the breakdown of distinctions: "... created during carnival time a special type of communication impossible in everyday life. This led to the creation of special forms of marketplace speech and gesture, frank and free, permitting no distance between those who came in contact with each other and liberating (them) from norms of etiquette and decency imposed at other times."[1]

Governed as we are by "smiling billboards," while aroused citizenry debate the true meaning of the cultural figure *bimbo* on the Morton Downey show, it seems that television has given us a "carnival" peculiarly appropriate for late Capitalism. I would not pretend to have this form of life figured out. But it is interesting that Bakhtin himself does not consider the "carnival" to be a completely bleak condition. In the relaxation of constraints, there sometimes is a new mystery to be found. I am not convinced that secrecy and disclosure are rhetorical forms either. But whatever they are, Nixon's own maudlin self must be considered a strange case. Here, after all, is a figure whose compulsive bursts of further and further disclosure only serve to provoke greater mystery.

But lest I get carried away (perhaps literally), we might remind ourselves that in an age of "carnival" the maudlin self can never be heroic. But if not heroic, what? Whether Checkers is a game or Checkers is a puppy-dog, the quality they have in common answers our question. It is a spirit of play; is it not?

---

[1]Mikhail Bakhtin, *Rabelais and His World*, trans. Helene Iswolsky (Cambridge: Cambridge University Press, 1968), p. 10.

III

EPILOGUE

EPILOGUE
THE ORATORICAL TEXT:
THE ENIGMA OF ARRIVAL

DILIP PARAMESHWAR GAONKAR

If there is one sentiment this conference volume unequivocally announces, it is the arrival of textual studies in rhetorical criticism and its substantive twin, public address. Five of the six formal papers and the corresponding critical responses deal with a single speech text and attempt to render what is known as a "close reading." Moreover, the untranscribed discussion that followed the presentation of papers at the conference centrally revolved around the theme of textual studies. Even when other important themes emerged in the course of discussions — the constitutive function of rhetoric (Ivie/Brummett), polysemy and critical pluralism (Campbell/Linkugel and Rowland), the temporal dimensions of oratory (Condit/Farrell), the need to rethink the concept of rhetorical effect (Browne/Lucaites), and the oratorical refigurations of ideology (Cox/Hariman) — each of these themes, demanding and deserving attention on their own, came to be mediated through a general preoccupation with the nature and function of oratorical text. Apparently, then, this volume participates in a trend towards textual studies identified and endorsed in recent essays by Michael Leff and Stephen Lucas.[1]

Since the arrival of the oratorical text was at the center of the conference, I will begin by exploring the enigma of its arrival, an arrival long in the making. Then, having set the papers in this volume in a disciplinary context, I will turn to the papers themselves. In this second part of my essay, I hope to identify some of the critical issues that emerge from this effort to place the text at the center of attention.

---

[1]Michael C. Leff, "Textual Criticism: The Legacy of G.P. Mohrmann," *QJS* 72 (1986): 377-389; Stephen E. Lucas, "The Renaissance of American Public Address: Text and Context in Rhetorical Criticism," *QJS* 74 (1988): 241-260.

THE FUGITIVE TEXT:
RESISTANCE AND DEFERRAL

Resistance to the Text

There has been considerable resistance against taking the oratorical text seriously. In 1957, W. Charles Redding issued a call for textual studies in public address, but it went largely unheeded.[2] Thus, thirty years later, Lucas, while noting a significant recent trend towards textual studies, was hard pressed to identify more than a handful of clear instances of "close reading" of speech texts,[3] and Medhurst's survey of Ph.D. dissertations (reported in this volume) underscores Lucas's point. Under the circumstances, it is safe to assume that there has been some sort of operant resistance — theoretical, methodological, and possibly ideological — that has stubbornly kept students of public address from "getting into" or "getting close to" their texts. Conversely, if textual studies now appear to be a developing trend, as this volume indicates, it is safe to assume that practicing critics have found ways to reduce, or at least confront, this resistance. Further, one might assume that in diminishing this resistance, critics must have re-conceived the oratorical text, and in the process, invested it with new commitments — theoretical, methodological, and possibly ideological — that could alter the shape and substance of the critical enterprise itself.

In any case, the status of the oratorical text has changed dramatically. Once upon a time, it was denied claims to "permanence and beauty" (Wichelns), described as consisting of "aphoristic crumbs" that sustain the popular mind (Wrage), and ascribed a certain kind of thematic and (by implication) ideological simplicity and transparency (Baskerville).[4] Now Leff invites us to view

---

[2]W. Charles Redding, "Extrinsic and Intrinsic Criticism," *Western Speech* 21 (1957): 96-103. A revised version of this essay is reprinted under the same title in *Essays on Rhetorical Criticism* ed. Thomas R. Nilsen (New York: Random House, 1968), 98-125.

[3]Lucas, "Renaissance of American Public Address," 259, endnote 44.

[4]Herbert A. Wichelns, "The Literary Criticism of Oratory," in *Studies in Rhetoric and Public Speaking in Honor of James Albert Winans* (New York: Century, 1925), 181-216; Ernest J. Wrage, "Public Address: A Study in Social and Intellectual History," *QJS* 33 (1947): 451-457; Barnet Baskerville, "The Critical Method in Speech," *Central States Speech Journal* 4 (July, 1953): 1-5.

oratorical texts, at least the "masterpieces," as products of a
temporal art form, however ephemeral those products. For Lucas,
the oratorical text is a primary site where the historical constraints
and linguistic practices of a particular world intersect and are
inscribed. For Karlyn Campbell, another distinguished practitioner
of textual studies, the oratorical text represents and embodies the
reflexive self-sufficiency of an originary rhetorical/critical act.[5]

Thus, it would seem that the oratorical text has come a long
way, journeying through the vicissitudes of our disciplinary
consciousness, and in the course of that journey, it has been
transformed from the fugitive flotsam and jetsam of popular
chatter into an autonomous cultural form. This transformation is
not an accident. It is not a sudden and unexpected lifting of the
conceptual fog and an immediate recognition of the proper object
of critical study that was always already there. On the contrary,
the discovery of the oratorical text is a decidedly ideological
moment (no less so than the enunciation of the neo-Aristotelian
paradigm during the infancy of our discipline), an arrival carefully
choreographed and anticipated in the metacritical writings of some
of our leading critics—Black, Campbell, Leff, Lucas, and the late
Professor Mohrmann.

The long delay in the arrival of textual studies requires some
explanation. Lucas says the delay is "nothing short of astonishing."
"How can it be," he laments, "that we are in our seventh decade
as an academic discipline and have yet to produce a body of rich
critical literature providing authoritative textual studies of...ac-
knowledged masterpieces."[6] But Lucas is being somewhat coy.
Everyone is by now familiar with the classic diagnosis and
explanation which originated with Redding, the first of the
"textualists," and which later critics, including Lucas himself, have
adopted in variant forms.

As a contributor to the 1957 *Western Speech* symposium on
"Criticism and Public Address," Redding asked the following
question: "Is it possible that rhetorical scholars have too often
moved out of rather than more deeply into their own subject?" For

[5]Karlyn K. Campbell, "The Nature of Criticism in Rhetorical and Communication
Studies," *Central States Speech Journal* 30 (1979): 4-13.
[6]Lucas, "Renaissance of American Public Address," 247.

Redding, delving more deeply into the subject meant "getting into" or giving a "close reading" of an oratorical text. Redding laments—the lament being the dominant genre of meta-critical discourse in our field—that rhetorical critics, unlike their innovative literary counterparts (that is, the "New Critics"), do not take hold of the text. They fly from it into the biographical and historical context ("about three-fourths of the space is typically devoted to historical and biographical information, with sometimes as little as one-tenth allotted to rhetorical analysis of speeches"), and if ever they return to the text after their exhaustive entanglement with the context, it is only surface encounter.[7]

Redding also offers an explanation for this marginalization of the text. He goes back to the source—Wichelns' inaugural essay, "The Literary Criticism of Oratory" (1925)—the essay that "literally created the modern discipline of rhetorical criticism."[8] The story Redding traces from this origin is now a well established part of professional lore, but, to follow the course of my argument, it requires yet another brief restatement here: Wichelns was attempting to secure for rhetorical criticism an identity separate from its literary counterpart, a task made urgent by the disciplinary politics of legitimating the newly established Speech Departments. In an often quoted passage, Wichelns explains that speech criticism is unique because it is concerned neither with "beauty" nor "permanence", but with effect. That is, the critic ought to regard the speech as "a communication to a specific audience," and his or her proper business is "the analysis and appreciation of the orator's method of imparting...ideas" to a specific audience.[9] In developing this position, Wichelns adopts pretty much the same strategy Hudson had employed two years earlier in specifying the boundaries of rhetoric by contrasting it with poetry.[10] In short, Hudson and Wichelns offer a conception of oratory as "the art of influencing men in some concrete situation" and of the orator as a "public man...influencing the men of his time by the power of his

---

[7]Redding, "Extrinsic and Intrinsic Criticism," 100.
[8]Mark S. Klyn, "Toward a Pluralistic Rhetorical Criticism," *Essays on Rhetorical Criticism,* 154.
[9]Wichelns, "Literary Criticism of Oratory," 209.
[10]Hoyt H. Hudson, "The Field of Rhetoric," *The Quarterly Journal of Speech Education* 9 (1923): 177.

discourse."[11] From such a perspective, speeches are fully intelligible only when placed in their immediate social and historical context. Therefore, critics must reconstruct the immediate context as best they can in order to judge the efficacy of the speech. As Wichelns puts it in another memorable phrase, the critic must "summon history to the aid of criticism."[12]

How Wichelns' inaugural essay came to be transformed from a provisional effort into a rigidly codified methodology and how that methodology prompted mechanical and unimaginative critical studies is a tale of woe told many times, and not without glee by later scholars. The tale is usually told by stringing together a series of striking but disconcerting phrases from leading authorities that depress the field to supplementary status as hand-maiden to history. The most chilling of such torn phrases belongs to Marie Hochmuth Nichols as she asks with utmost humility: "What are the historians doing that may well be supplemented by the work of the rhetoricians?"[13] Oratory, thus, fades into the master narrative of history.

What is central to Redding's diagnosis, a diagnosis generally upheld by later scholars, is the claim that the oratorical text came to be marginalized as a direct consequence of slavish adherence to a faulty theory and an equally faulty methodology. What Redding did not consider was the nature of the object studied. Perhaps the oratorical text itself resisted and repelled close reading, or at least it did so as long as one adhered to traditional views concerning its nature and function. In any case, efforts to revise neo-Aristotelianism proved that a mere change in theory and method was insufficient to solve the problem.

The Deferral of the Text

As is well-known, the faulty theory was replaced by a plethora of competing theories, all of them generally committed to the view of rhetoric as "symbolic inducement," a notion so enlarged that it could encompass virtually any theoretical stance—constructivist,

---

[11]Wichelns, "Literary Criticism of Oratory," 212-13.

[12]Wichelns, "Literary Criticism of Oratory," 199.

[13]Marie Hochmuth Nichols, *Rhetoric and Criticism* (Baton Rouge: Louisiana State University Press, 1963), 25.

phenomenological, hermeneutical, structuralist, dramatistic, or whatever. And the monistic methodology gave way to a nearly unanimous endorsement of "methodological pluralism," with everyone blithely citing Burke's dictum that a critic should "use all that is there to use" in making a critical object intelligible.[14] And yet, despite this proliferation of theories and methods, the day of the text did not arrive.

This deferral of the text is evident as one reviews the efforts to revise the conceptual bases of rhetorical criticism. In this essay, I cannot pursue all of the developments that followed from the reaction to neo-Aristotelianism, but two important positions illustrate the problem clearly—the "history of ideas" approach sponsored by Wrage and his students, and Black's seminal effort to construct an alternative frame of reference.

Wrage's revisionist program clearly subordinates the text. In his essay, "Public Address: A Study in Social and Intellectual History" (1947), Wrage takes a functionalist view of public address and privileges the "ideational content" of speeches: "Public address does not exist for its own sake...its value is instrumental.... The basic ingredient of a speech is content. The transmission of this content is its legitimate function. It is a vehicle for the conveyance of ideas."[15] Wrage asserts (in yet another attempt to legitimate our discipline) that a study of public address can "contribute in substantial ways to the history of ideas,"[16] since an intellectual history exclusively devoted to "monumental works" and to tracing the influence of ideas from one major thinker to the next is "hopelessly inadequate as a way of discovering and assessing those ideas which find expression in the market place."[17] The social life of ideas in contention is best understood by attending to what Wrage calls "fugitive literature", of which the public speech is an important species.

In a fundamental sense, Wrage remains within the neo-Aristotelian framework, since he regards speeches as situated

---

[14]Kenneth Burke, *The Philosophy of Literary Form* rev. ed. (New York: Vintage Press, 1957), 21.

[15]Wrage, "Public Address," 453.

[16]Wrage, "Public Address," 453.

[17]Wrage, "Public Address," 451.

discourses. But he extends the notion of "rhetorical influence" (much as Lucaites invites us to do in his response to Browne) by treating the oration as a nexus in the struggle and evolution of ideas. This extension requires a shift in critical focus from a "speaker-centered" to an "idea-centered" orientation.

Nevertheless, the resistance to the text not only persists, but now becomes a conscious part of the critical program. For Wrage, the speech text has no intrinsic interest.[18] A speech is merely a document for deciphering the configuration of ideas struggling to shape the public mind and sensibility. Wrage frequently refers to oratory as a "mirror." James Aune, in the essay included in this volume, suggests that the root metaphor that informs Wrage's perspective is that of a "window."[19] This is not the place to run through the conflicting implications of the two metaphors, the "mirror" and the "window," but in either case, oratory becomes a passive entity or site. The oratorical text is not a central locus in the struggle of ideas, but a "mirror" that reflects (or a "window" that overlooks) the struggle taking place somewhere else. Wrage does not appear to be interested in the mode of articulation and textualization of the struggle of ideas manifested in the oration itself. Orations are fugitive spaces only fleetingly inhabited by the true protagonists in Wrage's scheme—the ideas themselves.

The text is equally neglected by Wrage's two most prominent students, Barnet Baskerville and Thomas Nilsen. Baskerville's "transparency thesis" downplays the interpretive function of the rhetorical critic: "Speeches are seldom abstruse or esoteric (as poems and novels sometimes are). A speech by its very nature is, or should be, immediately comprehensible; hence the interpretive function of the critic is seldom paramount."[20] The deferral of the text persists in Nilsen, even as he attempts to correct Baskerville's rather narrow view of interpretation.[21] The interpretive function

---

[18]He sometimes refers to the study of public address as a supplement to the "intellectual history" proper.

[19]James Arnt Aune, "Public Address and Rhetorical Theory," in *Texts in Context: Dialogues on Significant Episodes in American Political Rhetoric* ed. Michael C. Leff & Fred J. Kauffeld (Davis, CA: Hermagoras Press, 1989), 43-51.

[20]Baskerville, "Critical Method in Speech," 1-2.

[21]Thomas R. Nilsen, "Interpretive Function of the Critic," *Western Speech* 21 (1957): 70-76. A revised version of this essay is reprinted in *Essays on Rhetorical Criticism,* 86-97.

that Nilsen ascribes to the rhetorical critic uses the speech text as a
mere point of departure. Nilsen's critic looks for and evaluates
(from a decidedly liberal point of view) larger patterns of thought
and action, such as the conceptions of man, society, and ideas
implicit in a given speech. Even Croft's discerning essay, "The
Functions of Rhetorical Criticism" (1956), does not break from
this cycle of deferring from the text.[22]

A more complex case arises when we turn to Edwin Black's
Rhetorical Criticism, A Study in Method (1965), perhaps the single
most important work in the revisionist tradition. In some important
respects, the book anticipates the emergence of textual criticism as
it is now practiced. Black demonstrates a command of and
sensitivity to the texts he studies and attends to them more
carefully than most other critics of the period. Moreover, his
efforts to deepen the interpretative function of rhetorical criticism
and his arguments for the use of "touchstones" in critical judgment
seem to focus attention on particular discourses. Nevertheless, in
this book, Black does not place the text at the center of the critical
enterprise. In the final chapters, where he sketches "an alternative
frame of reference," he moves decidedly in the direction of larger
discursive formations such as exhortation and argumentation, and
the critical studies found in the book do not rest in the study of
particular texts but tend to deal with texts as symptomatic of more
general rhetorical tendencies.

This point is clearly illustrated in what is perhaps the most
often cited section of the book—the critique of John Jay
Chapman's "Coatesville Address." This speech is notable because
of its previous obscurity; delivered to an audience of three in an
abandoned grocery store, the address commemorates the anniversary
of the brutal lynching of a Negro. While Black cites Chapman's
text in its entirety and interprets it in a way that keeps the text
before the reader's consciousness, his comments do not enter the
text in order to follow its internal dynamics, and thus his analysis
is quite different from the "close reading" practiced by recent
textual critics. Black rarely makes use of the text except for
negative purposes—to demonstrate why the neo-Aristotelian canons

---

[22]Albert J. Croft, "The Functions of Rhetorical Criticism," *QJS* 42 (1956):
283-291.

cannot account for its "strange and moving power." In fact, Black's positive thesis—that the speech seeks to shape our perception of the lynching as "ritual murder"—is secured without reference to the internal workings of the text. And his remarks on the significance of the speech conclude with a shocking revelation drawn from Chapman's biography. Only four years after delivering this plea for tolerance and humanity, Chapman, broken by the death of his son, gave vent to anti-German, anti-Catholic, and anti-Semitic prejudices, and "half mad, sank into death, hating."[23] This sort of endnote is not meant to hold the critic or the reader within the text; it takes us inexorably into the vicissitudes of the psyche and through the psyche into the culture that produces such an ambivalent character. So Black's critique quickly soars beyond the text as it locates the proper context for the discourse, a context that joins "a dialogue participated in by Jefferson, Tocqueville, Lincoln, Melville, Henry Adams, Samuel Clemens, and Faulkner—a dialogue on the moral dimensions of the American experience.... The context of the Coatesville address is less a specific place than a culture."[24] The quarrel with neo-Aristotelianism here is not so much a quarrel about the direct reading of the text as it is about establishing the proper context for judgment.

My point, of course, is not to object to Black's reading nor to complain about his critical perspective. Even the proponents of "close reading" would not do so, since as staunch pluralists they have never suggested that their approach constitutes the only path to good criticism. But the facts of the case here are important as a matter of disciplinary history. Black is an astute critic, highly sensitive to the nuances of the texts he studies. Nevertheless, his commentary on the Coatesville address quickly spins outward to its larger cultural context, and thereafter, his book turns to broader questions of theory and method and to more general discursive formations. Surely, these facts are testimony to the persistent resistance which the rhetorical text presented to the critic and the way that the early revisionist effort subordinated interest in the text to relatively abstract issues of theory and method.

---

[23]Edwin Black, *Rhetorical Criticism: A Study in Method* (Madison, WI: University of Wisconsin Press, 1978, 1965), 90.
[24]Black, *Rhetorical Criticism,* 83-84.

Thirteen years after the publication of the book, on the occasion of its re-printing, Black himself seems to acknowledge this point: "Behind the composition of *Rhetorical Criticism, A Study in Method* was an idea too dimly understood by its author to possess the book as firmly as it would if the book were to be written now. That idea is that critical method is too personally expressive to be systematized."[25] The emphasis here falls on the critic, but it obviously also entails a concentration on the process of reading that centers on the text itself. In an essay written a few years later, Black expands on this perspective, but by then the textual turn already had begun, and Black's position must be seen against a somewhat different background.

The Origins of Textual Criticism

This brief survey of the critical literature from Wichelns to Black indicates how the text seemed to resist critical inquiry under the historicist presuppositions of neo-Aristotelianism and how the theoretical concerns of later critics tended to defer interest in the text. But by the beginning of this decade a notable shift was apparent. A number of critics, grappling with traditional problems, had come to regard the text as the focal element in rhetorical criticism and had begun efforts to justify and explain this orientation. The origin and character of this effort is important as background to the studies contained in this volume.

About the year 1980 a remarkable coincidence of interest in the text emerges from inquiry into three distinct problems in the tradition: the fit between theory and practice in criticism, the apparent tension between historical and critical inquiry in public address studies, and the continuing concern about characterizing the rhetorical act itself.

The first of these concerns surfaces in a special issue of *The Western Journal of Speech Communication* published in 1981 as a sequel to a 1957 symposium on rhetorical criticism. The problem of the relationship between critical theory and critical practice emerges in an interesting way as one reads through the issue as a whole. In the opening essay, after reviewing publications in two

---

[25]Black, *Rhetorical Criticism*, x.

national and four regional journals over five years (1975-1979), Mohrmann concludes that the advent of new critical theories still had failed to bring critics into closer contact with their object of study: "In the earlier use of tradition, the critic is a circuit rider, forever circling around and about the herd, but never getting into its center. Yet if this critic seldom takes us into the text of the speech and its workings, the pretense in the contemporary adaptations and departures is no more satisfying."[26] Thus, in Mohrmann's judgment, the lack of fit between critical principles and practical criticism remained as notable in the heady days following the demise of neo-Aristotelianism as it did under the old regime.

In another essay, Edwin Black makes a more general argument concerning the theory/practice issue. Drawing on the work of linguist Kenneth Pike, Black distinguishes between two approaches to criticism:

> ...the theoretic or etic viewpoint, which approaches a rhetorical transaction from outside of that transaction and interprets the transaction in terms of a pre-existing theory: and the non-theoretic or nominalistic or emic viewpoint, which approaches a rhetorical transaction in what is hoped to be its own terms, without conscious expectation drawn from any sources other than the rhetorical transaction itself.[27]

Black clearly favors the emic approach grounded in the rhetorical transaction (or text), especially in the interpretive phase of criticism. He notes that the theory-driven etic approach "tends much more to be a confirmation than an inquiry...(and) is continually attended by the fallacy of question-begging."[28] In short, the deferral of the text is what vitiates the etic approach and the theory-driven studies that result from it.

In the essay that concludes the symposium, Leff develops and reinterprets Black's distinction between the etic and emic approaches and offers a proto-theoretical formulation in defense of textual studies. Leff accounts for the persistent deferral of the text

---

[26]G.P. Mohrmann, "Elegy in a Critical Grave-Yard," *Western Journal of Speech Communication* 44 (1980): 272.

[27]Edwin Black, "A Note on Theory and Practice in Rhetorical Criticism," *Western Journal of Speech Communication* 44 (1980): 331-32.

[28]Black, "Note on Theory and Practice," 333.

not in terms of excesses of etic theoreticism but rather as an unfortunate consequence of the bad fit between rhetorical theory and critical practice. Following the psychoanalytic analogy proposed by Black and combining it with the ethnographic analogy suggested by Geertz, Leff characterizes the interpretive process involved in criticism in terms of something that might be called an emic "theory of the case." This is a conception of theory that "functions not to generalize to or from cases, but within them."[29] Leff's reasoning is too complicated to be unpacked here, but it clearly makes the text the primary site of mediation between rhetorical theory and critical practice:

> Extrinsic principles do not resolve the problem of how to interpret a subject, but subjects do not interpret themselves. The act of interpretation mediates between the experience of the critic and the forms of experience expressed in the text. To perform this act successfully, critics must vibrate what they see in the text against their own expectation and predilections.[30]

Just about the time Leff was offering the text as the site of mediation between rhetorical theory and critical practice, Lucas was attempting to resolve the growing tension between the proponents of "rhetorical history" and the proponents of "rhetorical criticism" by recourse to the text.[31] Lucas dismisses the schism between the two as artificial and self-defeating. History and criticism cannot go their separate ways because the oratorical text and its context are inextricably intertwined. Through an analysis of Thomas Paine's *Common Sense,* Lucas shows the futility of either writing a rhetorical history of the text without a careful analysis of its internal structure and dynamics, or of composing such an internal critique without some grasp of the historical context. While Lucas' argument is too detailed and too fastidiously documented to be summarized here, it is clear that he privileges the text as the point of mediation between the competing claims of historical understanding and critical evaluation. If he is less explicit and emphatic about the centrality of the text than is Leff, there is

---

[29]Michael C. Leff, "Interpretation and the Art of the Rhetorical Critic," *Western Journal of Speech Communication* 44 (1980): 347.
[30]Leff, "Interpretation," 345.
[31]Stephen E. Lucas, "The Schism in Rhetorical Scholarship," *QJS* 67 (1981): 1-20.

little doubt that his argument moves in much the same direction.

Finally, Karlyn Campbell contributes to this "textual turn" in rhetorical criticism not only through her specific studies of important texts, but also by developing a kind of ontological justification for the enterprise. In her essay "The Nature of Criticism in Rhetorical and Communication Studies" (1979), she indicates some of the complexities involved in defining the object of our study as we proceed from "speaker-centered" to "idea-centered" to "text-centered" studies. Campbell claims that criticism, and by implication rhetorical criticism, is an autonomous activity. She advances two arguments on behalf of that claim. First, she presents a general argument that characterizes human beings as "symbol using animals" reflexively equipped with a critical impulse. Second, in an argument more relevant to our present concerns, Campbell derives the autonomy of rhetorical criticism from the autonomy of its objects, be they rhetorical acts, events, or transactions.[32] Thus, by positing rhetorical acts as self-grounded entities she is able to secure the autonomy of rhetorical criticism itself. Since texts are generally the sole material traces of bygone rhetorical actions and events, this mode of reasoning also leads to the privileging of the text, especially in practical criticism.

Such is the extraordinary convergence of ideas of some of our leading critics around 1980 that prepared the way for the arrival of the oratorical text. Now that it is here, what are we to do with it? For some hints and directions, we now turn to the essays in the present volume.

TEXTS IN CONTEXT

Since each of the papers in this volume has received adequate consideration from the assigned respondents, I will confine my remarks to general/theoretical issues raised by the conference as a whole, especially as those issues relate to the status of textual criticism and its implications. Two major areas seem to command attention. The first has to do with the changing status of theory itself as critical interest focuses on particular texts rather than on the discovery and organization of abstract theoretical principles.

---

[32]Campbell, "The Nature of Criticism," 5.

The second leads us into a more complex set of issues that follow
from the way the textual turn upsets traditional assumptions about
the relationship between texts and contexts. The textual turn
clearly implies greater autonomy for public address than does the
traditional conception, but far from abandoning interest in the
context, textual criticism may serve to complicate and enrich our
capacity to understand the interaction between texts and contexts.
Two complications of this sort seem to emerge from the conference,
and I will consider both: by opening rhetorical criticism to the
concept of polysemy, we might deepen our sense of the dynamic
relationship between public address and its ideological background
and by attending to the integrity of the text as a field of discursive
action, we might actually enhance our understanding of the non-
discursive background that surrounds and informs the text.

Against Theory

The proceedings at the conference evinced a marked indif-
ference, if not hostility, towards theory. This is evident in Robert
Scott's foreword. He invites a putative rhetorical critic to operate
from within the rich and somewhat inconsistent rhetorical tradition
that is "well over two thousand years old" rather than from within
the narrow confines of a single theory. For Scott the term "theory"
evokes (even in its "rather common and benign uses") negative
associations: the aura of a formula, the algorithmic lust, Cicero's
idle, talkative Greeklings, cooptation into the "knowledge industry,"
and mechanical reproduction. In contrast, the "tradition" evokes
all the right associations and even its inconsistency is viewed as its
"glory": "What we may call the tradition of rhetoric is many-
voiced, many-valued, and directed towards many ends."[33] Thus,
Scott recommends that we draw upon this richly pluralistic
tradition while negotiating our critical objects rather than subject
them to alien and reductive theories.

In a similar vein, Martin Medhurst takes issue with Roderick
Hart's insistence that conceptual innovation and theory construction
are an integral part of the critical enterprise. In a wide-ranging

---

[33]Robert L. Scott, "Against Rhetorical Theory: Tripping to Serendip," *Texts in
Context,* 1-9.

critique issued in 1986, Hart argues that contemporary public address scholarship needs to move beyond its preoccupation with immediate data towards some sort of general theoretical understanding—and hence, the critic should be "concerned insistently and exclusively with the *conceptual record*" as opposed to a "complete historical record."[34] Medhurst's brief response is one of exasperation which sharply dismisses Hart's position as being utterly out of date: "To insist only on theory-based or theory generative studies is to be playing Cardinal Barberini in the age of Galileo."[35] This spirit seemed to pervade the conference as a whole. Its ethos was generally one of overwhelming fatigue with theory that finally provoked Aune to complain against unwarranted "theory bashing," a complaint that went without sympathetic response from the participants.

What is more telling, however, is the attitude towards theory displayed in the critical essays. Only Robert Ivie attempts to ground his essay in a fairly explicit theoretical framework, specifically a framework derived from Kenneth Burke's writings on metaphor and motive. And only Ivie negotiates a discursive formation ("Johnson Administration's Vietnam War Rhetoric") of greater scope than a single speech text. The remaining five critics go about their business without anchoring their approach within any specific theoretical position. Nor is there any conscious attempt to view the oratorical text as a site of mediation between rhetorical theory and critical practice. The critical focus is on the particular text itself, even when, as in the case of both Cox and Condit, it is viewed as symptomatic of a larger ideological configuration. However, this is not to suggest that the essays are devoid of conceptual interest or influence. Condit explores the implications of Jurgen Habermas' notion of "civil privatism" while charting the internal dynamics of Nixon's "Checkers Speech". Stephen Browne's notion of "rhetorical judgment" has a discernible

[34]Roderick P. Hart, "Contemporary Scholarship in Public Address: A Research Editorial," *Western Journal of Speech Communication,* 50 (1986): 284.

[35]Martin J. Medhurst, "Public Address and Significant Scholarship: Challenges of the Rhetorical Renaissance," *Texts in Context,* 29-42.

affinity to Ronald Beiner's views on "political judgment."[36] Browne, in fact, finds in Edmund Burke's "Speech on Conciliation" an extended discursive manifestation of what Beiner would regard as an exemplary enunciation of "political judgment." Cox displays a command of the interdisciplinary literature on "time and temporality," especially as they relate to the narrative flow of discourse. Among the respondents, Tom Farrell imaginatively invokes Bakhtin, and Linkugel and Rowland draw on the literature concerning myth. Thus, we may safely assume that the textual orientation does not necessarily lead to conceptual insularity. At the same time, these critics are not subservient to an alien conceptual scheme. Condit does not offer a Habermasian reading; nor does Browne offer a Beinerian reading. One of the distinctive achievements of these essays is that abstract notions, such as "civil privatism," "rhetorical judgment," and "temporality," are richly instantiated through the readings. The abstract concepts acquire a certain density as they are made to journey through the text.

In the long run, this mode of discursively grounding abstract notions may have significant theoretical implications. The essays in this volume, despite their implied reluctance to theorize, may be pointing in the direction anticipated by Black and Leff. Though none of the authors explicitly address this issue, the thickening of concepts through grounded critical readings has serious implications for "concept formation," a prerequisite for theory construction. Therefore, if textual studies become dominant in our field, which is a distinct possibility, they are likely to reconfigure the relationship between rhetorical theory and critical practice rather than simply "marginalize" theory.

Polysemy and Critical Pluralism

Critical pluralism continued its unassailed reign as the dominant disciplinary piety at the conference. The ritual invocation of this

---

[36]Ronald Beiner, *Political Judgment* (Chicago: Chicago University Press, 1983). Although Browne does not mention Beiner here, his familiarity with Beiner's work is evident in the essay he co-authored with Michael Leff, "Rhetoric and Political Judgment: Edmund Burke's Paradigm," in *Argument and Social Practice: Proceedings of the Fourth SCA/AFA Conference on Argumentation* eds. J.R. Cox, M. Sillars, and G. Walker (Annandale, VA.: Speech Communication Association, 1985), 193-210.

piety was partly accentuated by the format—a formal paper followed by a prepared response, resulting in polite but competitive reading of the same text. The respondents presented various textual and extra-textual reasons for fashioning their alternative readings, such as: a different historical frame within which to view the speech (Wenzel), a different estimate of the ideological configurations that constrained the orator (Hariman), different motives or strategies that could be ascribed to the orator (Linkugel and Rowland), and a different assessment of the figural elements in the speech (Farrell). Aside from these specific justifications for offering alternative readings, there is also a tacit assumption in these essays that underwrites the very possibility of alternative or multiple readings—namely, the polysemous character of the oratorical text.

The idea of polysemy has received considerable attention in the recent literature on "cultural studies."[37] Now it is making its way into the lexicon of rhetorical criticism. Simply put, the code of a polysemous text is such that it can be read competitively and even oppositionally by different audiences. While there may be a dominant interpretation inscribed within a text as a constitutive part of its production, that interpretation cannot fully arrest the natural polysemy of language. Hence, the text is potentially open to alternative readings, and privileged cultural texts can become sites of intense ideological struggle over meaning.

The application of this model of the polysemous text to oratory has far reaching implications. It opens fundamental questions about the status of the oratorical text. Can we still regard the oratorical text as a simple, readily comprehensible message as Wrage and Baskerville did? Or must we regard the meaning of the text as something to be determined only after the application of much hermeneutic effort and argument.?

The traditional distinction between poetry and oratory frequently invoked and rejected by rhetorical critics may cast some light here. According to this distinction, the language of poetry is ambiguous (radically polysemous) by design, while the language of oratory aspires by necessity to a certain directness of address. Hence, the oratorical text as a rule is no more polysemous than a

---

[37]See, John Fiske, "Television: Polysemy and Popularity," *Critical Studies in Mass Communication,* 3 (1986): 391-408, and references cited therein.

contextually bound commonplace utterance. If any hermeneutic labor is required to unpack an oratorical text, it consists primarily in placing the text in its proper (original) context. To invoke the distinction made by Barthes, the oratorical text is preeminently a "readerly" text rather than a "writerly" text.[38] Its code/s are unobtrusive and simple. It seems to refer, even while concurrently crafting an ethical proof or making an emotional appeal, to a world beyond itself. It is precisely in this sense that Wrage and Baskerville conceive of the oratorical text as simple and functionally transparent.

To be sure, what is "simple" or "obvious" is itself an ideological construction. But to say this is not to say something new and startling. The oratorical text insofar as it partakes of common sense and mobilizes the commonplace has never been anything but an ideological artifact, if we conceive of ideology in a broadly sociological sense. What textual criticism can bring to light is not the ideological character of the oratorical text but rather the possibility of unsettling the ideologically fixed and taken for granted meanings of such texts by recourse to the notion of polysemy. Thus, the logic of polysemy when applied to the oratorical text generates a new set of problems for rhetorical criticism. One might say that textual criticism aspires to reconstitute oratory from a "readerly" to a "writerly" text. The implications of this transformation of the oratorical text that is being attempted here in a rather mild and rudimentary form remain largely unknown and need further exploration.

Rhetoric and Reality

The extent to which rhetoric can shape and reshape our perception of political and historical reality is partly at issue in each of the six exchanges. These exchanges suggest some new versions of how the problematic relationship between rhetoric and reality is textually negotiated and articulated. The traditional approach (even during the heyday of the "great speaker" model) privileged the "reality" end of the equation by conceiving rhetorical discourse as functionally related to the "situation." According to

[38]Roland Barthes, *S/Z: An Essay* tr. Richard Miller (New York: Hill and Wang, 1974).

this view, the inventional freedom and the dispositional play of the orator are deeply circumscribed by the "exigencies" and "constraints" imposed by historical and material conditions.[39] The very idea that oratory is radically situated discourse robs it of a certain kind of autonomy and influence.

This delimited notion of the power of rhetoric does not dominate the essays collected in this volume. Campbell shows how Anna Dickinson, through the power of her discourse, was able to transform the historically contested life and legend of Jeanne d'Arc into an ideologically palatable story of a "woman with whom nineteenth-century Americans could identify."[40] Cox argues that the "moral power" of "I Have A Dream" speech consists in the successful critique it develops against the ideology of "gradualism" ("the tranquilizing drug of gradualism") prevalent during the "turbulent years following the Supreme Court ruling in *Brown v. Board of Education* (1954)."[41] In a revisionist reading of Burke's "Speech on Conciliation," Browne argues that the speech was "far more than a hopeless but elegant appeal for imperial concord" in the Parliamentary debates over the American question. Instead the speech should be read as a vindication of "Whig ideology in its moment of crisis."[42] In a similar fashion, Condit and Osborn ascribe to the discourses under their review a tangible power to influence and refigure the ideological terrain from which they originated.

Surprisingly Ivie, while diagnosing a clear case of rhetorical failure — the Johnson administration's unsuccessful campaign to rally public support for the Vietnam war — implies the greatest faith in the constitutive power of rhetoric. Ivie explains that failure in terms of the administration's inability to extract itself from the inherited and convenient rhetoric of containment. On this account, the administration was captive to a rhetoric that was woefully inadequate to "sustain the national will long enough to prevail in

[39]For a functionalist view of rhetoric, see Lloyd F. Bitzer, "The Rhetorical Situation," *Philosophy and Rhetoric* 1 (1968): 1-14.

[40]Karlyn K. Campbell, *"La Pucelle d'Orleans* Becomes an American Girl: Anna Dickinson's 'Jeanne d'Arc," *Texts in Context,* 91-111.

[41]J. Robert Cox, "The Fulfillment of Time: King's "I Have A Dream" Speech (August 28, 1963)," *Texts in Context,* 181-204.

[42]Stephen Browne, "Burke's "Speech on Conciliation": The Pragmatic Basis of Rhetorical Judgment," *Texts in Context,* 55-80.

Viet-Nam,"[43] but it was unable to overcome this problem because
it could not invent and exploit a more rhetorically appropriate set
of root metaphors. What is striking about Ivie's analysis, (something
that deeply troubles the respondent, Brummett,) is that it almost
completely brackets the historical and geo-political considerations
that led to the American entanglement and failure in Vietnam. Ivie
moves so decisively and exclusively on the discursive plane that
Brummett feels compelled to remind him of Kenneth Burke's
notion of the "recalcitrance" of reality, no matter how symbolically
charged and mediated that reality may be.

Neither Brummett nor I believe that Ivie is unaware that the
dialectic of history (the cold war and the retreat of colonialism)
had something to do with the Vietnam debacle. What is problematic is a critical procedure that completely neglects that
dialectic. In Ivie's paper there is no methodological gesture that
tells us, to borrow the language of Foucault, how he conceives the
relationship between discursive practices and non-discursive practices (say, institutional realities).[44] Ivie is examining an intriguing
set of now "declassified" discourses — behind the scenes exchanges
of "memoranda, reports, speech drafts, and other documents
written by and for the President and his advisors and reflecting
upon the administration's perception of the available means of
persuasion."[45] Precisely because Ivie is opening up new discursive
objects for rhetorical investigation, we need to know all the more
urgently the presumed connection between those objects and what
Foucault calls *enunciative modalities.* Three are identified: the
status of the speaker, the sites from which the statements are made,
and the positions of the subjects.[46] Ivie's essay gives the impression

---

[43]Robert L. Ivie, "Metaphor and Motive in the Johnson Administration's Vietnam
War Rhetoric," *Texts in Context,* 121-141.

[44]Michael Foucault, *The Archaeology of Knowledge* tr. A.M. Sheridan Smith (New
York: Pantheon, 1972).

[45]Ivie, "Metaphor and Motive," *Texts in Context,* footnote 21.

[46]For instance, in the medical discourse medical statements cannot come from
anybody. The doctor occupies a privileged status. First, he is the statutorily defined
person who has the right to make them. Second, his statements originate at certain
institutional sites like hospital and laboratory. Third, the position of the doctor as the
subject varies according to what he is doing — perceiving, observing, describing, teaching,
etc. See, Dilip Parameshwar Gaonkar, "Foucault on Discourse: Methods and Tempta-
tions," *The Journal of the American Forensic Association* 19 (1982): 246-57.

that the relationship between the verbal artifacts and the conditions of their production is either unproblematic or that its problematic character has already been negotiated and integrated into our disciplinary consciousness. But this is manifestly not the case.

The issue cannot be resolved by a mere methodological gesture (not uncommon in rhetorical and cultural studies) that acknowledges the existence of non-discursive practices, but proceeds to unpack discursive practices in relative isolation. The pressing task, for which "textual studies" are ideally suited, is to offer an understanding of "contexts" (non-discursive formations) through a reading of texts (discursive formations) while allowing the text to retain its integrity as a field of action. The fate of textual studies devoted to so public a medium as oratory will clearly depend on how well we succeed in deciphering what is outside the text by charting what is inside the text without altogether reifying the outside/inside dichotomy.

IV

TWO NEWLY-EDITED
SPEECH TEXTS

"ANNA E. DICKINSON'S "JEANNE D'ARC"[1]

1. Among the names, to which Time has decreed Eternity, is that of Jeanne D'Arc.

2. With reason.

3. Consider, the time in which she lived; the needs of her day; the work she wrought; the life she lived; the death she died.

4. First of all: — France.

5. In 1316, an infant girl was the rightful heir to the French Crown.[2]

6. Her uncle,[3] who should have been her actual, as he was her legal protector, had her thrust to one side; had himself crowned by the power of the sword.

7. The people, believing in that day, — as in many a day since — that right is made by might, accepted this verdict. A law, of which Germany was the birthplace, and heathenism, the date, was summoned to the support of this robbery.[4]

8. The affair was settled.

9. But, mark you, legitimacy sacrificed in the person of a young girl, left the door wide, for manly usurpations, and, illegitimate claims. Edward the 3rd of England[5] was quick to see his opportunity, — thrust his hand through this loop-hole, to grasp at the French Crown.

---

[1]From a holograph in the Anna Dickinson Papers, Library of Congress, Mss. 17,984, Reel 17, container 14, 471-507. Capitalization has been made consistent, and punctuation has been altered slightly to conform to more contemporary usage.

[2]Jeanne (1312-49), daughter of Louis X (1289-1316) and of Margaret, daughter of Robert II, duke of Burgundy, who was convicted of adultery and strangled (1315).

[3]Philip V (1293 or 1294-1322), king, 1316-22, was followed by Charles IV (called the Fair, 1294-1328), king, 1322-28, who was followed by Philip VI (1293-1350) of Valois, king, 1328-50, who invoked the Salic Law to set aside both Charles IV's daughter and Edward III of England, the son of Charles's sister.

[4]Between 1316 and 1328, as a result of the events described in n.3, a principle was established whereby women were excluded from succession to the French throne, and between 1328 (accession of Philip VI) and 1437 (Charles VII's triumphal entry into Paris) its corollary, that descent from the daughters of French kings could not be admitted as a claim to the royal succession, was accepted. These came to be called the Salic Law of Succession, inaccurately associated with laws of the Salian Germans.

[5](1312-77), King of England, 1327-77.

10. From this ensued a war of 120 years.[6] A war, extending through the reigns of five English and five French kings, during which, the great realm of France was twice lost, and twice re-won, by Frenchmen.

11. A war, that began by denying—right—to a woman, was ended, by a woman.

12. A war, the outset of which was the sacrifice of legiti-macy in the person of a young girl, was closed, victory gained, peace established by another young girl.

13. Thus, the "Whirligig of Time brings in his revenges."[7] Thus, by a species of Divine adjustment, which we do not now comprehend, the Scales of Justice—held in the hand of God—swing down, even, at last.

14. This war went on with varying measures of success,—but always of success—to the English; with varying measures of defeat,—but always of defeat—to the French, till, at last, in 1427, Bedford,[8] the then English regent, wrote to his master, Henry of England,[9]—"I am about putting in practice a scheme which, if successful, will ultimate in the destruction of France as an independent power,—will reduce it, as a vassal, to your Crown."

15. What was this scheme? England was master of the entire of the Northern Province of France—with the exception of a few insignificant fortresses. Charles[10] still held the centre, with a portion of the Southern Province of his own domain. Orleans was his last stronghold, and was in such position, that, whoso held it, had an open door, through which he could pass to the possessions of England—those in the North, or, to the possessions of France—those in the Centre and South.

---

[6]The series of wars known as the Hundred Years War began in 1337 and ended in 1453.

[7]William Shakespeare, *Twelfth Night,* Act V, Scene 1, ln. 388.

[8]During Henry VI's early years, England was under a protectorate of his uncles John of Lancaster (1389-1435), duke of Bedford, regent in France, and Humphrey, Duke of Gloucester.

[9]Henry VI (1421-71), King of England, 1422-61, 1470-71.

[10]Charles VII, the Dauphin (1403-61), King of France, 1422-61, whose reign saw the end of the Hundred Years War.

16. Bedford, desiring to go to the South of France, saw that it was necessary, ere advancing, to have this key of Orleans in his keeping.

17. To this end, he massed a great army over against the city: — twenty-three thousand as Hume,[11] the historian of England asserts; twice and thrice that, as the French chroniclers maintain. He summoned, from posts of far off duty, his chiefest generals to head this army. He scattered money, like rain, through the ranks.

18. As for France, it did what it could.

19. It threw into this city a few of its scattered and marauding bands; — (its excuses for an army.) The people, already famishing, stripped themselves a little more closely, and fed, a little more narrowly, that these defenders might have supplies for brief months, or weeks at least. The young nobles flung themselves into the city; with the determination, to save it, or, to die.

20. "Dim, is the rumor of a common fight,
Where host meets host, and many names are sunk.
But of a single combat, Fame spoke clear."

21. This contest, by reason of the peculiarity of the position of Orleans, by reason of the magnitude of the issue at stake, by reason of the combatants, had all the interest of a duel, and all the intensity of a duel to the death: — A duel wherein France and England were the principals, while all Europe looked on.

22. Here was the last stand to be taken for French Nationality,[12] and, it was taken — nobly.

23. Orleans comprehended, that if she fell, she dragged down with her, her King and her country, and she said: — Nothing shall subdue me."

24. But, there be limits to human endurance, and by and by, Orleans stretched out meagre and trembling hands, crying for help.

25. To the King.

---

[11]David Hume (1711-76), Scottish philosopher and historian, published an exhaustive *History of England* (1754-62).

[12]It was Michelet who in 1833 first used the word *nationalité* [and]...who so frankly identified Joan with France (Warner 1981, 265-66).

26. The King was packing his belongings, making his preparations to flee from his country, turning his back upon the people who were dying for him, — that he might save his own worthless life.[13]

27. To the Army.

28. The Army was broken into bands of robbers, its motto being, "each man for himself."

29. To the People. — To France. But what could France do? France — whose highways were deserted, whose fields were barren, whose cities were desolate, and whose villages had ceased? High and low, rich and poor, master and servant, noble and serf were alike, helpless to aid or save their country, in this its hour of direst need and utmost extremity.

30. The end of all seemed near.

31. Suddenly — through this darkness a light shone. Suddenly, there went sounding down, through this sorrow, and gloom, and despair, a voice that cried — "I am come from God to save you!" And all the people said, "Amen! For vain is the help of man."

32. The people never begin to pray, till they are afraid to hope.

33. This voice, that brought comfort to the fainting hearts of men, was a woman's voice: — that of a girl, young and beautiful, and unselfish, and wise with that wisdom which, through all ages, entering into holy souls, has made them prophetic, and friends of God.

34. In all history, there is no character whose course can be more readily and easily traced, than that of this young girl.[14]

35. Over four hundred authentic histories have been written of her. Her enemies, who, by their process of condemnation in 1431, thought to consign her to eternal infamy, have thereby built her enduring monument.

36. They summoned witnesses from all parts of the Empire, from the greatest noble to the lowest peasant, to testify concerning her, — and this testimony, sworn and proven, lies tonight

---

[13]Modern scholarship provides a more favorable evaluation of his character (Gies 1981, 40).

[14]"The primary sources are abundant and diverse, unique for a medieval personage and rare for a historical figure of any premodern period" (Gies 1981, 2; Warner 1981, 6).

among the State Papers of France, for whoso to examine, that has need or desire.[15]

37. Thus, when one speaks of her and her work, one does not speak of a myth, of a legend, of a tale that is told. One does not say, "Perhaps it was thus," "Maybe it was that," "Perchance it was another." One simply says, — so it was.

38. She was born in the little village of Domremy, in Lorraine — which was then, as it has been full often since, swept by contending armies, — in the year 1411.[16]

39. Her parents were peasants, — poor — but, with the independence that always comes from actual ownership of the soil.

40. For herself, she lived a life chiefly out of doors, that was simple, strong, vigorous, active, wholesome.

41. Beyond this, friend and foe, poet and historian, alike tell us of her goodness, her kindness, her charity. — Her seriousness and earnestness, amounting to sadness.

42. So kind was she, — as they tell us, — as to take the bread from her mouth, to give to some hungry traveller, who came to her father's door, — as, to get off her little bed at night, to sleep upon the floor, that some weary wayfarer might have rest, for a few hours, — as to give all of her scanty childish store, with the work of her hands, to the poor, the sick, and the suffering of the village.

43. So pious was she, with the piety of her day and generation, as not to be content to seek the church only at stated intervals, but, upon sunny morning, or twilight evening, or high noon, she could be found prostrate at altar or shrine.

44. "She," — said her old priest, "was the only one in the village who never missed confession, and who had never anything to confess."

45. So serious, and sad, and thoughtful was she, as to provoke the wonder of her elders — with whom alone she would associate, for when she went abroad with her young companions, under the free arch of the skies, — while they played, she walked by herself in silent meditation, and when they laughed, she prayed.

---

[15]The record of the trial, the rehabilitation, and related documents were first published by Jules Quicherat (1841-1849).

[16]Her date of birth is unknown, probably 1412 or 1413.

46. Not only this,—but the village in which she lived was one to add to this habit of mind and seriousness of thought. It was a village—a little village it is true, but it was situated at the crossing of two high roads, and these roads, the vastly travelled ones, between the kingdoms of France and the kingdoms of Germany. Thus, whoso journeyed,—knight, soldier, pilgrim, beggar, peasant, priest,—everybody came that way, travelling newspapers, —bringing with them, stories of the great contest raging outside,— a contest wherein they were all profoundly interested,—stories of which grew sadder and sadder, as the years went on, to those who loved the cause of the rightful King.

47. Among the listeners I venture to assert, none gave such an ear, such a heart of heed, as those of this young girl.

48. Through all of her after life,—at the head of her army, disputing with learned Doctors, dictating terms of peace to nations, crowning a king,—through it all, she showed plainly that her sentiment for France was not merely a sentiment, her feeling was not simply feeling,—but was a divine passion of patriotism.

49. Her patriotism was her religion. Her religion was her life.

50. How, then, must these stories of the sorrow, the wrongs, the want, the anguish of France have affected one who believed her country to be a portion, and the favored portion of the kingdom of God? Who regarded her King but as the viceregent of the Most High upon earth.

51. How?

52. Manifestly they made her lose her life to find it again.[17]

53. She so loved France; she so sorrowed in its sorrow; she so longed to live for it, to suffer for it, to die for it at need, that by and by this one supreme thought took absolute possession of her being. Things small, things petty, things base, things that are for self and self alone, or nearly touching self:—the life of today, the what to eat, the wherewithal to be clothed, the roof to shelter us—matters that interest one and all of us, good friends,—by and by such matters as these, were crushed to death in her, by a mightier than they, and, from their grave, her soul plunged to depths, and rose to heights, where it found God.

---

[17]Matt. 10:39; Mark 8:35; Luke 9:24.

54. Hume tells us that her undisciplined mind grappling with difficulties that were beyond its comprehension mistook the ravings of passion for divine inspiration.

55. Schiller,[18] — whose tragedy is full of the most exquisite poetical conceits, but, which as history, is a romance, pure and simple, from end to end — Schiller represents her as a nondescript in creation. A being neither angel nor human.

56. Shakespeare[19] trails his great genius in the filth of a national prejudice, and daubs out of it the picture of a rude, coarse, vulgar, disgusting charlatan.

57. Michelet[20] and Lamartine[21] speak of her as Frenchmen almost invariably speak of women: — with the outward courtesy that veils inward contempt.

58. —And Miss Catherine Beecher[22] (who has written a somewhat exhaustive and exhausting article upon her) discovers that these voices and visions, of which we have heard so much, were the results of disease; a distempered condition of the body: affecting the organs of sight and sound.

59. For myself — I believe in these visions, — but, — I believe they were but the reflex of her own soul.

60. I believe she was called to her work. — Not by voices. By signs, by wonders in the air. No. I believe *she* was called, just as you and I are called, since I know full well that every soul that ever yet was sent into the world, had its work appointed of God, and the voice of conscience, to drive it on.

---

[18]Friedrich von Schiller (1759-1805), German dramatist, who wrote *Die Jungfrau von Orleans,* first performed in 1801.

[19]*Henry VI, Part I* (1623).

[20]Jules Michelet (1798-1874), a historian of the French romantic school, whose *Jeanne d'Arc* appeared in volume 5 (1844) of his major work *Histoire de France* (1833-67), then separately published in 1853.

[21]Alphonse Marie Louis de Lamartine (1790-1869), French poet, novelist, statesman, whose "Jeanne d'Arc" first appeared in *Le Civilisateur, Journal Historique* (April-May 1852).

[22](1800-78), educator, who argued in *The Evils Suffered by American Women and American Children: The Causes and the Remedy* (1846) that inadequate air and exercise and murderous fashions had so ruined women's health that most dreaded maternity. The article on Joan, which I cannot locate, may have been occasioned by the fact that Joan was a favorite figurehead for woman's rights activists, e.g. Sarah Moore Grimké translated Lamartine's biography, which was published as *Joan of Arc: A Biography* (1867).

61. She had goodness in a generation of infidelity,—she had genius in a time of commonplace—above all she had Faith. She believed in France, in her King, in Heaven's interposition in behalf of its own,—and this goodness, this genius, above all this faith, made her the fit leader and helper of a faithless King, a shattered army, a dispirited and heart broken people.

62. Meanwhile, the needs of France grew and grew, and her desire to serve France kept pace with its needs.

63. By and by she could keep silence no longer.

64. One night, then, she stopped her father's neighbor,—a poor laboring man,—as he was returning from his toil, and putting her arm upon his arm said,

65. —"I tell thee, there is one—standing right here,—within sound of our voices,—who, within the year, will raise the siege of Orleans, and see that the Dauphin is crowned King. What hast thou to say to that?"

66. Manifestly the girl wanted to take the thought out of herself, mark its effect upon another.

67. As to this other,—he was an ignorant, superstitious, kindly fellow, living in the midst of ignorance and superstitution, and it by no means astounded him. He took it, in good part.

68. She, gaining courage thereby, went her way to her father and mother, and no longer said, "It is a girl," but, "I myself will do this thing."

69. And the good, commonplace father and mother did just about what good, commonplace fathers and mothers would have done, in all ages since then:—the mother blinded her eyes and wore her knees with tears and with prayers, and the father said,

70. "Thou go with the army? Thou march with these soldiers? Why, sooner than that, I will drown thee with these hands."

71. For her, none of these things moved her. The great battle, between her love and her genius, her duty and her affections, had been fought long before, in the inner depths of her nature. They might break her heart. They could not sway her purpose, nor her soul.

72. From this point on, it is clear that the girl marked her path from her father's door to the King—and beyond, and followed it, step by step.

73. First of all, how to reach the Dauphin, whom she would serve.

74. She thought:—she said then, "I will go halfway to the Governor of the Province, the great man of the district, Robert de Baudricourt.[23] He shall hear me. He shall forward me to the King."

75. To this end, she enlisted in her service her good uncle, Durand Laxart, who loved her, and believed in her, and sent him on this mission to the knight.

76. Fancy the scene!

77. A magnificent castle. In it, a man grown gray with years, covered with honorable orders. A knight, a courtier, a scholar, a gentleman.

78. Into this superb presence comes another man. A peasant, clad in homespun, wooden shoes on his feet, his hands burdened with toil,—and this man says to this man that he comes thence as "an ambassador!" An ambassador from *whom?*

79. From another peasant! A child! a young girl who cannot write her own name, nor read it, after it is written!—and this girl, this child, this ignorant peasant says that "She will raise the siege of Orleans, and see that the Dauphin is crowned, King"—That where kings and armies and potentates and powers have failed, she will succeed.

80. Why, across all this dimming distance of time, you and I can yet imagine the sort of smile that came to the knight's face as he said,—

81. "Go thy way, good fellow, box thy niece's ears, and send her home."

82. He went his way. He did not box his niece's ears, nor send her home. He was blessed to see, back of the girl's face and the woman's form, the august soul that was to work such results in the world, and when she said,—

83. "Take thou me to the governor," he took her. But the governor would not see her. Shut the door in her face.

84. She, nothing daunted, went her way to the house of the next women in the town,—the wife of the blacksmith,—and there took up her abode, waiting the knight's pleasure.

85. And while she there waited, she talked much,—and all her talk was of France. She shed innumerable bitter tears,—and all her tears were for France. She prayed incessantly,—and all her prayers

---

[23]Captain of the Dauphin's forces at Vaucouleurs.

were for her wretched King, and his yet more unhappy land.

86. She so talked, she so wept, she so prayed, that the people of the village, the country folk round about, crowded to see and hear her, and one and all, swept and swayed by some subtle power and magnetism they could not comprehend, went their way from her presence, complaining against the Governor, over in his castle, for withholding "Divine aid, that should be forwarded to the King."

87. They so talked, the wonder so spread, as finally to reach the ears of a young knight, Jean of Metz,[24] who rode that way with his old squire, to whom he said,—

88. "Come, my squire, let us turn a little out of our path, and see this girl."

89. Which was done, accordingly.

90. And it is plain, from the outset, what effect the girl had upon the knight, for there yet [sic], in letters extant—simple, sweet, manly letters—that the young fellow wrote to his mother and sisters, telling them of the marvellous [sic] girl, and of the wonderful influence she had on whoso approached her.

91. So he staid [sic] and talked with her about many things, and at last, said to her,—

92. "What is it, thou dost desire, Jeanne? What wouldst thou do? What is all this mystery?"

93. To which she,—

94. "I am sent of God to this governor,—Robert de Baudricourt, over yonder in the great castle,—to tell him he must forward me to the King. But he will not listen. He shuts the door in my face! And yet, I must reach the Dauphin before Easter Morning, if I have to go to him, upon my knees, for neither kings nor princes, nor the daughter of the King of Scotland (who was the ally of France) can in any way aid or serve him. I alone can save him. For so my Lord has ordained."

95. And you and I can yet hear the laugh, that came from the gay young fellow, as looking at her, and then at his old squire, he asked,—

96. "Thy lord? Who is thy lord, Jeanne?"

---

[24]Jean de Metz or Jean de Nouillompont.

97. "God."

98. At that, the young knight and the old squire,—stretching out their mailed hands,—took her young, slight palm in their grasp and swore to conduct her to the King, or whithersoever she would.

99. "When wilt thou go?" said they.

100. "Rather today than tomorrow," she answered.

101. She realized that when a man is dying, there is need of dispatch.

102. "Wilt thou go in that dress?"

103. "I will be thankful for another."

104. Nothing should stand betwixt her and her work. The woman's dress would expose her to difficulty, danger, insult, perchance, death itself.

105. Meanwhile, the Governor, moved by all this, had written to the Dauphin. The Dauphin, doubtless swayed by a variety of emotions, had sent back word "forward her to us," and so, all things conspiring, the King, commanding her presence, the knight and squire swearing to conduct her, the people believing in her, she was sent on her way; and, as she was about riding forth, clad in complete armor, the Governor, de Baudricourt himself going into his armory, taking a sword from the wall, putting it into her hand, said,—

106. "Go! Go and let come what thou canst accomplish!"

107. Evidently the knight thought it was a very small affair the girl was to do.

108. Why, it was a vast enterprise, even, to begin.

109. She had to get over one hundred and four leagues of territory,—the old French league being twice as long as the present one,—every town, every village, every fortress of which was in the hands of the enemy,—the English and Burgundian forces. She had to cross eight rivers, and innumerable streams, every one of which was bridgeless. She had to go upon a journey, which, from the fatigue, exposure, exhaustion, hunger, thirst, cold, would have taxed the strength of a strong man.

110. More than this, she had to go, a girl, young, beautiful, alone, with seven knights and men-at-arms, in a day when men held woman's honor but as thistle-down, to be blown down the winds, and yet,—as these same men afterwards testified, under oath,—tho' they rode all day on horse at her side, and stretched themselves out to sleep by her side in the open fields at night, no

thought ever came to them concerning her, other than though she
had been an angel.

111. At last, she reached the town where lived the King,[25] —
but the King had changed his mind,—would not see her. He sent
her to an inn, and commissioners to her.

112. But she had naught to say, to them.

113. Then, he forwarded some, to her old home, to inquire
into her past life, and impatient, ere these could return, sent other
commissioners to her.

114. But she replied to these, as to the first,—

115. "I have naught to say to you. Take me to the King. I will
answer him."

116. Till at last the King said, "We will receive her. Let her
come in."

117. And so,—as the old chronicles tell us,—the impoverished Court made itself fine to receive the peasant girl. It got out
its splendid robes, and its cloth-of-gold, and its magnificent jewels,
and arrayed itself therein. It had fifty candles, twelve feet high,
burning in the room. It had three hundred knights in complete
armor waiting in the antechamber, and the Dauphin said,—

118. "If she come of God, she will recognize us in disguise,"
and so put him into plain armor, and mingled with his Court. "If
she come of the devil—she will pick out my handsomest
courtier," and himself selecting the knight, had him dressed in his
own robes, placed his Crown upon his head, mounted him, in his
Chair of State, and had her summoned to audience.

119. And here, say those who will find in this girl everything,
save, what she was, a creature of genius, of power and patriotism,
say those, who will see in her a mere blind tool in the hand of
fate, "here be two incidents in her career that plainly demonstrate
the truth of our theory."

120. They tell us, as she was riding across the drawbridge, to
come into the castle, where the King was waiting to receive her, a
brutal man-at-arms, struck by the beauty of her face, and the
singularity of her dress, said to a comrade,—

121. "Who is that?"

---

[25]Chinon castle.

122. "Jeanne D'Arc," was the answer. "The maid, you know, who has come to the help of the King."

123. The man with horrid oaths, and hideous blasphemy, made some threat against her womanhood.

124. They tell us she paused, drew bridal rein, turned and looked at the man, and, in a voice, thrilling and terrible, cried out—

125. "Ah, by my God, thou blasphemest Him! And thou, so near to death." And in a little while thereafter, they tell us the man fell into the river, and was drowned.

126. Need of a miracle, here? Why so good, and so serious, and so earnest a soul must, of necessity, have borne its testimony against blasphemy and indecency, and, for the rest, Time must always have seemed short, and the grave near, to one who lived in constant thoughts of Eternity.

127. Coming then, into the presence of the King and his Court she was by no means deceived, by this mock dauphin on his throne. She knew her rightful lord. She knelt at his feet. She claimed him as her own.

128. Again, need of a miracle?

129. Why, she had lived for four days in the same town with him,—a little town,—a town of one street. Every knight of his court had been into her presence,—all their talk had been of the King,—she must have heard him described, a thousand times.

130. For myself I believe that from the moment she came into the presence of the King and the Court, they saw, of what stuff she was made, and for what work she was ready, but it was necessary to prepare the minds of the common people, to fight under her banner, in this last desperate enterprise for the salvation of France.

131. So they held councils, and had questions and cross questions aplenty, and her answers full of that rarest of all genius, the genius of Common Sense, were scattered broadcast across the land.

132. Through this, six thousand men, from the midst of the multitudes who had swarmed to the place, had enlisted under her banner. The people, finding that a final effort was to be made in behalf of Orleans, gathered, of their scanty remaining store of provisions, to lend to the starving wretches of the town.

133. She, then, being first of all appointed Commander-in-Chief of the King's forces, was clad in shining white armor. A so-called sacred sword put into one hand. A so-called sacred banner,

into the other, and so, with her army, her escort, her provisions, she rode on her way,—the last hope of the last stronghold of France.

134. They marched all day, and they marched by night, through many days and nights, and at last found themselves at a little village, a few leagues distant from Orleans, and there waited till the officers of the town could come out to meet her.

135. On this side the city, the English siege lines were of such strength, as to compel her army to go about by a long and circuitous route, and so come into the place from the other side.

136. By and by the officers of the town came out to meet her. Her army went on its way. She, and her escort, and her provisions, came down the river to a little place just opposite Orleans, and wind and tide favoring, entered unmolested in.

137. "How!" say you, "unmolested?" "Where, then, were the English? Why did they not prevent?"

138. She was as well known in the one camp as in the other, but with a difference.

139. The French said,—

140. "She comes of Heaven!"

141. The English said,—

142. "She comes of Hell."

143. The French cried, "She is God's special interposition in our behalf!"

144. The English could not accept that theory, for God, you know, is always on our side. Nevertheless, the Devil is a formidable adversary, and they preferred (wisely enough) staying behind their entrenchments, to meeting him in the open field.

145. And so, coming into that city at eight o'clock of the pleasant summer evening, 1428, what did she bring to it?

146. A great army to fight their battle?

147. No.

148. A commanding general whose name, of itself, would be a tower of strength in their midst?

149. No.

150. A King, to arouse their enthusiasm?

151. No.

152. She brought two hundred men-at-arms. She brought some food for starving mouths. She brought herself.

153. But, in that last bringing, she literally brought, "beauty

for ashes, the oil of joy, for mourning, and the garment of praise, for the spirit of heaviness" [Isa. 61:3].

154. The people, crowding the house tops, darkening the windows, blocking the doorways, swarming in the streets, looking at this marvellous, beautiful, inspired face, as it rode up, cried,

155. "Ah! She is sent indeed, of Heaven. We are saved!"

156. And the next day she began active enterprise in their behalf, and for their salvation, by calling together a council of war and putting before it her plan of a campaign.

157. "Her plan of a campaign?" says someone. "What did she know of such matters? It is self evident that it was the generals, the officers, the men who understand these things who planned the campaign, and she, by her youth, and sex, and enthusiasm merely inspired the men to fight."

158. Let us see if that statement will hold water.

159. The siege of Orleans had begun in October 1428. This was April 1429.

160. This was the same city, these the same officers in command, this the same army, this the same besieging English line. Not an item had changed, save only, that this girl had come into the town.

161. The officers had had everything their own way for six months. They could plan as they pleased, and fight as they pleased. What had they gained by it?

162. They had gained, precisely, six months of waiting—and starvation.

163. She, then, standing in their midst laid down her plan of a campaign.

164. Said she, "We will take our men, burning with hope, at white heat of enthusiasm, will weld them into one compact body, will beat this down upon the nearest and weakest of the enemy's forts. Taking this will cut their line,—will inspire our men to greater deeds,—will be an entering wedge to victory."

165. Why her whole plan was simply that, what Napoleon put into practice centuries later, through which, he made himself temporary master of the world. It was to take his army, large or small, make one compact mass of it, hurl this upon the frailest point, in the line of the enemy, and so breaking it in two, have the whole thing at his mercy, to be taken, in detail.

166. Of the man, the world says, "What august power! What

commanding genius!"

167. Of the woman, under precisely similar conditions, it cries, "Why what a lucky accident it was, she should happen to hit upon that plan."

168. So she presented it, and the Governor of the City, the Count Dunois,—the ablest officer, bravest soldier, most cultured scholar, elegant gentleman of the Court of Charles the 7th,—said Dunois, and such men as he, as became true greatness—

169. "All we have to propose has come to nothingness. We have no fresh plan to offer. Here is a new one. We stand to back it, and see what comes of it."

170. Said the little ones,—

171. "It is not to be thought of for one instant."

172. They had never thought of it. But, when the council had broken up, and the great men and the great woman had gone on their ways, these lesser souls, gathering themselves together said,—

173. "Good! Capital! Tomorrow when she is where she ought to be, in her own house, we will take her plan, and the men she has inspired, and will march out, and pick the laurels of this tree of her planting."

174. So the next morning, early, they took the men, they took the plan, and went their way to its fulfillment.

175. They went out swelling to victory.—And they came home again!

176. She, lying upon her bed, at high noon, asleep,—exhausted by the long toils of the past month,—was wakened by the sorrowful tumult in the street, by voices that cried under her window,—

177. "Awake! Arouse! The French line has advanced! Has attacked! Is defeated! Is in full retreat at the gates of the city, the enemy at its heels!"

178. She heard;—she awakened;—she answered!

179. She sprang from her bed,—she dashed into her armor,—she fled down the stairways,—she vaulted into her saddle, and tearing her banner from the window where it floated, put spurs to her horse, and rode from the Western gate of the city to the Eastern gate—the gate of Burgundy,—across the whole length of the town ere her old squire had fairly cased himself in armor.

180. Riding, then, among these scattered, beaten fugitives, she swept around them eye and voice of command; and the men

recognized — (what men always have and always will recognize to the end of time) — the eye and the voice of the Master Soul, where it blazes, and when it speaks.

181. They gathered about her; they closed in after her; they followed her through the gate of the city to the fort from whence they had fled a half hour before, and in another half hour, they literally took it by storm. Five hundred Englishmen had been left dead under their bloody swords and spears.

182. So quick, so terrible, so resistless had been the assault, that the English, in the near forts did not venture to the rescue of their comrades, and even Bedford, the great English commander, did not care, as Hume himself confides, to meet this girl in the open field with the sword.

183. That, in short, was the story of that day — and, of the next, and the next.

184. Through this, the major officers stood to support her, the minor ones to oppose her, till at last these said, "Enough! Let us make an end!"

185. Thursday, a Saint's Day, (she, devout, on her knees in her own chamber in prayer) these malcontents gathered themselves together in a council from which Dunois had been excluded, of which she was supposed to know nothing.

186. Being so gathered, the one suggested one reason; — another another; — a fifth, a fifth; — a tenth, a tenth for — "Delay," till her army, which was already half way over its course, should reach its destination, and they with its assistance, should accomplish some great thing.

187. This being done they were about making up their council, when she, who was supposed to know naught of it, came knocking, knocking, at the door, and entering in, said to them —

188. "Gentlemen, you have been at your council, I have been at mine. Believe me, the councils of men shall come to naught, but, that of my God, shall stand. I will attack the enemy, tomorrow."

189. So the next morning when the sun rose, she rose. She clad herself in armor, and came riding through the city streets to the city gates; — to find them locked and barred against her, their keeper, with the keys in his hand, his guard about him.

190. "Let me through!" she cried.

191. "It is against the orders of the council," he answered.

192. "Let me through!" she repeated.

193. "The generals have otherwise decided," was the response.

194. The generals were not there, and the council was not there,—but the army was there, and the people were there, and when she cried to them, "Let us go through!" they went through!

195. They battered the gate to atoms. They swarmed across the bridge to attack the last stronghold of the enemy:—The Tournelles—two great towers that lifted themselves up over against the city, connected by a drawbridge.

196. Here the English—(learning wisdom through disaster)— had gathered in the men from the outlying forts, and so massed them in these two towers as to force them out upon the open and exposed drawbridge.

197. Here, then, they fought that day as Englishmen know how to fight! As men, who struggled, not alone for life, but for immortality!

198. Against this seemingly impregnable fortress, against this desperate and heroic foe, the French line beat from seven of the morning 'till one of the afternoon,—and beat in vain.

199. She, then, finding her men were losing heart and hope, that she could not rally them, flinging her sword to one soldier, her banner to another, ran, and with her own hands seizing a ladder, put it against the walls of the fort, and mounted it, battle axe in hand, shouting to her men to come onward.

200. They heard!—They followed!—They answered! but not soon enough. An archer, taking too sure aim, let fly an arrow from the wall, striking her here (in the breast) making a wound a finger length broad, the arrow head coming out behind.

201. She fell, fainting, to the bottom of the trench. Her men ran,—seized her,—tore her from under the very advancing feet of the foe, and carrying her away to a green and quiet spot, stood about her, to watch her die.

202. But, presently, life came back to her, and with life, the consciousness of intolerable pain. The tears were wrung from her eyes,—but remembering herself—herself once more, with her own hand, she tore the arrow from the wound, with her own hand dressed it, and ordered her men to carry her back to the front.

203. But through this, the minutes had grown to hours. The soul gone, how could the body fight? The French line was in full retreat. It thought her dead.

204. She, looking across the field saw that this was no defeat, saw that it was a panic. She recognized, what military men in all ages have recognized, that under the whole shining surface of the sun, there is naught so senseless as a panic in an army.

205. But, finding she could not sway the generals—to her mind—with that quickness of thought that pertains to genius, and goes to its mark, like the lightning of God, she said—

206. "At least, let the men sit down to supper. They have had naught to eat, nor to drink, this day."

207. Thereby she gained two points; strength, for the men, to fight the battle she meant to wage that night; time for them, sitting there coolly to see what it was, from which they had fled, what it was they were to face.

208. The generals did not fathom her plans. They were not willing for the men to fight, they were more than ready to let them feed. So they were put down to their suppers.

209. Through this, she went by herself in prayer, and this done, and that done, she came among them once more—to find them refreshed and inspired. New men.

210. As to these English in their two towers, they expected no second assault. They thought the day well and honorably won. They had flung aside their arms, and put off their armor. They were feasting, and reveling, and rejoicing themselves in a false security, when the solitary sentry, from the wall cried,—

211. "Behold!"

212. And lo, here was seen creeping up through the gathering twilight of the spring evening, seemingly a new army, and at its head the woman they thought dead, hours before, came living and commanding the living.

213. There could be no two results. Such an assault. Fighting, —struggling,—contending,—inch by inch of the way,—the English were forced out upon the overcrowded drawbridge.

214. Here, then, fully exposed, the French fire cutting through and through them, the French arrows whizzing across and across them, she, from where she stood, saw, that the timbers were cracking, the bridge giving way, and, with a blessed instinct of mercy, ran forward, and cried to [William] Glasdale, the English commander,—

215. "Surrender, thou and thy men, and ye shall have mercy! You shall not be put to the point of the sword."

216. And Glasdale, who had promised that if she ever fell into his hands, he would burn her as a witch, responded, with brutal oaths and blasphemy,—and,—at the instant,—the timbers burst! The bridge gave way! The hundreds on hundreds there gathered, sank into the river beneath, and as Glasdale himself went down, and the dark waters closed over his blaspheming head, she cried, for his dying ears to hear,—

217. "Ah, how I pity and pray for thy soul!"

218. The other tower was soon taken.

219. The siege of Orleans was ended.

220. It had lasted for six months ere she came to the city. This, was the night of the sixth day, after she entered it.

221. The next day was the Sabbath. She would permit no fighting. She compelled the whole army to stand still, while the shattered remnants of the English forces marched away.

222. Monday, while the place was in the midst of its rejoicing, she went her way to the King.

223. She was received with all honor. She was loaded with gold and with favors. The dissolute young courtiers, for once in their lives, paid respect to genius, and to goodness,—but they recommenced their councils.

224. One said,—"She shall go with me, into Normandy, to reconquer my possessions there."

225. Another said,—"Nay, not so, selfish fellow, my castle and lands in Brittany are greater than thine. She shall go with me, there."

226. Others said, "She shall go upon no private enterprise. She shall fight the battle of the King."

227. As for the King, about whom was the whole ado, he said, "Enough has been done. Let us eat, drink, and be merry."

228. As for her, she saw the first need of the King was to be King, indeed. The first want of the empire was a head.

229. There was a superstition, rife through all France—from the highest noble to the lowest peasant, to the effect, that the rightful heir to the throne, could nowhere be properly crowned, and anointed, save, in the great cathedral of the City of Rheims.

230. Every French King had there been crowned,—Charles, alone, excepted.

231. Charles the 6th had died in 1422. This was 1428. The Dauphin had not been crowned in the place appointed, since it,

and all the country round it, was in the hands of his powerful enemies,— the English and Burgundian forces.

232. Grave doubts were everywhere entertained of the Dauphin's legitimacy;— doubts that Bedford, the English regent, the most astute prince of his time did his best to intensify. He had already sent to England for young Henry. It was a race, between the two, whoso should first reach this city of Rheims, and there be crowned. Henry of England or Charles of France, would be recognized by the great body of the people as their rightful head.

233. The King did not know his own danger. His knights and nobles were too blind, selfish, or indifferent, to tell him thereof.

234. Jeanne D'Arc, a peasant, comprehended the superstitions of the peasants. A child of the people, understood what would touch the hearts of the people. A soldier, knew what would rouse the courage of soldiers, so, that, coming into the presence of the Dauphin, she said, —

235. "Sire, if thou wouldst forever set at rest, this whole question of loyalty, and legitimacy, in France, if thou wouldst bring knight, soldier, peasant, as one man to fight under thy standard, go thou thy way, as all thy forefathers have gone, before thee, to this city of Rheims, and there be crowned. The first step will be half the journey. The very effort to start will prove, thou has the right to go, and will bring thy people to thy support."

236. The King cried,—

237. "No! — Madness!"

238. The Court cried,—

239. "No! — Folly."

240. She said, —

241. "Aye!"

242. And when power speaks, weakness yields. She carried them on their way.

243. And, to sum up in brief that story of journey through a hostile country,— she came to fortresses and took them; she came to strongly walled and garrisoned places, and took them; at Patay, she fought the first battle in eight years of ceaseless battle wherein France had stood victorious in the open field. Nay, here was not alone defeated, here was positively annihilated the vast power, sent from England years before for the subjugation of the French.

244. From this point on, it was, as she had predicted: — the march of the King was one triumphal progress.

245. The fortresses let down their drawbridges at his approach. The towns and cities, flung their keys and their allegiance at his feet. The people crowded the roadsides, shouting at his approach.

246. The King had, literally, "come to his own."

247. Reaching the city of Rheims, it was to find the gates thrown wide, the English army marched away, the citizens rejoicing to receive them.

248. The morning Jeanne d'Arc entered that city, she climbed the apex of her life. She reached the summit of her existence.

249. Everyone of us, you and I, my friend, have had, or, will have, our day, from which we date.

250. This was hers.

251. That morning, she dictated a letter to Burgundy, that ultimately brought peace between the King and his great rebellious subject. She dictated a letter to Bedford decreeing terms of settlement that were scoffed at that day, but that in comparatively brief space of time were accepted to the last letter. Entering the city, though in the procession were knights, and nobles, and men with even royal blood in their veins, she took precedence of them all. She marched at the right hand of the King.

252. In the Cathedral where he was crowned, she still held her post of honor at his right hand.

253. The King, crowned, sent for her homely, old, peasant uncle, and delighted to have him sit at the same table, and, as the greatest mark of favor he could show him, fed out of the same dish with him. He sent for her peasant father and peasant mother, ennobled and knighted them. He loaded her with honors, and with gold. In every magnificent pageant of Camp and Court in all Europe, no figure stood as resplendent, as that, of this young girl.

254. 'Twas a dizzy height.

255. Did she lose balance, there? Was it necessary, to place behind her, as behind Caesar, (in his triumphs,) a slave, to whisper, "remember, thou, too, art but human?"

256. She was a peasant. She was a girl of eighteen. She had all France at her feet, and was the marvel of Europe. What was her ambition?

257. The King, throned and established, she came into his presence, and said,—

258. "Sire, I have somewhat, to ask of thee."

259. And the King said,

260. "Speak on."

261. He would have given her, then, the half of his kingdom.

262. Then she said —

263. "I pray thee, sire, that thou wouldst let me go back, to my old home. Thou hast no longer need of me, here. The siege of Orleans is raised; — The English army is dispersed. Thou, thyself, art crowned. Burgundy is considering terms of truce with thee. Thy knights and thy nobles are crowding to thy standard. What remains to be done, can soon be done, and without farther aid of mine. I pray thee, then, that thou wouldst let me return; — that I may enter once more, under my mother's roof, to tend my father's sheep. Grant me this, sire, I beseech of thee, since I have naught more to ask of thee."

264. The soldier's work, was done. The patriot's labor, was ended. The woman's heart cried for home.

265. "No," said the King.

266. "Not to be thought of!" cried the knights. Thou hast gathered this army; thou has inspired it; thou has led it to victory. Stay, thou, then with it, till is accomplished, what is so nearly done.

267. She prayed, — she entreated, — as a good and loyal subject, she yielded to the commands of the King.

268. But, it was noted that from this time, a great sadness fell upon her, and that she no longer originated plans. She was content to execute the orders of others.

269. Still, she marched and she fought. Wherever, a forlorn hope was to be led, wherever, a desperate encounter was to be headed, there, was she. But one day, in front of the walls of Paris, in endeavoring to save from destruction an attack she had not alone not planned, but against which she had protested, she and her men were driven back.

270. Coming from this defeat to the little town of Saint Denis, she was welcomed by the King and his Court!

271. Though it is so long ago, ages ago, the actors in the scene dead, and turned to dust, and the most of them, forgotten, — tis enough to make the indignant tears to start to one's eyes, to read what treatment was accorded her.

272. The King, whose brow she had crowned, whose throne she had established, whose kingdom she had saved, at this, her first disaster, turned upon her, with heartless jeers and revilings. The courtiers, in too many cases, hated her for her power, and were

envious of her success, and they made the most of the opportunity, to reveal their bad feelings. The people, the common soldiers, loved her, as of old.

273. For herself, though she knew she was surrounded by enemies, that her King would prove faithless, for herself, she never faltered to the end, — and the end was near.

274. Compiègne was attacked.

275. The Duke of Burgundy had brought the entire of his army from Germany, where it had been successful, and planted it over against the city. The commandant of the town, [Guillaume] de Flavy, a rough and brutal soldier, hated her, and made no secret of his enmity.

276. Undeterred by this she did, as she had done in other cases. She took a handful of men, flung herself into the city, promising the citizens she would save them, or would die, with them.

277. At five o'clock in the afternoon of the day after she came into the town, she took six hundred men-at-arms, and marched across the drawbridge, to attack a portion of the Burgundian line.

278. Twice she drove them before her. The third time, she and her followers, were driven back. They were, however, retiring in good order, when another section of the Burgundian line went about, to get between them and the bridge, shut them within two forces, and so, grind them to powder.

279. The men saw. They lost hope. They lost courage. They broke ranks, and fled like sheep, to the bridge.

280. She, finding she could not lead them to victory, would cover them, in retreat. She rode from her post at the head, to the rear. She fought, as even her malignant enemies, the old English chroniclers assert, as ten men might have fought. She fought, till she saw her last soldier on the bridge, her last soldier across it, then, she put spurs to her own horse to ride forward. His fore feet [sic] were poised to bear down upon the bridge, when the cruel governor, de Flavy, gave the signal! The drawbridge swung into mid-air. Jeanne d'Arc was alone. Surrounded, by ten thousand enemies! Soon, she was torn from her horse, and in the hands of her foe.

281. What treatment was accorded her?

282. She was a soldier, an officer, a prisoner of war. She had never done aught to forfeit the treatment due such an one. In every case, she had been a most magnanimous enemy. What, then, was

done with this heroic and hapless soul?

283. The man-at-arms who captured her surrendered her to de Signy. De Signy sold her to [John of] Luxembourg, Luxembourg sold her to Burgundy,[26] Burgundy sold her to the English, and her traitorous countrymen, and the English who had failed to capture her, were not ashamed of the bargain. There was paid for her,—the King of England transmitting it through his coffers at Rouen,—the sum of ten thousand livres.

284. They passed her, from prison to prison, from keeper to keeper, till at last she was lodged in the great castle of the city of Rouen, in which place, already, lived Henry, the young English King. They gave her as jailer—the secular arm holding her, for the church to try—the Earl of Warwick,[27] he, who is written down in history, as the pink and flower of the chivalry, of his time.

285. What did he do for her?

286. The men who constructed it,—at his command—afterwards, testified under oath, that they made for her an iron cage, too low, for her to stand upright, therein, too short, for her to stretch herself, at length. They chained her, about her neck, about her waist, about her hands, about her feet. They fastened these, iron links, to the iron bars of her cage.

287. They thrust this cage, into a dungeon under water, into which no ray of daylight ever could penetrate. They put three brutal men-at-arms within, two outside her dungeon, to watch her, to insult her, to waken her from brief and troubled slumbers, to tell her the executioner was coming, to carry her to torture, and to death. They almost starved her.

288. Worse than this, such men as the Count of Luxembourg, the Earl of Warwick, the Bishop of Beauvais,[28] were not ashamed to come into her dungeon, and while men-at-arms held up torches to shine upon her face, to laugh at, and revile her, where she lay.

289. Nay, the great John of Luxembourg, making a mock of her, said,—

290. "Ah, Jeanne, I have come to buy thee, of these English,—

---

[26]Philip the Good.

[27]Richard de Beauchamp, Earl of Warwick (1382-1439), served as tutor to Henry VI from 1428 to 1437, when he was appointed lieutenant of France and Normandy.

[28]Pierre Cauchon, d. 1442, president of the ecclesiastic court that convicted Jeanne d'Arc at Rouen in 1431.

to pay thy ransom, to let thee go free. What! So silent? Hast thou
no thanks, to offer me, for that?"

291. And she, where she lay, helpless, yet, heroic, looking at
him with undaunted eyes, answered. —

292. "Thou mockest me! Thou canst not, if thou wouldst.
Thou hast sold me to the English. They will burn me. That I know,
right well. But, though they destroy me, and one hundred thousand
more, they will be swept from France, for so God has ordained."

293. At that, the Count tore the dagger from his belt to stab
her to death, but the Earl of Warwick dashed hand and dagger to
one side, saying, —

294. "Not so easy a death. She is to be saved, for the stake,
and the burning."

295. They exhausted ingenuity, in trying to find testimony
against her — and failed. Among other efforts, they sent to her old
home to buy it, and were naught else known in her favor, this
would suffice. These English emissaries went into a country
desolated by war, to bare fields, to empty cupboards, to cold
hearthstones, to hungry mouths, — they went with hands, full of
gold, — and they couldn't find in all the village, nor in the region
round about, man, woman, nor little child, so poor, as to sell the
truth, against her.

296. I tell you there is no calumny, not one, that can stand
against the words — beloved by the poor.

297. At last, they brought her to trial.

298. I can give you no transcript of that work. Had I a brush,
dipped into the blackness of darkness, on the one hand, thrust into
all the splendor of God's own sunlight, on the other, I could not
paint that scene.

299. Ninety judges on the bench; — the clearest intellects, the
finest brains, of all France. The whole power, of the Inquisition, to
back them.

300. The girl, absolutely alone, — save for her soul and her
God. But these, sufficed.

301. The trial, lasted for months. There were in the aggregate,
hundreds of questions, put, and answers, received, and the strangest
part of this strange trial is, that these marvellous [sic] answers can
be accepted without doubt, cavil, or question, since they have come
to us, not on the record of friend, defender, or supporter. The very
men who condemned her to die had the record written out for you

and for me to read.

302. Piling [sic] her scaffold, they built their own monument, of infamy.

303. But of these amazing answers, I pick, but one or two. Wonderful, I pray you to remember, only, as all are wonderful. Types, of the whole.

304. Said one of her judges,—

305. "Art thou in the grace of God, Jeanne d'Arc?"

306. They thought did she say "Yes," they would accuse her of presumption. Did she say "No," they would accuse her of heresy.

307. In either case, they had her.

308. Mark, how she went between them,—

309. "If I am not in the Grace of God," she answered, "may he take me there. If I am, may he keep me."

310. And, for this effort to prove her a witch;—from the multiplicity of questions, here are one, or two.

311. Said one of her judges,—

312. "Thou wast sure, Jeanne d'Arc, to wear a ring upon thy hand,—a ring to which thou didst talk, didst kiss, over which thou didst pray, before going into battle. Manifestly 'twas an evil thing, given thee by the enemy of souls. Thou dost not dare to deny it."

313. "Ah," she answered, the tears rising to her tender eyes, "'Tis true I did—I do wear such a ring. I did so talk to it, so kiss it, so pray to it, before going into battle. It was because it had the name of Jesus carved upon it,—because it had been given me by my mother,—because it was full of memories of childhood, and of home."

314. "But," said another, "thy standard! That was an evil thing. Thou wast heard again, and yet again, to tell thy men that standard would gain them victory, anywhere. All they had to do, was to look at it."

315. "No," she cried, the soldier speaking there. "No. I told them no such thing. I told them to follow that standard, whenever and wherever it led to the front, to the hottest part of the battle, and for all witchcraft, I carried it there myself."

316. "But," said they, "thou didst take it into the Cathedral, where the King was crowned. In all that magnificent pageant thine was the only banner. What did that miserable, tattered piece of silk, and hacked and hewn bit of wood, do there? Thou didst not dare leave it out of thy grasp. Thou wast afraid thy Master would

come else, to capture thee."

317. "Carry it there?" she cried,—and the answer would go
to the heart of every soldier, at least. "Carry it there I did, as was
most meet. Since my banner had been where there was danger,
and suffering, and struggle, and death, it was fit that it should go
where there was honor and glory."

318. As to the effort to compel her, to submit her inspiration
to the judgment of the Pope,—knowing, full well, that as the Pope
was the ally of England, on that ground, he would decide against
her; that, since she had maintained that men should obey the
orderings of God in their own souls, rather than the commands of
any man, on that second count, she was foredoomed. I pray you,
who care to estimate this girl, and her character aright, to remember that before the word "Protestant" was spoken in Europe,
before Luther was dreamt of, this child, this peasant, this Catholic,
facing prelates of her own church, life and death hanging on the
balance, answered them, after this wise:

319. "As to my work, my battles, my signs, these were the
toils of human hands. I am content to submit them to the judgment
of the Pope, and his Council, men great in power, yet, human
beings like myself. But for mine inspiration—it came of Heaven. I
yield it, to Heaven, alone. I refuse to recognize the right of any
man to interfere between the soul, and its God."

320. And, at last, weary of injustice, and anguish, she cried,—

321. "I am come from God. I have naught to do here. Dismiss
me to God, from whence I came."

322. Finding, that even perverted law could not trap her, they
resorted to strategy. They brought her, face to face, with torture
and death, and, in their presence, read her a something called a
recantation;—a something, by which, she promised, to go back to
her home, to resume her peasant's gown, and that,—if the Pope so
decided,—she would stay there,—would no longer fight the battles
of the King.

323. Can you not imagine the girl's thought? as she listened.
How she must have said to herself,—"it will take time for this to
reach the Pope,—time, for him to consider it,—time, for it to be
sent back, here. Meanwhile, if I sign it, I gain freedom thereby. I
can finish the battles of the King,—they are nearly done! After
that, what matter!"

324. —"Read it, again."

325. It was read, again.

326. 'I will sign it."

327. But, instead of putting this paper under her hand, they placed another, wherein she accused herself of every crime and enormity—(for remember she could not read a word)—and, smiling as she took the quill, she traced at the foot of the parchment, a circle, and marked within it, the sign of the cross,—for the hand, that had beaten down the power of all England, could not sign its own name,—and then, stood up for sentence, supposing it would be one of dismissal.

328. It was read to her.

329. "Thou art condemned, to be carried back to thy dungeon, there, to eat the bread of sorrow, and to drink the waters of bitterness, till, thou shalt die."

330. And even at that, the soldiers, and her own false countrymen crowding the streets, gathered up stones to fling at the priest on the scaffold, crying,—

331. "Ah false priests! Ye are not earning the King's money. You are not doing as you were bid! You are letting her live! She is to die! She is to be burned! She is to be burned!"

332. And at that, the priests coming down from the scaffold, going among the people, laughed and nodded as they went by, saying,

333. "In good season. In good season. In good season. We will have her again."

334. So, she was carried back, to her dungeon.

335. And on the eighth morning, as she would rise from her bed, she found lying beside it, not the peasant gown she had sworn to resume,—and on which hung her life,—but the steel links of the armor, she had promised never to wear again.

336. She knew that to clothe herself in that armor would be to dress herself in her shroud;—to enter those steel links, would be to enter the open door of her tomb, and so standing, she cried again and again for her peasant garments and they were withheld, till, to save herself from insult, from danger, nay, from absolute violation, she put it on.

337. 'Twas but a trap in which to catch her. Spies had been watching. They ran with hasty steps to tell the Bishop of Beauvais. And she, where she stood in the gloom of her dungeon, could hear the Bishop's feet sounding on the flagstones of the courtyard

outside, could hear his voice, jarring the solemn stillness of the Sabbath morning, as he cried to the Earl of Warwick, where he hung from an upper window, "Aha! We have caught her!"

338. And the next day she was carried out to her death.

339. The story goes on to tell us, how she was brought from her dungeon, and put into a cart. The one officer of the jail who had been kind to her on the one side, the monk, who was faithful to death, on the other. How the cart moved down the narrow street to the open marketplace of the city, crowded with reviling soldiers who literally spat upon her as she went by.

340. At the one side, a high scaffold. On it, the Bishop of Winchester, the Bishop of Beauvais, the knights, and prelates, and officers who were in the town.

341. At the other, a scaffold, equally high. On it, a stake, faggots, the executioner.

342. Outside, swelling and surging like waves of the sea, the people of the city of Rouen, for whom she would have died, come to witness her burning.

343. And here, at the selfsame moment of her life, she manifested herself, supreme. Dying, she conquered the living.

344. She knelt in her cart, in the crowded street. She prayed for these her enemies, accusers, judges, murderers. For this, her executioner. For the reviling soldiers about her. For the King, the army, the nation that had forgotten her. For herself, that she might hold fast, to the awful end.

345. What power was it, think you, that speaking from dying life and dying eyes, brought to such results?

346. That made the Bishop of Winchester, who in "dying made no sign," turn his face to the wall, unable to witness the sight?

347. That made the Bishop of Beauvais who, a short half hour before, had read her death sentence, cover his face with his hand, so that those who stood watching, could see the tears drip down the back of it?

348. That made the yelling, cursing, reviling soldiers pause to listen, and, as the prayer went on, drop their swords and spears, and seizing one another's arms, cry out, "Ah, look at her! Listen to her! See her! See a Saint of God we are about to burn!"?

349. That sent her with steady, unwavering feet,—up the gallows stairs? That chained to the stake, the smoke, stifling and

blinding her, the cruel flames cracking her bones, and shrivelling her flesh, made her in dying, remember the living who had forgotten himself?

350. She saw where the flames ran out to seize the robe of the faithful monk who stood by her side, and tearing loose her scorching, withering hands, thrusting them forth, she cried,

351. "Go down, my father. Go down and save thyself. But stand where thou canst hold the blessed cross before me, and speak, I pray thee, words of comfort, to me, to the end."

352. Then, those who stood, looking and listening, in awe-struck stillness, could hear, issuing from the flames and the smoke, naught save confused sounds: — broken murmurings of a voice: — a soul, speaking to its God, in death.

353. Then, silence.

354. She had fought a good fight. She had finished her course. She had kept the faith.[29]

The End

---

[29]2 Tim. 4:7.

"I'VE BEEN TO THE MOUNTAINTOP"[1]

MARTIN LUTHER KING, JR.

1. Thank you very kindly, my friends. As I listened to Ralph Abernathy and his eloquent and generous introduction, and then thought about myself, I wondered who he was talking about. (Laughter) It is always good to have your closest friend and associate to say something good about you. And Ralph Abernathy is the best friend that I have in the world.

2. I'm delighted to see each of you here tonight in spite of a storm warning. You reveal that you are determined (Voice says, "Right!") to go on anyhow. (Voices agree) Something is happening in Memphis, something is happening in our world. And you know, if I were standing at the beginning of time with the possibility of taking a kind of general and panoramic view of the whole of human history up to now, and the Almighty said to me, "Martin Luther King, which age would you like to live in?" I would take my mental flight by Egypt, and I would watch God's children in their magnificent trek from the dark dungeons of Egypt through— or rather across—the Red Sea through the wilderness on toward the Promised Land, and in spite of its magnificence I wouldn't stop there. I would move on by Greece and take my mind to Mt. Olympus, and I would see Plato, Aristotle, Socrates, Euripides and Aristophanes assembled around the Parthenon, (applause) and I would watch them around the Parthenon as they discussed the great and eternal issues of reality, but I wouldn't stop there. (Voices agree. One voice says, "Come on, talk to us.") I would go on even to the great heyday of the Roman Empire, and I would see developments around there through various emperors and leaders, but I wouldn't stop there. (Voice says, "Keep on.") I would even come up to the day of the Renaissance, and get a quick picture of all that the Renaissance did for the cultural and aesthetic life of

---

[1]Transcription verified by Michael Osborn, Professor of Communication Studies, Memphis State University, from an audiotape of the speech as it was delivered at Mason Temple, Memphis, Tennessee, on the evening of April 3, 1968. Copyright ©1968 by the Estate of Martin Luther King, Jr. Used by permission of Joan Daves.

man, but I wouldn't stop there. I would even go by the way that
the man for whom I'm named had his habitat, and I would watch
Martin Luther as he tacks his 95 Theses on the door at the Church
of Wittenberg, but I wouldn't stop there. I would come on up even
to 1863, and watch a vacillating President by the name of Abraham
Lincoln finally come to the conclusion that he had to sign the
Emancipation Proclamation, but I wouldn't stop there. (applause) I
would even come up to the early 'thirties, and see a man grappling
with the problems of the bankruptcy of his nation, and come with
an eloquent cry that "We have nothing to fear but fear itself," but
I wouldn't stop there. Strangely enough I would turn to the
Almighty and say, "If you allow me to live just a few years in the
second half of the twentieth century, I will be happy." (applause)

3. Now that's a strange statement to make because the world
is all messed up, the nation is sick, trouble is in the land, confusion
all around. That's a strange statement. But I know somehow that
only when it is dark enough can you see the stars. And I see God
working in this period of the twentieth century in a way that men
in some strange way are responding. Something is happening in
our world. The masses of people are rising up, and wherever they
are assembled today, whether they are in Johannesburg, South
Africa; Nairobi, Kenya; Accra, Ghana; New York City; Atlanta,
Georgia; Jackson, Mississippi; or Memphis, Tennessee, the cry is
always the same: "We want to be free!" (applause. Thunder sounds
in the background)

4. And another reason that I'm happy to live in this period is
that we have been forced to a point where we are going to have to
grapple with the problems that men have been trying to grapple
with through history but the demands didn't force them to do it.
Survival demands that we grapple with them. Men for years now
have been talking about war and peace but now no longer can
they just talk about it. It is no longer the choice between violence
and nonviolence in this world, it's nonviolence or nonexistence.
That is where we are today. (applause) And also in the human
rights revolution, if something isn't done and done in a hurry to
bring the colored peoples of the world out of their long years of
poverty, their long years of hurt and neglect, the whole world is
doomed. (applause. Voice says, "All right.") Now I'm just happy
that God has allowed me to live in this period, to see what is
unfolding, and I'm happy that He has allowed me to be in

Memphis. (applause)

5. I can remember...I can remember when Negroes were just going around as Ralph has said so often, scratching where they didn't itch and laughing when they were not tickled. (applause) But that day is all over. (applause) We mean business now, and we are determined to gain our rightful place in God's world. (applause) And that's all this whole thing is about. We aren't engaged in any negative protests and in any negative arguments with anybody. We are saying that "We are determined to be men, we are determined to be people." We are saying, (applause)...we are saying that "We are God's children." And if we are God's children we don't have to live like we are forced to live.

6. Now what does all of this mean in this great period of history? It means that we've got to stay together. We've got to stay together and maintain unity. You know, whenever Pharaoh wanted to prolong the period of slavery in Egypt, he had a favorite, favorite formula for doing it. What was that? He kept the slaves fighting among themselves. (applause) But whenever the slaves get together, something happens in Pharaoh's court and he cannot hold the slaves in slavery. When the slaves get together, that's the beginning of getting out of slavery. (applause) Now let us maintain unity.

7. Secondly, let us keep the issues where they are. (Voice says, "Right.") The issue is injustice. The issue is the refusal of Memphis to be fair and honest in its dealings with its public servants who happen to be sanitation workers. (applause) Now we've got to keep attention on that. That's always the problem with a little violence. You know what happened the other day, and the press dealt only with the window-breaking. I read the articles. They very seldom got around to mentioning the fact that one thousand three hundred sanitation workers are on strike, and that Memphis is not being fair to them, and that Mayor Loeb is in dire need of a doctor. (cheers and applause) They didn't get around to that.

8. Now we're gonna march again and we've gotta march again in order to put the issue where it is supposed to be, and force everybody to see that there are thirteen hundred of God's children here suffering, sometimes goin' hungry, going through dark and dreary nights wondering how this thing is gonna come out. That's the issue. And we've got to say to the nation, "We know how it's coming out." For when people get caught up with that which is right and they are willing to sacrifice for it, there is

no stopping point short of victory! (applause)

9. We aren't going to let any mace stop us. We are masters in our nonviolent movement in disarming police forces. They don't know what to do. I've seen them so often. I remember, in Birmingham, Alabama, when we were in that majestic struggle there, we would move out of the 16th Street Baptist Church day after day. By the hundreds we would move out, and Bull Connor would tell them to send the dogs forth, and they did come. But we just went before the dogs singing, "Ain't gonna let nobody turn me around." (cheers) Bull Connor next would say, "Turn the firehoses on." And I said to you the other night Bull Connor didn't know history. He knew a kind of physics that somehow didn't relate to the transphysics that we knew about, and that was the fact that there was a certain kind of fire that no water could put out. (applause. Voice says, "Tell it like it is.") And we went before the firehoses. We had known water. If we were Baptist or some other denominations we had been immersed, if we were Methodists and some others we had been sprinkled, but we knew water. That couldn't stop us. (applause) And we just went on before the dogs and we would look at them, and we'd go on before the water hoses and we would look at it, and we'd just go on singing "Over my head I see freedom in the air." And then we would be thrown in the paddy wagons, and sometimes we were stacked in there like sardines in a can. And they would throw us in and old Bull would say, "Take 'em off," and they did. And we would just go on in the paddy wagons singin' "We Shall Overcome," And every now and then we'd get in jail and we'd see the jailers looking through the windows being moved by our prayers, and being moved by our words and our songs. And there was a power there which Bull Connor couldn't adjust to. And so we ended up transforming Bull into a steer, and we won our struggle in Birmingham. (applause)

10. And we've got to go on in Memphis just like that. I call upon you to be with us when we go out Monday.

11. Now about injunctions—we have an injunction and we are going into court tomorrow morning to fight this illegal, unconstitutional injunction. All we say to America is, "Be true to what you said on paper." (applause) If I lived in China or even Russia or any totalitarian country, maybe I could understand some of these illegal injunctions. Maybe I could understand the denial of certain basic first amendment privileges because they haven't

committed themselves to that over there. But somewhere I read of the freedom of assembly. Somewhere I read of the freedom of speech. Somewhere I read of the freedom of the press. Somewhere I read that the greatness of America is the right to protest for right. And so just as I say, we aren't going to let any injunction turn us around. We are going on. We need all of you.

12. And you know, what's beautiful to me is to see all of these ministers of the gospel. It's a marvelous picture. Who is it that is supposed to articulate the longings and aspirations of the people more than the preacher? Somehow the preacher must have a kind of fire shut up in his bones, (Voice says, "Yes, Sir.") and whenever injustice is around he must tell it. (Voices say, "Yeah.") Somehow the preacher must be an Amos, who said, "When God speaks, who can but prophesy." Again with Amos, "Let justice roll down like waters, and righteousness like a mighty stream." Somehow the preacher must say with Jesus, "The spirit of the Lord is upon me because He has anointed me." And He's anointed me to deal with the problems of the poor. And I want to commend the preachers, under the leadership of these noble men: James Lawson, one who has been in this struggle for many years, he's been to jail for struggling, he's been kicked out of Vanderbilt University for this struggling, but he's still going on fighting for the rights of his people. (applause) Reverend Ralph Jackson, Billy Kyles, I could just go right on down the list but time will not permit. But I want to thank all of 'em, and I want you to thank them, because so often preachers aren't concerned about anything but themselves. (Voices of agreement)

13. And I'm always happy to see a relevant ministry. It's all right to talk about long white robes over yonder in all of its symbolism, but ultimately people want some suits and dresses and shoes to wear down here. (cheers and applause. Voice says, "Yes, yes, yes.") It's all right to talk about streets flowing with milk and honey, but God has commanded us to be concerned about the slums down here and His children who can't eat three square meals a day (applause) It's all right to talk about the New Jerusalem, but one day God's preacher must talk about the New New York, the New Atlanta, the New Philadelphia, the New Los Angeles, the New Memphis, Tennessee. (applause) This is what we have to do.

14. Now the other thing we'll have to do is this: Always

anchor our external direct action with the power of economic
withdrawal. Now we are poor people. Individually, we are poor
when you compare us with white society in America. We are
poor. Never stop...forget that collectively, that means all of us
together, collectively we are richer than all the nations in the
world with the exception of nine. Did you ever think about that?
(Voice says, "Right on.") After you leave the United States, Soviet
Russia, Great Britain, West Germany, France — and I could name
the others — the American Negro collectively is richer than most
nations of the world. We have an annual income of more than
thirty billion dollars a year, which is more than all of the exports
of the United States, and more than the national budget of
Canada. Did you know that? That's power right there if we know
how to pool it. (applause)

15. We don't have to argue with anybody. We don't have to
curse and go around acting bad with our words. We don't need
any bricks and bottles. We don't need any Molotov cocktails. We
just need to go around to these stores, (Voice says, "Yes sir") and
to these massive industries in our country and say, "God sent us by
here to say to you that you're not treating His children right.
(Voice says, "That's right") And we've come by here to ask you to
make the first item on your agenda fair treatment where God's
children are concerned. Now if you are not prepared to do that we
do have an agenda that we must follow. And our agenda calls for
withdrawing economic support from you." (applause)

16. So as the result of this we are asking you tonight to go
out and tell your neighbors not to buy Coca Cola in Memphis.
(applause) Go by and tell them not to buy Sealtest milk,
(applause) tell them not to buy — what is the other bread? —
Wonder bread. What is the other bread, Jesse? Tell them not to
buy Hart's bread. As Jesse Jackson has said, "Up to now only the
garbage men have been feeling pain. Now we must kind of
redistribute the pain." (applause) We are choosing these companies
because they haven't been fair in their hiring policies, and we are
choosing them because they can begin the process of saying they
are going to support the needs and the rights of these men who are
on strike, and then they can move on downtown and tell Mayor
Loeb to do what is right. (applause)

17. And not only that. We've got to strengthen black institutions. I call upon you to take your money out of the banks

downtown and deposit your money in Tri-State Bank. (applause) We want a bank-in movement in Memphis. Go by the savings and loan associations. I'm not asking you something we don't do ourselves in S.C.L.C. Judge Hooks and others will tell you that we have an account here in the savings and loan association from the Southern Christian Leadership Conference. We are telling you to follow what we are doing, put your money there. You have six or seven black insurance companies here in the city of Memphis. Take out your insurance there, we want to have an insurance-in. (applause)

18. Now these are some practical things that we can do. We begin the process of building a greater economic base, and at the same time we are putting pressure where it really hurts. And I ask you to follow through here. (applause)

19. Now let me say as I move to my conclusion that we've got to give ourselves to this struggle until the end. Nothing would be more tragic than to stop at this point in Memphis. We've got to see it through. (applause) And when we have our march you need to be there. If it means leaving work, if it means leaving school, be there. (applause) Be concerned about your brother. You may not be on strike, but either we go up together or we go down together. (applause) Let us develop a kind of dangerous unselfishness.

20. One day a man came to Jesus and he wanted to raise some questions about some vital matters of life. At points he wanted to trick Jesus (Voice says, "That's right") and show him that he knew a little more than Jesus knew, and throw him off base. Jesus showed him up because he was a lawyer and he was raising a question that any lawyer should know. And finally the man didn't want to give up and he said to Jesus, "Who is my neighbor?" Now that question could have easily ended up in a philosophical and theological debate. But Jesus immediately pulled that question from mid-air, and placed it on a dangerous curve between Jerusalem and Jericho. (chuckles of appreciation from crowd.) And he talked about a certain man who fell among thieves. And you remember that a Levite (Voices say, "Sure") and a priest passed by on the other side. They didn't stop to help him. And finally a man of another race came by. (Voice says, "Yes sir!") He got down from his beast, decided not to be compassionate by proxy, but he got down with him, administered first aid, and helped the man in need. Jesus ended up saying, this was the good man,

this was the great man, because he had the capacity to project the "I" into the "thou," and to be concerned about his brother.

21. Now you know we use our imagination a great deal to try to determine why the priest and the Levite didn't stop. At times we say they were busy going to a church meeting, an ecclesiastical gatherin', and they had to get on down to Jerusalem so they wouldn't be late for their meeting. At other times we would speculate that there was a religious law that one who was engaged in religious ceremonials was not to touch a human body twenty-four hours before the ceremony. And every now and then we begin to wonder whether maybe they were not going down to Jerusalem — or down to Jericho rather — to organize a Jericho Road Improvement Association. (Laughter) That's a possibility. Maybe they felt that it was better to deal with the problem from the causal root rather than to get bogged down with an individual effect.

22. But I'm going to tell you what my imagination tells me. It's possible that those men were afraid. You see, the Jericho road is a dangerous road. (Voice says, "That's right. That's right.") I remember when Mrs. King and I were first in Jerusalem. We rented a car and drove from Jerusalem down to Jericho. And as soon as we got on that road I said to my wife, "I can see why Jesus used this as the setting for his parable." It's a winding, meandering road. (Voice says, "Yeah, yeah.") It's really conducive for ambushing. You start out in Jerusalem, which is about twelve hundred miles — or rather twelve hundred feet — above sea level, and by the time you get down to Jericho fifteen or twenty minutes later you are about twenty-two hundred feet below sea level. That's a dangerous road. In the days of Jesus it came to be known as the Bloody Pass. You know it's possible that the priest and the Levite looked over to that man on the ground and wondered if the robbers were still around. (Voices agree, "Yeah.") Or it's possible that they felt that the man on the ground was merely faking. (Voice says, "Uh-huh") and he was acting like he had been robbed and hurt in order to seize them over there, lull them there for quick and easy seizure. (Voice says, "Oh, yeah.") And so the first question that the priest asked, the first question that the Levite asked, was, "If I stop to help this man, what will happen to me?" But then the good Samaritan came by, and he reversed the question: "If I do not stop to help this man, what will happen to him?"

23. That's the question before you tonight. Not, "If I stop to

help the sanitation workers, what will happen to my job?" Not, "If I stop to help the sanitation workers, what will happen to all of the hours that I usually spend in my office every day and every week as a pastor?" The question is not, "If I stop to help this man in need, what will happen to me?" The question is, "if I do *not* stop to help the sanitation workers, what will happen to them?" That's the question. (Long applause)

24. Let us rise up tonight with a greater readiness. Let us stand with a greater determination. And let us move on, in these powerful days, these days of challenge, to make America what it ought to be. We have an opportunity to make America a better nation, and I want to thank God once more for allowing me to be here with you. (Voice says, "Yes sir.")

25. You know, several years ago I was in New York City, autographing the first book that I had written. And while sitting there autographing books, a demented black woman came up, and the only question I heard from her was, "Are you Martin Luther King?" And I was looking down writing, and I said, "Yes." The next minute I felt something beating on my chest. Before I knew it, I had been stabbed by this demented woman. I was rushed to Harlem Hospital. It was a dark Saturday afternoon. And that blade had gone through, and the X-rays revealed that the tip of the blade was on the edge of my aorta, the main artery, and once that's punctured you drown in your own blood. That's the end of you. It came out in the *New York Times* the next morning that if I had merely sneezed, I would have died.

26. Well, about four days later they allowed me after the operation, after my chest had been opened and the blade had been taken out, to move around in the wheelchair in the hospital. They allowed me to read some of the mail that came in, and from all over the states and the world kind letters came in. I read a few but one of them I will never forget. I had received one from the President and the Vice-President. I've forgotten what those telegrams said. (Voice says, "Go ahead, now. Go ahead.") I had received a visit and a letter from the governor of New York but I've forgotten what that letter said. (Voice says, "Yes sir") But there was another letter (Voices say, "All right") that came from a little girl, a young girl, who was a student at the White Plains High School, and I looked at that letter and I'll never forget it. It said simply. "Dear Dr. King, I am a ninth grade student at the

White Plains High School." She said, "While it should not matter, I would like to mention that I'm a white girl. I read in the paper of your misfortune and of your suffering, and I read that if you had sneezed you would have died. I'm simply writing you to say that I'm so happy that you didn't sneeze."

27. And I want to say tonight...(applause) I want to say tonight that I too am happy that I didn't sneeze, because if I had sneezed (Voice says, "All right") I wouldn't have been around here in 1960 when students all over the South started sitting in at lunch counters. And I knew that as they were sitting in they were really standing up for the best in the American dream and taking the whole nation back to those great wells of democracy which were dug deep by the founding fathers in the Declaration of Independence and the Constitution. If I had sneezed (Crowd replies, "Yeah") I wouldn't have been around here in 1961 when we decided to take a ride for freedom and ended segregation in interstate travel. If I had sneezed (Crowd says, "Yes") I wouldn't have been around here in 1962 when Negroes in Albany, Georgia, decided to straighten their backs up. And whenever men and women straighten their backs up they are going somewhere because a man can't ride your back unless it is bent. If I had sneezed (Long applause)...if I had sneezed I wouldn't have been here in 1963, when the black people of Birmingham, Alabama, aroused the conscience of this nation and brought into being the civil rights bill. If I had sneezed, (applause) I wouldn't have had a chance later in that year in August to try to tell America about a dream that I had had. If I had sneezed, (applause) I wouldn't have been down in Selma, Alabama, to see the great movement there. If I had sneezed, I wouldn't have been in Memphis to see a community rally around those brothers and sisters who are suffering. (Voices say, "Yes sir.") I'm so happy that I didn't sneeze.

28. And they were telling me...(applause) Now it doesn't matter now. (Voice says, "Go ahead.") It really doesn't matter what happens now. I left Atlanta this morning, and as we got started on the plane—there were six of us—the pilot said over the public address system, "We are sorry for the delay, but we have Dr. Martin Luther King on the plane, and to be sure that all of the bags were checked and to be sure that nothing would be wrong on the plane, we had to check out everything carefully, and we've had the plane protected and guarded all night."

29. And then I got into Memphis, and some began to say the threats, or talk about the threats that were out of what would happen to me from some of our sick white brothers. Well, I don't know what will happen now. We've got some difficult days ahead. But it really doesn't matter with me now because I've been to the mountaintop. (applause) And I don't mind. Like anybody I would like to live a long life. Longevity has its place, but I'm not concerned about that now. I just want to do God's will, and He's allowed me to go up to the mountain, and I've looked over and I've seen the Promised Land. I may not get there with you, but I want you to know tonight that we as a people will get to the Promised Land (applause) So I'm happy tonight, I'm not worried about anything, I'm not fearing any man. Mine eyes have seen the glory of the coming of the Lord. (Long applause, cheers.)

THE CONTRIBUTORS

JAMES ARNT AUNE is assistant professor of speech at St. Olaf College, Northfield, Minnesota. His publications focus on the relationship between rhetorical theory and political philosophy.

STEPHEN H. BROWNE is assistant professor in the Department of Speech Communication at Pennsylvania State University, University Park. His research focuses on the analysis of rhetorical practice in the eighteenth century.

BARRY BRUMMET is associate professor of communication at the University of Wisconsin, Milwaukee. His research interests include theory and critical approaches to the work of Kenneth Burke, the rhetoric of popular culture, and media criticism.

KARLYN KOHRS CAMPBELL is professor of speech communication at the University of Minnesota. She is the author of *The Rhetorical Act* (1982), and of a two-volume work on the rhetoric of woman's rights/woman suffrage movement, *Man Cannot Speak For Her* (forthcoming).

CELESTE CONDIT is assistant professor of speech communication at the University of Illinois, Urbana. Her essays focus on the role of rhetoric in processes of social change and stability. She is author of *Decoding Abortion Rhetoric: Communicating Social Change.*

J. ROBERT COX is associate professor of speech communication at the University of North Carolina at Chapel Hill. His publications focus on rhetorical and argumentation theory and on contemporary social movements. He co-edited the volume *Advances in Argumentation Research and Theory* for the American Forensic Association (1982).

THOMAS B. FARRELL is professor of communication studies at Northwestern University. His research has focused on the intersection of classical rhetoric and critical theory. His publications have addressed rhetorical problems in invention and judgment in conversation, technical systems in discourse, and political ritual. He is completing a book called, *The Norms of Rhetorical Culture: Heritage and Possibility.*

DILIP GAONKAR is assistant professor of communication arts at the University of Wisconsin, Madison. His research interests include contemporary rhetorical theory, rhetoric of inquiry, and history of rhetoric.

ROBERT HARIMAN is associate professor of speech communication at Drake University. His research focuses on rhetorical theory and political discourse. His essays have appeared in *Quarterly Journal of Speech, Social Epistemology, Journal of the History of Ideas,* and *Rhetorica.*

ROBERT L. IVIE is professor of speech communication at Texas A&M University. His publications focus on the rhetoric of war, especially the relationship of metaphor to rhetorical invention in the cold war era. He is author of *Congress Declares War: Rhetoric, Leadership, and Partisanship in the Early Republic* (1983) and *Perspectives on Cold War Rhetoric: Ideology, Metaphor, and Strategy* (forthcoming).

FRED J. KAUFFELD, co-editor of this volume, is professor of communication arts at Edgewood College, Madison, Wisconsin. He has written on topics in rhetoric and the philosophy of language.

MICHAEL C. LEFF, co-editor of this volume, is professor of communication arts at the University of Wisconsin, Madison. He is the editor of *Rhetorica: A Journal of the History of Rhetoric* and has published numerous articles on rhetorical theory and criticism.

WIL LINKUGEL is professor of communication at the University of Kansas. He has written in the history of American public address, and is best known for his work on the apologetic genre of discourse and the history of women's rhetoric. He is the co-author of a rhetorical biography of Dr. Anna Howard Shaw.

JOHN LOUIS LUCAITES is assistant professor of speech communication at Indiana University. His publications focus on the relationship between rhetoric, power, and socio-political legitimacy. He is the editor of *Great Speakers and Speeches* (forthcoming, 1989) and is currently co-editing a volume of essays on the rhetoric of Martin Luther King, Jr.

MARTIN J. MEDHURST is associate professor of speech communication at Texas A&M University. He is co-editor of *Rhetorical Dimensions in Media* and publishes regularly in the areas of Presidential rhetoric, media criticism, and criticism of religious discourse. He presently serves as book review editor for the *Quarterly Journal of Speech.*

MICHAEL OSBORN is professor of communication at Memphis State University. His publications have centered on the rhetorical metaphor, and his work on this theme has been honored by the Douglas Ehninger Distinguished Rhetorical Scholar award and by a Golden Anniversary Monograph award presented by the Speech Communication Association.

ROBERT ROWLAND is assistant professor of speech communication at the University of Kansas. He has written extensively on argumentation and public decision-making, the state of discourse in the public sphere, as well as narrative and mythic approaches to criticism. He is the author of *The Rhetoric of Menachem Begin: The Myth of Redemption Through Return.*

ROBERT L. SCOTT is professor of speech communication at the University of Minnesota. He has written or edited five books and forty scholarly essays. His principal interest is in the philosophical foundations of rhetoric. In 1970 he shared with Donald K. Smith a James A. Winans/Herbert A. Wichelns Memorial Award for Distinguished Scholarship in Rhetoric and Public Address.

JOSEPH W. WENZEL is associate professor of speech communication at the University of Illinois in Urbana-Champaign. His publications focus on the theory and criticism of argumentative discourse. He was editor of the *Journal of the American Forensic Association,* 1983-86, and has served as associate editor of other communication journals.

DAVID ZAREFSKY is professor of communication studies and Dean of the School of Speech at Northwestern University. His research focuses on the nature of American public discourse during two eras of social unrest, the 1850's and the 1960's. His book, *President Johnson's War on Poverty: Rhetoric and History,* received the Speech Communication Association's Winans-Wichelns Award for distinguished scholarship in Rhetoric and Public Address.